THE PSYCHOLOGY OF HUMOR AT WORK

This is the first book to look at the psychological processes that enable humor to affect people and teams in the workplace. It recognizes that humor plays many roles beyond making people feel happier and more productive, and acknowledges humor's potential darker side as well.

Bringing together a small but growing field of study, the book features chapters around core psychological topics such as perception, creativity and stress, while also addressing organizational issues such as leadership, teamwork and social networks. The collection concludes with chapters on the role of humor in recruitment processes, as well as how humor consultants work with organizations.

Each chapter in *The Psychology of Humor at Work* not only provides a comprehensive review of what is known in that area, but also considers future directions for research and practice. It will prove fascinating reading for students, practitioners, and researchers in organizational psychology, human resource management and business and management.

Christopher Robert is an Associate Professor of Management in the Trulaske College of Business at the University of Missouri, Columbia. His research focuses on humor at work, as well as cross-cultural management, work groups and teams, and conflict.

"*The Psychology of Humor at Work* makes a significant contribution to our understanding of humor in the workplace across a wide range of contexts. This is an important book for anyone who wants a deeper understanding of the serious business of humor."

– ***Chuck Gulas***, *Wright State University, USA*

"The authors bring perfect order to the paradoxes inherent in research on humor in the workplace, humor being both 'simultaneously everywhere and nowhere' and 'extraordinarily complex but also very simple.' They do this by presenting a clear and valuable outline of crucial research questions, empirical findings and prevailing theories and models; and by convincingly encouraging researchers to just go ahead, embracing the above ambiguities."

– ***Lita Lundquist***, *Professor Emeritus, Department of Business and Politics, Copenhagen Business School, Denmark*

Current Issues in Work and Organizational Psychology
Series Editor: Arnold B. Bakker

Current Issues in Work and Organizational Psychology is a series of edited books that reflect the state-of-the-art areas of current and emerging interest in the psychological study of employees, workplaces and organizations.

Each volume is tightly focused on a particular topic and consists of seven to ten chapters contributed by international experts. The editors of individual volumes are leading figures in their areas and provide an introductory overview.

Example topics include: digital media at work, work and the family, workaholism, modern job design, positive occupational health and individualised deals.

New Frontiers in Work and Family Research
Edited by Joseph G. Grzywacz and Evangelia Demerouti

Time and Work, Volume 1: How Time Impacts Individuals
Edited by Abbie J. Shipp and Yitzhak Fried

Time and Work, Volume 2: How Time Impacts Groups, Organizations and Methodological Choices
Edited by Abbie J. Shipp and Yitzhak Fried

Burnout at Work: A Psychological Perspective
Edited by Michael P. Leiter, Arnold B. Bakker, and Christina Maslach

Towards Inclusive Organizations: Determinants of Successful Diversity Management at Work
Edited by Sabine Otten, Karen Van Der Zee, and Marilynn Brewer

Well-being and Performance at Work: The Role of Context
Edited by Marc van Veldhoven and Riccardo Peccei

Employee Recruitment, Selection, and Assessment: Contemporary Issues for Theory and Practice
Edited by Ioannis Nikolaou and Janneke K. Oostrom

Idiosyncratic Deals between Employees and Organizations: Conceptual Issues, Applications, and the Role of Coworkers
Edited by Matthijs Bal and Denise Rousseau

The Psychology of Humor at Work
Edited by Christopher Robert

THE PSYCHOLOGY OF HUMOR AT WORK

Edited by Christopher Robert

Routledge
Taylor & Francis Group
LONDON AND NEW YORK

First published 2017
by Routledge
2 Park Square, Milton Park, Abingdon, Oxon OX14 4RN

and by Routledge
711 Third Avenue, New York, NY 10017

Routledge is an imprint of the Taylor & Francis Group, an informa business

British Library Cataloguing in Publication Data
A catalogue record for this book is available from the British Library

Library of Congress Cataloging in Publication Data
Names: Robert, Christopher, 1972- editor.
Title: The psychology of humor at work / edited by Christopher Robert.
Description: 1 Edition. | New York : Routledge, 2017. | Series: Current issues in work and organizational psychology | Includes index.
Identifiers: LCCN 2016028211 | ISBN 9781138944947 (hardback : alk. paper) | ISBN 9781315671659 (e-book)
Subjects: LCSH: Wit and humor—Psychological aspects. | Stress (Psychology)—Prevention. | Work—Humor.
Classification: LCC BF575.L3 P79 2017 | DDC 152.4/3—dc23
LC record available at https://lccn.loc.gov/2016028211

ISBN: 978-1-138-94494-7 (hbk)
ISBN: 978-1-138-23236-5 (pbk)
ISBN: 978-1-315-67165-9 (ebk)

Typeset in Bembo
by Keystroke, Neville Lodge, Tettenhall, Wolverhampton

This book is dedicated to my kids, Emma and Zack, who are a constant source of humor, pride, and wonder. And to my adored wife, Amanda Rose, who tolerates my bad jokes.

CONTENTS

CONTRIBUTING AUTHORS

Joseph A. Allen, Department of Psychology, University of Nebraska at Omaha, Omaha, Nebraska.

Julia B. Bear, College of Business, Stony Brook University, Stony Brook, New York.

Melanie Booth-Butterfield, Department of Communication Studies, West Virginia University, Morgantown, West Virginia.

Cynthia, A. Cerrentano, Harold Washington College, Chicago, Illinois.

Cecily D. Cooper, School of Business Administration, University of Miami, Coral Gables, Florida.

John Crowe, Department of Psychology, University of Nebraska at Omaha, Omaha, Nebraska.

Serge P. da Motta Veiga, Kogod School of Business, American University, Washington, DC.

B. Alan Echtenkamp, Time Warner Inc., New York.

Emuna Eliav, Faculty of Industrial Engineering and Management, Technion-Israel Institute of Technology, Haifa, Israel.

Lisa M. Finkelstein, Department of Psychology, Northern Illinois University, DeKalb, Illinois.

Nale Lehmann-Willenbrock, Department of Experimental and Applied Psychology, Vrije Universiteit Amsterdam, Amsterdam, The Netherlands.

Ella Miron-Spektor, Faculty of Industrial Engineering and Management, Technion-Israel Institute of Technology, Haifa, Israel.

John Morreall, President, Humorworks, & Department of Religious Studies, College of William & Mary, Williamsburg, Virginia.

Christopher Robert, Robert J. Trulaske, Sr. College of Business, University of Missouri, Columbia, Missouri.

Scott U. Seyrek, Robert J. Trulaske, Sr. College of Business, University of Missouri, Columbia, Missouri.

Elora C. Voyles, Department of Psychology, Northern Illinois University, DeKalb, Illinois.

Melissa Bekelja Wanzer, Department of Communication Studies, Canisius College, Buffalo, New York.

James D. Westaby, Program in Social-Organizational Psychology, Teachers College, Columbia University, New York.

1

HUMOR AT WORK

Often experienced, seldom studied

Christopher Robert

I have been talking about humor in the workplace for over a decade with friends, strangers, colleagues, reporters, and pretty much anybody who will listen. When I tell people that I study humor at work, they generally express surprise, curiosity, shock, and excitement. The typical response is "Really? (pause), Huh (far away look). That's cool!" It's a terrific conversation starter, with most people wanting to know things like "how do you study that?" and "what do you find?" People from all sorts of different backgrounds become engaged and excited about the topic.

Why does the topic of humor at work elicit such strong reactions? It is safe to say that everybody experiences humor at work, and that most people experience humor frequently and in a wide range of forms and work contexts. Moreover, those experiences are often laden with emotions, both positive and negative, which make the topic immediately salient and personally relevant. I suspect that the ubiquity of humor behavior in work contexts, in combination with its emotional relevance, result in people giving a lot of thought to humor at work, its complexities, and its impact on their lives.

Although most people recognize that humor can have some downsides when used as a vehicle for aggression or belittling others, the overwhelming majority of individuals perceive humor to be a fundamentally positive and important aspect of work life. My colleague Scott Seyrek and I recently asked about 100 working adults from the US to write a paragraph or two describing what humor at work means to them (see Chapter 10 where we discuss this study in more detail). Although the depth and intensity of their responses varied, they paint a remarkably consistent picture of humor at work as a deeply meaningful phenomenon. Below are some illustrative quotes:

> Humor is essential to my sanity at work. I always tell people, if you can't find humor in a situation, then life just isn't worth living.

> The importance of humor cannot be denied.
>
> If not for the humor between us (co-workers), I would not return to this job.
>
> Humor is essential to a well-rounded life.
>
> Humor in the workplace is vital.
>
> Humor is a necessity in life.
>
> Humor is important for individuals not to take themselves too seriously.
>
> Without humor life wouldn't be the same. Without it you could easily fall into depression, anger, or even commit suicide.
>
> It's easier to trust someone and rely on them for help (and vice versa) when you feel like you know that person a little, and humor is a great way to at least develop working friendships.
>
> I am significantly younger than the people I work with and so I find that humor can be a really powerful way of crossing the "bridge" of age.
>
> If it weren't for my co-workers and our shared sense of humor I would undoubtedly be bored out of my mind.
>
> Humor at work is extremely important to me as I am coming from a former job where humor was not in the workplace.
>
> Humor is very necessary to my day-to-day experiences at work.
>
> Humor is completely key for me in most facets of my life, especially when it comes to working.
>
> I believe that humor at work is essential for success in the workplace.
>
> I work with children and they do make me laugh often. This is a part of the job that I love.
>
> Humor at work is beneficial to everyone, as long as it is innocent fun.
>
> Humor doesn't play a big role in my current job, because we get reprimanded if we basically even have a two-minute conversation with a co-worker. It makes the day really dull and long. Not being able to be light-hearted at work makes me feel like we are all being watched all the time and we'll get an email or phone call from one of the managers just for asking how someone's day is. It makes it really depressing. I feel like everyone just kind of goes into their own cubicle and shuts themselves off from everyone else because that's the only way to get by. I hate that.

In stark contrast to the last quote, in which the individual laments the fact that management has basically prohibited social interaction, and humor in particular, one individual expressed an entirely different perspective:

> I really don't think humor is too important in the work place, at least for me. My goal in most working situations is to get the job done and make money, the personalities and sense of humor of my co-workers or supervisors don't

> mean much to me. However, it is nice when they do have a sense of humor, because it makes the work less boring and more entertaining, which I suppose is beneficial to unmotivated workers. At my previous job, the type of humor my co-workers enjoyed was often offensive and led me to eventually quit and move to a new job.

Although this was certainly a valid and well-considered response, the existence of such a starkly different perspective on humor actually reinforces the near universality of a positive perception of workplace humor. Indeed, the frequent use of descriptors for workplace humor such as "necessary," "beneficial," "key," "essential," "vital," and "powerful" help serve to illustrate that people perceive humor to be an indispensable feature of a healthy and positive workplace.

Given the strength and depth of peoples' feelings about workplace humor, it seems ironic that humor has received very little attention in the research literature as a fundamental psychological process in workplace contexts. In his comprehensive volume on the psychology of humor, Rod Martin (2007, p. 361) noted that "very little psychological research of any kind has been conducted on the general topic of humor in the workplace." In the ten-or-so years since the publication of Martin's book, with some important exceptions that will be discussed later (Robert & Seyrek, this volume), this has not changed much. In fact, in their recent meta-analysis on humor in the workplace, Mesmer-Magnus, Glew, and Viswesvaran (2012) were only able to identify 49 independent empirical studies that fit their search criteria to examine leader or subordinate humor and some correlates (e.g. job satisfaction).

For rough comparison purposes, consider the vast number of empirical studies that have been conducted on other topics in organizational psychology. A quick search for empirical articles in peer-reviewed journals in the Psyc Info database, cross-listed with the term "organization," yielded 6,008 articles on job satisfaction, 5,424 articles on leadership, 20,433 articles on groups, 3,770 articles on stress, 1,043 articles on creativity, and 1,502 articles on emotion. In comparison there were only 95 articles on humor, which is similar in relative magnitude to sexual harassment (159), incivility (75), noise (67), and abusive supervision (61). Indeed, it might be possible to develop a good understanding of a literature of this size over margaritas on a ten-day beach vacation.

I am not trying to argue that any of these topics should *not* be extensively studied by researchers, or that topics such as noise and abusive supervision are unimportant. But I wonder, given that humor is such a ubiquitous human phenomenon, and that people have such strong reactions to humor at work, why so little love for humor in the organizational literature?

I suspect there are four reasons. First, I think there is a tendency to regard humor, almost by definition, as lacking seriousness, and thus unimportant. If one's first instinct is to think about humor at work as merely "cracking a few jokes," it is easy to regard it as fundamentally insignificant or irrelevant. But as I have argued elsewhere (Robert & Wilbanks, 2012), humor is likely to impact people at work through its many small and subtle effects that accumulate over time. Relatedly, as noted by Linstead (1985) and Martin (2007), because humor is such a common feature of our everyday lives and interpersonal interactions, people might assume that it is already well understood.

Second, humor is an extremely flexible and complex phenomenon. It hides in plain sight by being leveraged in so many different contexts, and taking on so many faces. Humor can be light-hearted or serious, silly or sophisticated, and blunt or subtle, and it can be used to soothe, anger, stimulate, calm, support, or belittle. For researchers, who generally prefer to isolate, define, and tightly operationalize the phenomena they wish to study, finding a place to start might feel daunting. By choosing to study it from one particular vantage point, researchers might believe they are failing to do the topic justice. How do we grab on to a phenomenon that seems to be simultaneously everywhere, but nowhere in particular?

Third, humor phenomena have not been well integrated into the organizational literature. Indeed, much of the empirical work that has been done on humor in the workplace comes from disciplines outside of the core organizational psychology and organizational behavior literature, such as communication, anthropology, sociology, and even medicine. On one hand, this creates a certain degree of richness that is valuable, particularly for understanding the breadth of humor phenomena. On the other hand, the use of methodological and theoretical paradigms that are unfamiliar to organizational researchers makes it more difficult for the findings to be easily integrated into the body of existing knowledge, and might make organizational researchers feel like humor is not a topic that they "own."

Finally, I suspect that scholars have been hesitant to pursue the topic of humor in the workplace because it might be unclear exactly how humor might be effectively leveraged in workplace contexts. That is, assuming that humor can have numerous positive impacts in the workplace, as most people assume, how do we inject, infuse, or inspire humor in order to benefit from those effects? Organizational scholarship has a long tradition of considering the applied potential of theories and research findings, but it might be difficult to generate practical advice that does not feel obvious. As I have noted elsewhere (Robert, Dunne, & Iun, 2015), the popular and practitioner literatures that address humor tend to take a straightforward perspective on workplace humor: the use of positively-toned or "nice" humor at work should be encouraged, but be mindful of "mean" humor and its destructive power. This conventional wisdom feels overly simplistic, and perhaps disconnected from the specific contexts in which humor is used.

This book is designed to help address these issues. I chose to organize this book around core organizational processes that are likely to be impacted by humor, and/or which have been addressed in the literature on humor in organizations. These include leadership, person perception, social networks, creativity, stress, groups and teams, and recruiting. The final two chapters take a somewhat broader view by examining the approaches that are taken within the relatively new field of humor consulting, and by discussing paradoxes that inhibit research attention to humor, humor theory, and the relationship between humor and culture.

The authors of the chapters are part of a small (but illustrious!) group of scholars with interests in humor in organizations, who have conducted research on humor in organizations, or who are willing to consider the role of humor in their subject area (e.g. Westaby and Echtenkamp's examination of the role of humor within dynamic network theory, and da Motta Veiga's examination of humor in recruiting). I was pleased and humbled to have these authors agree to my invitations to contribute chapters, because the value of this book is derived from their knowledge, expertise, creativity, and energy. You will find that each chapter not only provides a comprehensive review of what is currently known about each content area, they also offer insightful, and nuanced considerations of humor that have important implications for theory, research, and practice. To provide you with an overview of the book, below are some thoughts about each of the book's remaining chapters.

Overview of chapters

In Chapter 2, Cooper addresses humor and leadership: a topic that has arguably received more attention in the small literature on humor in organizations than any other. Her chapter includes an in-depth analysis of qualitative data she collected through interviews with individuals employed in a wide variety of organizations. Building on these data, Cooper argues that leader-member exchange (LMX) theory provides a useful lens through which to view the social exchange of humor between leaders and their subordinates. Specifically, she argues that subordinates' *perceptions* of the leader's hedonic tone are the key drivers of leader humor's effects, and that each subordinate might perceive the leader's humor differently. Importantly, she develops the hedonic tone concept, and argues that a leader's humor is not only interpreted based on whether it is positive or negative in general tone, but also in terms of whether it is spontaneously generated and relevant to work (rather than distracting). This perspective represents a valuable contribution to the literature, which has generally been leader-centric, and focused on the leader's general use of humor or humor style (i.e. an "average leader perspective"), and on the simple "positive versus negative" humor dichotomy. Cooper's framework suggests that leader humor and its impact is best thought of in terms of a dynamic interplay between leader, subordinate, context, and nuances of humor content, and that humor has an impact on organizations through its ongoing effects on the leader-subordinate relationship.

In Chapter 3, Finkelstein, Cerrentano, and Voyles explore humor's seldom-examined role in person perception, and tackle a very fundamental question: How does an individual's use of humor color the way we perceive that individual? By thoroughly reviewing both seminal and recent research on person-perception and integrating that work with their own research, the authors argue that a "halo of humor" is likely cast around individuals who use humor. The notion of a halo of humor suggests that people who use humor tend to be perceived more positively (at least when using positive humor styles), and that they exhibit a host of other positive traits. Clearly, the existence of a halo of humor has important ramifications for how we interact with individuals such as clients, customers, and vendors, and has implications for many workplace processes such as selection, performance appraisal, promotion, and compensation. This chapter also raises interesting theoretical and practical issues that are ripe for empirical examination. These include issues surrounding causality and directionality in the nature of humor in person perception (e.g. humorous and friendly are related traits, but are friendly people always humorous or vice versa?), the role of affect in humor's impact on person-perception (i.e. does humor impact our perceptions of others *because of* the way it makes us feel?), and whether peoples' beliefs in the fixed versus malleable nature of traits impact whether instances of humor impact perceptions of other related characteristics. Finally, one of the most interesting ideas raised by the authors concerns the impact of humor on metaperceptions: how does my use of humor impact what I think other people think of me, and thus my subsequent behavior?

In Chapter 4, Westaby and Echtenkamp examine the role of humor in organizational networks. Traditional network theory examines characteristics such as strong and weak ties between individuals, and the centrality of individuals within a network of relationships. This approach might suggest that humor is best conceptualized as an independent variable, and that positive humor strengthens network ties, whereas negative humor damages network ties. In contrast, the focus of this chapter is on the application of dynamic network theory (Westaby, 2012) to humor. Instead of focusing on the network itself, dynamic network theory focuses on individual goal striving (e.g. an individual's motivation to use humor at work), and how supportive versus de-affirming network ties can either facilitate and support goal striving behavior, or work against that behavior. Moreover, the dynamic network theory approach suggests that humor behavior might cause a "rippling of emotions" back through the network, such that positive emotions are experienced directly or indirectly by individuals in a supportive role relative to the successful humorist's goals, and negative emotions are experienced by individuals in de-affirming roles. In other words, the dynamic network perspective views humor as both affected by the network, and as affecting the network itself. The authors provide an extended example of how the dynamic network perspective might differ from a traditional social network perspective, emphasizing how various network roles might cause direct and indirect effects of humor. They also offer examples of how a dynamic network perspective might be valuable for examining humor's role in a number of specific contexts (e.g. conflict management).

In Chapter 5, Eliav, Miron-Spektor, and Bear dig deeply into the relationship between humor and creativity. The authors provide an up-to-date and thorough review of the existing literature, which has demonstrated a correlation between humor use, or the sense of humor, and creativity. However, the most notable contribution of this chapter is the way they flesh-out this relationship, by providing an in-depth analysis of the psychological processes involved in the link between humor and creativity. These processes are represented in an elegant theoretical model (see Figure 5.1), which depicts a number of important moderating and mediating processes. The authors argue that humor and creativity share a number of important properties, particularly with regard to shared or similar cognitive processes relating to complexity, novelty, and abstract thinking. But the chapter and the theoretical model also incorporate emotional and social processes as important mediators of the humor–creativity relationship, and the authors' consideration and detailed analysis of the social and emotional effects of humor in the creativity process represent a novel perspective in this literature. Moreover, the chapter identifies a number of important possible moderators of the humor–creativity relationship, including humor type, humorist status, gender, and the relational context. These ideas represent excellent foundations for future research in this relatively wide-open area of inquiry. In particular, I think the authors' brief discussion of the temporal context offers some particularly ripe ideas for future research.

One of the more common arguments people make in support of workplace humor is that it can help reduce stress. In Chapter 6, Booth-Butterfield and Wanzer review the existing literature addressing the humor–stress relationship in organizational contexts, including some of their own important work on the topic. However, they also make a number of important observations about how workplace humor is unique relative to humor used in other contexts. For example, they note that work settings place a number of constraints on humor use, such as constraints imposed by the relative status or power or actors, which is not necessarily present in other social contexts where individuals can make their own rules governing the appropriate use of humor. Similarly, work contexts require that individuals interact with others who they do not necessarily choose to interact with, and often within a legal environment that might influence humor behavior (e.g. laws pertaining to harassment). The authors develop arguments for how and why humor impacts stress primarily in terms of its ability to help individuals cope, and suggest that problem- and emotion-focused coping are the key mediating mechanisms between humor and stress. Importantly, the authors note that although the existing literature has generally focused primarily on the impact of *responses* to humor on stress, their chapter highlights the importance of humor *enactment* as a key stress-reducing behavior, which has received relatively little attention in the research literature. The authors suggest a number of promising directions for future research, most notably in areas such as examining the efficacy of humor training (i.e. can people be taught to enact humor effectively?), and exploring the boundary between effective or beneficial humor, and humor that exacerbates problems.

Crowe, Allen and Lehmann-Willenbrock address the issue of humor use in group and team contexts in Chapter 7. Their perspective draws substantially from work on team meetings (including some of their own), and they argue (convincingly) that humor in team meetings represents an important "interaction ritual" (Collins, 2004) which allows group members to synchronize their efforts and promote effective team functioning. Specifically, they present a model which suggests that humor that results in humor–laughter patterns (which others might call "humor episodes," e.g. Robert & Wilbanks, 2012) result in constructive team interactions including new ideas, which in turn lead to team performance. Indeed, their approach is somewhat reminiscent of Connie Gersick's (1988, 1989) seminal work on pacing and transitions within teams. They also emphasize the notion that the humor used by team leaders might have a particularly strong impact on the team by virtue of the leader's centrality in the group, and they point out that leader humor might be used to both solidify the leader's power and to reduce social distance within the team. This observation highlights the fact that humor can be a highly nuanced behavior that can seemingly play contradictory roles for a given person at different times. The authors conclude with some excellent suggestions about directions for future research, including exploration of the antecedents of workplace humor (i.e. where does it come from?), the relationship between humor and the broader notion of "workplace fun," and research on both gender and power issues.

In Chapter 8, da Motta Veiga addresses the possibility that humor might influence both the job search and recruitment processes. Unlike the topics addressed in the preceding chapters, for which *some* previous work has been done that examines humor, da Motta Veiga notes that humor's role in job search and recruitment has been basically unexplored. In that spirit, he calls for future research that examines both processes individually, as well as research that examines both the seeker and recruiting organization simultaneously. In particular, he notes that humor might be used both as a stress-reducing strategy that can help job seekers cope with the stress of the job search process, and as a method of impression management. For organizations, humor can be used to signal organizational culture, and as a way of generating positive affect that can be associated with the organization. I think one of his more interesting observations is that there is likely an important dynamic component to the use of humor in job search and recruiting, whereby, for example, humor use by recruiters might impact the job seeker immediately, but also might impact the job seeker's attitudes and behaviors toward other employers as the search process unfolds.

For Chapter 9, I asked John Morreall to take a different perspective on workplace humor than was taken in the previous chapters. Based on considerable depth of experience as both a scholar and as an author and consultant in the area of workplace humor, I asked him if he would provide an overview of how workplace humor consultants approach the task of introducing humor and its applied potential to organizational audiences. Morreall provides a historically situated review of how humor has been viewed in the past, and suggests that an appreciation of how humor might have beneficial effects in workplace contexts is a relatively new phenomenon. He provides numerous examples of how companies have adopted various approaches to adopting humor in the workplace, noting both humor's promise as well as barriers to its acceptance. He concludes the chapter by describing different ways that humor consultants approach their interactions with organizations, and with some bios of well-known humor consultants that illustrate the different types of backgrounds that have drawn people into this area.

In Chapter 10, Scott Seyrek and I take a broader view on humor by noting two paradoxes in the study of humor in the workplace that we argue have limited research attention to the topic. We argue that "humor is everywhere and nowhere," and that "humor is extraordinarily complex, but also very simple." These paradoxes reflect the notion that humor probably has an impact on lots of different organizational phenomena, and that even though the subjective experience of humor feels simple (i.e. a positive feeling), the theoretical explanations for how humor works are likely to be quite complex. We suggest that much like the literature on affect in the workplace, which developed primarily in the 1980s and 1990s, we need to acknowledge and embrace these paradoxes if the field is going to progress. The result might be a theoretically and empirically messy literature, but the field of workplace humor will need to endure the mess before some order can arise from the chaos. Toward this end, we discuss humor theories that might be applied to future work, and describe some of the better exemplars of work that has been done in this area. In addition, we address the particularly thorny issue of culture's impact on humor, and include some results from a study we conducted that examined humor themes across American, Chinese, and Indian cultures.

Conclusion

Although there have been some exemplary contributions in recent years, as a field, the study of humor at work is still very much in its infancy. As a consequence, we also know relatively little about how humor can be leveraged in organizational contexts. Practical advice and applied implications seem to be limited to the encouragement of positive humor, and discouragement of negative humor. More detailed and appropriately complex theoretical approaches to the study of humor, and perhaps even intervention-based research, should help provide both better and more practical advice for how humor can be leveraged in organizations to improve both individual outcomes and organizational functioning. In the remaining chapters, the authors address some of the more promising avenues for future research into workplace humor.

References

Collins, R. (2004). *Interaction ritual chains*. Princeton, NJ: Princeton University Press.

Gersick, C. J. G. (1988). Time and transition in work teams: Toward a new model of group development. *Academy of Management Journal*, 31(1), 9–41.

Gersick, C. J. G. (1989). Marking time: Predictable transitions in task groups. *Academy of Management Journal*, 32(2), 274–309.

Linstead, S. (1985). Joker's wild: The importance of humor in the maintenance of organizational culture. *The Sociological Review*, 33, 741–765.

Martin, R. A. (2007). *The psychology of humor: An integrative approach*. Amsterdam: Academic Press.

Mesmer-Magnus, J., Glew, D. J., & Viswesvaran, C. (2012). A meta-analysis of positive humor in the workplace. *Journal of Managerial Psychology*, 27, 155–190.

Robert, C., & Wilbanks, J. E. (2012). The wheel model of humor: Humor events and affect in organizations. *Human Relations*, 65, 1071–1099.

Robert, C., Dunne, T. C., & Iun, J. (2015). The impact of leader humor on subordinate job satisfaction: The crucial role of leader-subordinate relationship quality. *Group and Organization Management*. Advance online publication. doi: 10.1177/1059601115598719.

Westaby, J. D. (2012). *Dynamic network theory: How social networks influence goal pursuit*. Washington, DC: American Psychological Association.

2

HUMOR AND LEADERSHIP

Cecily D. Cooper

When looking across the research on humor in organizations, the topic that has generated the most interest is the role of humor in leadership. Research generally finds that leaders who use humor elicit results such as enhanced workgroup performance (Avolio, Howell, & Sosik, 1999), creativity (O'Quin & Derks, 1997), and helping behaviors (Cooper, 2002). Humorous leaders also engender positive employee attitudes and are viewed as more effective overall by those they oversee (Priest & Swain, 2002). This small but burgeoning area of research has been summarized in a number of literature reviews (Cooper & Sosik, 2012; Duncan, Smeltzer, & Leap, 1990; Romero & Cruthirds, 2006) and some theoretical articles (Cooper, 2005, 2008; Robert & Wilbanks, 2012). The reviews consistently acknowledge the positive implications of leader humor and unanimously agree that humor is a valuable interpersonal skill for leaders. Since these reviews are current, I am not going to offer a similar review in this chapter.

Rather, I would like to take this opportunity to share some data from a qualitative study I conducted very early in my academic career. The thoughts, observations, and stories shared by participants in these interviews shaped my perspective of leader humor at that time. These insights remain relevant because research on leader humor has not progressed significantly since. For example, though we know that leader humor elicits certain positive outcomes, research has yet to test how the effects of humor are transferred (i.e. mediated) or what any boundary conditions might be. Many opportunities exist for empirical advancements and the themes from these interviews help illustrate some possible future directions. Although humor was not defined for the informants of the study reported herein, for the purpose of this chapter, *humor* will be considered as any event shared by an agent with another individual (i.e. a target) that is intended to be amusing to the target and that the target perceives as an intentional act (Cooper, 2005). In other words, this chapter focuses on interpersonal humor rather than "sense of humor" which is an individual difference (Martin & Lefcourt, 1984). This chapter has two goals. First, I will present results and insights from a qualitative study on humor and leadership which represents the foundations of my thinking on humor. Second, drawing from these insights and other observations of the literature on leader humor, I offer an agenda for future research while also acknowledging key challenges scholars must address.

Qualitative study

This study relied on 36 informants representing various types of jobs and organizations. I used Glaser and Strauss's (1967) grounded theory approach to analyze the interviews (see also Creswell, 1998). A grounded theory is one that is "inductively derived from the study of the phenomenon it represents" by using qualitative research methods in which "data collection, analysis, and theory stand in reciprocal relationship with each other" (Strauss & Corbin, 1990, p. 23). The interviews on which this study was based were from a data collection effort for a more broadly-focused study. Correspondingly, the sample is quite diverse in terms of occupation, background, and demographics.

The respondents in the sample spoke to me as a favor, or as a favor to the person who referred me, and were not necessarily interested in discussing humor. This approach was advantageous for two reasons. First, it helped control for participants' self-selecting to participate because they were strong advocates for or against workplace humor. Second, much of the data gathered was very personal and sometimes quite sensitive. Because participants knew me, personally or through a referral, I believe they were more willing to share their stories and feelings. The informants held positions in public and private organizations including a large metropolitan police department, a county school board office, a small building construction firm, a real estate agency, a large aerospace company, a small marketing consulting firm, a branch of the United States military, a large public accounting firm, a high tech startup, and others. They had been with their organizations from four months to 33 years and in their current positions from four months to 25 years.

Data collection

In accordance with a grounded theory approach, I used a semi-structured interview format. Questions were mostly open-ended. The initial questions asked, such as "Can humor be productive at work?" and "What factors determine whether humor is acceptable at work?" were broader than later questions which directly asked them about other factors relevant to humor in the workplace, such as organizational culture, power, work performance, and situational norms. Interviews lasted from 35 minutes to an hour. I recorded and transcribed all of the interviews, yielding a few hundred pages of data, and then used a qualitative data analysis package to code the data. I analyzed the interviews in three stages.

Analysis

Stage 1: Conduct and analyze the first 29 interviews

I conducted 15 initial interviews to assess the face validity of the questions. After reading these initial transcripts, I inserted an additional set of questions for subsequent interviews that were designed to prompt the subject to explicitly talk about their attraction for, and perception of, people they work with who express humor well or not. I then conducted 14 more interviews with the original questions plus these additional questions. After transcribing and coding these 29 interviews, it was apparent that the issue most important to respondents was how leaders used humor and the effects that a leader's humor can have on subordinates. Of the 29 respondents, 24 explicitly spoke about this issue. No other issue was mentioned as frequently.

Stage 2: Adapt interview questions to understand leader humor

At this point, I wanted to gather an even deeper understanding of: 1) how leaders used humor with their subordinates; 2) the various effects of this humor; and 3) the boundary conditions which were relevant to this issue. Thus, I adapted a portion of the interview schedule again to focus respondents specifically on leader humor. These new questions asked respondents to think of two managers, one who used humor well and another who used humor poorly. Then, I asked many follow-up questions prompting them to compare the two managers (e.g. "Do you consider the performance of these managers to be any different from each other?" and "Would you go out of your way to do a work-related favor for either of these people?"). I interviewed seven respondents in this stage. I stopped after seven interviews because I reached a saturation point (Creswell, 1998).

Stage 3: Analyze all 36 interviews for information relevant to leader humor

At this point, I re-coded and analyzed all of the remaining interview data. I specifically looked for information related to leaders using humor with their subordinates. The respondents discussed many such examples. Eighteen of the 36 respondents spoke about themselves in their role as leader using humor with their subordinates. Although most discussed how they try to use humor in a positive or useful way, three of these respondents also gave anecdotes of times when their humor did not seem to be well-received. In addition to these examples, respondents identified and discussed a total of 41 other leaders they worked with or had previously worked with and described how these leaders used humor and its impact on subordinates.

The descriptions and anecdotes of these 41 leaders fell into one of four categories. The humor expressed by the leader was either considered: 1) good or enjoyable in

TABLE 2.1 Examples of descriptions of leaders' humor

Good humor (18 leader descriptions fell into this category)	[He is] a pretty serious guy, but every now and then he just breaks out with something that's just really funny. It just catches you off-guard and the whole room laughs. Or it just puts a smile on your face. [His humor] is effective. (30)
	[Her humor] was quick. It was funny. It was frequent. She came up with interesting twists. (36)
	Tom's a sales manager [who is very effective in using humor]. He reports to me. And, in turn, he oversees four sales reps in the office and he's responsible for production himself. So his immediate subordinate is Mark and his counterpart on the service side is a service manager by the name of Chris. Yeah, Chris is funny, but not nearly as gregariously funny as Tom. (25)
Bad humor (15 leader descriptions fell into this category)	[Her humor is] sarcastic. It's always at somebody else's expense – "well that was well done" (sarcastic tone) . . . those kinds of things, just putting a barb in the end of it. (27)
	Well, besides [making sexual jokes] he would make jokes about Mexicans. He would just really make you uncomfortable. He's the kind of person who would make jokes and everybody was just kind of quiet afterwards. It's like I can't believe he just said that, you know. He was just clueless. He was just really crude in his jokes. (35)
No humor (7 leader descriptions fell into this category)	He has no humor at all. Really devoid. [He just doesn't use humor.] (33)
	She just doesn't tend to use [humor]. She may laugh if someone else says something funny, but she just doesn't seem as receptive to it. (30)
	She has [no humor] . . . she just doesn't have humor. [She's] not really unhappy. She just doesn't joke around. (34)

some way; 2) hurtful or inappropriate; 3) non-existent (i.e. the leader never used humor); or 4) mixed (i.e. at times the leader's humor could be either hurtful or enjoyable). Since only one of the leaders discussed represented the "mixed" category, I dropped this category from my analysis and proceeded coding with the other three leader categories: good humor, bad humor, and no humor. Examples of descriptions falling into each of these categories appear in Table 2.1. The interview data ultimately reflected the relationships outlined in Figure 2.1. In the next section, I will discuss these findings, including representative quotations from the interviews to more fully illustrate results. I differentiate the quotes from various respondents by including a number at the end of each quote that corresponds to one of the 36 interviewees.

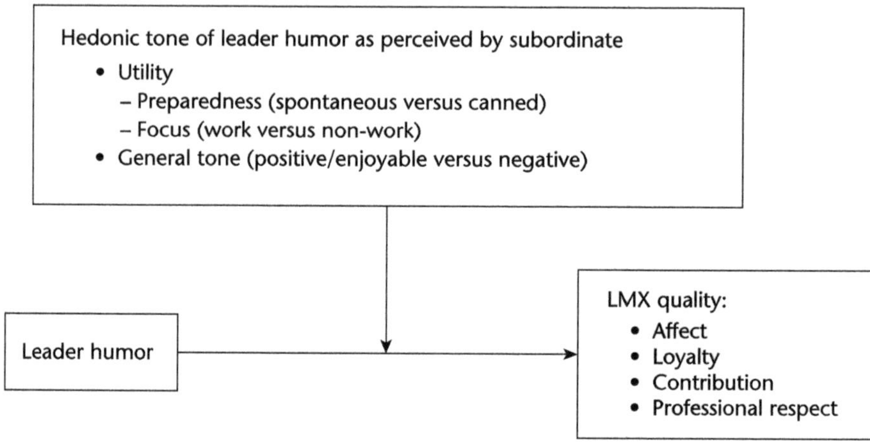

FIGURE 2.1 The moderating impact of hedonic tone on leader-member exchange (LMX) quality.

Interview themes

The humor-related issue that quickly presented itself as most relevant to the respondents in the sample dealt with humor shared between leaders and subordinates. The interviews revealed that leaders' use of humor at work influenced the establishment and maintenance of their relationships with subordinates. Many respondents stated things such as, "a manager can use [humor] to be a more effective manager." (34) One respondent who owns a small consulting firm discussed how she used humor as a management tool with her employees by saying, "I think that when management utilizes [humor] that it can increase teamwork and comfort zone and an acceptance level and all this. I just think it is unbelievably important." (8) Similarly, an individual who was recently promoted from senior accountant to manager in a large public accounting firm believed that:

> As a manager in my firm, I think [proper use of] humor becomes more important, especially in sticky situations where I'm . . . delivering some constructive criticism to an employee or subordinate . . . It kind of softens the blow of what I have to deliver to them. It just makes the environment more positive. (1)

After I began to read and code the interviews, I started to develop a framework for understanding these interpersonal dynamics involving humor, leaders, and subordinates. Since leaders and subordinates were the focus of study, I, naturally, referred to the leadership literature to inform the analysis. Although aspects of certain leadership theories corresponded to the data, there was still an inherent mismatch between most leadership theories and the respondents' stories. The mismatch stemmed from the fact that traditional leadership theories reflect an average leadership style perspective. In other words, they are based on the assumption that managers have an average leadership style that they use with all subordinates which, then, generates a general response from these subordinates.

The interview data, rather, indicated that leaders' use of humor did not elicit a similar reaction across all subordinates. Instead, it became clear from the stories of respondents that a leader's humor can have *differing* effects on each of that leader's subordinates depending upon the subordinates' appreciation of that humor. For example, an attorney recounted the following story:

> We had a meeting at the end of a large transaction . . . and one of the associates that's in a similar position to mine was given a present by one of the senior partners that he worked with and it was a leash. And everybody else at the meeting thought it was hilarious, because he was always available 24 hours a day, seven days a week to do everything he was supposed to do. And even I laughed at it, because I was hoping I wasn't the one who had to be available all that time. But he did not find the humor in it and I think found it to be quite negative. I think it probably made him look at that manager, at the senior partner quite differently after he was given that present. [The partner] was trying to be funny with it. (14)

Because of these differing effects, I began to conceptualize the consequences of leader humor at the dyadic level. I then referred back to the leadership literature to find a theory with a dyadic component and directed my attention to leader-member exchange (LMX) theory to help inform the data analysis.

LMX refers to the nature of the relationship between a leader and a subordinate characterized by varying levels of "physical or mental effort, material resources, information, and/or emotional support exchanged between the two parties" (Liden, Sparrowe, & Wayne, 1997: 48). LMX theory contends that when subordinates begin working for a particular leader they go through a period of role-development in which the leader influences their resulting role through a series of interpersonal exchanges (Graen, 1976). This informal process results in differentiated role definitions of subordinates, and, correspondingly, in varied leader-member exchanges (Dienesch & Liden, 1986). Although some leaders differed in their general propensity to express humor at work, their use of humor influenced the relationships with each of their subordinates differently. In summary, the interviews implied that leader humor plays a role in LMX quality.

Additionally, although studies investigating antecedents of LMX frequently look at the congruence in behaviors or values of the two parties (e.g. Bauer & Green, 1996; Day & Crain, 1992), the current research focuses on the use of humor by the leader and the subordinate's appreciation of this humor. Previous research demonstrates leaders have more discretion in using humor and, therefore, set the tone for whether humor expression is acceptable (Coser, 1960; Lundberg, 1969). The perspectives of respondents concurred with this research:

> [The hierarchical level of the employee matters in terms of how humor is perceived] without a shadow of a doubt . . . You look to the leader as

> being the person who has the most responsibility for the establishment and the maintenance of the . . . professional climate. (9)

> [The expression of humor] becomes a hierarchical event. In other words, you know if the person at the top doesn't express . . . humor, then the people below that don't have the guts. It would be considered inappropriate or disrespectful, if they express humor . . . If there are people who are above me, I let them handle the cues [for whether humor is acceptable]. (29)

When considering leader humor, respondents identified two aspects of leader humor as relevant factors in determining LMX quality: 1) whether the leader used humor; and 2) the hedonic tone of that humor as perceived by the subordinate.

Humor use

Humor only influenced the exchange relationship to the extent that the leader actually shared humor with the subordinate. By sharing humor with the subordinate, the leader could have a positive or negative influence, improving or degrading the relationship between the two parties. If a leader did not use humor at all or used it only infrequently, then the benefits and risks associated with humor use did not exist. One respondent who worked for an executive placement firm described a leader in his organization who did not use humor: "I think her rapport [with her subordinates] could be a lot better with humor [if she was] a little less serious all the time. I think her rapport could be a lot better." He even continued on to distinguish that this leader did not use humor badly, she "just doesn't really use it at all." He considered her lack of humor to have a different impact than a leader who used humor badly, because: "Someone who uses [humor] badly, consistently – you just don't want to be around them." (30)

Thus, the remaining analysis will focus on leaders who actually use humor with their subordinates and the implications associated with that use of humor.

Hedonic tone

Although leader humor usually improves the quality of the exchange (as I will discuss in the next section), the hedonic tone of the leader's humor, as judged by the subordinate, is a key contingency. Perceived hedonic tone (i.e. whether the subordinate finds the humor to be pleasant or unpleasant) is primarily determined by two aspects of leader humor: 1) the *utility* of the humor (i.e. whether the subordinate perceives the humor to be useful in some way); and 2) the *general tone* of the humor (i.e. whether the subordinate finds the humor positive/enjoyable or negative). To clarify, hedonic tone refers to the subordinate's reaction to the leader's general style of humor expression, not to one particular humor instance. Some instances may resonate more with the subordinate than others; however, the interviews implied the subordinate's overall opinion of whether the leader's humor is generally pleasant or unpleasant is the most important consideration.

Utility refers to whether the subordinate perceives the leader's humor as useful in a capacity related to work, for example, by decreasing conflict, releasing tension, increasing morale, or communicating a message. Respondents typically did not appreciate humor that detracted from the work process. Notably, this criterion for judging humor is unique to the workplace- respondents implied that utility did not similarly matter for assessing humor in non-work (i.e. non-task related) situations. Analysis of the interviews identified two aspects of the humor that affected subordinate perceptions of utility: 1) the *preparedness* of the humor (i.e. whether the humor was spontaneous or canned); and 2) the *focus* of the humor (i.e. whether the humor was related to work or non-work issues).

When considering the preparedness of the humor, interviewees indicated that spontaneous, not canned, humor was the type most frequently used and most appreciated at work. Of the 36 respondents, 15 spoke about canned humor at work. Of these 15 respondents, 12 said they did not like canned humor at work: nine of them believed that canned humor had more risk of being offensive than spontaneous humor, whereas, the other three respondents simply thought sharing canned humor at work was a "waste of time." These respondents thought that canned humor was not as acceptable in the workplace, compared to non-work environments, because it either detracted from the work process or the work environment. Of the three respondents that liked canned humor at work, two mentioned it could be useful in presentations, and one said practical jokes were the norm where he works but only when work is "slow." Therefore, even in the case of these three respondents, they appreciated canned humor but only to the extent that it served a purpose at work. Given this information, it seems that, other aspects of leader humor being equal (i.e. focus and general tone), subordinates appreciate spontaneous humor at work more so than canned humor. Infrequent use of canned humor by leaders may be acceptable, but should be employed with discretion.

The second characteristic of humor that influenced subordinates' perceptions of utility was focus. The majority of humor that respondents discussed in the interviews was work-related, concerning either the task at hand, interpersonal dynamics in the office, or the like. When at work, respondents appreciated this work-related humor to a greater extent than humor that was not related to work. 18 of the 36 respondents spoke about their preferences for work-related versus non-work related humor. Of these 18, 11 mentioned that the majority of humor at work is about work. These 11 individuals also believed that humor not related to the work situation had more risk of being offensive. Of the seven respondents that thought non-work humor at work was okay: one was referring to the use of imitations (of television characters) at work, two were referring to humor about sports or politics, and only four believed that humor about very personal topics (e.g. family, dating, etc.) was okay. Yet, even these four respondents stipulated that this humor occurred with people at work whom they were very close to personally.

The previous two humor characteristics, level of preparedness and focus, appear to generalize across subordinates. More specifically, the responses implied that subordinates generally appreciate spontaneous humor more so than canned humor and work-related humor more so than humor not related to work, all other things being equal. The third factor, however, general tone, is the characteristic likely to exhibit the most variability across subordinates, because it reflects the subordinates' appreciation of the leader's humor (this will be illustrated in the next section). For any given leader, subordinates of that leader may react to the leader's humor idiosyncratically. In other words, a leader can express humor that one or more of the subordinates thinks is enjoyable, but may be simultaneously offensive to others.

One additional clarification regarding hedonic tone is noteworthy. Although humor can exist in various forms including sarcasm, practical jokes, teasing, etc. (see Berger (1976) for a typology) regardless of form, hedonic tone appeared to be the only characterization of humor that generalized across respondents. Reaction to a leader's humor was not determined by the humor type (e.g. practical jokes, teasing) but the three dimensions of hedonic tone presented earlier.

The irrelevance of humor types was most obvious when some of the respondents discussed examples of sarcasm at work. Many of the interviewees, generally, did not like the use of sarcasm and described instances of negative reactions to its use. For example, one respondent gave a second-hand account of a leader using sarcasm when telling a subordinate about a raise the subordinate had been awarded:

> instead of trying to relay the message in a positive way, he fouled up . . . Why would you make some sort of sarcastic comment like that versus . . . giving him some positive feedback to make . . . the associate or employee feel like they had earned it?" (21)

Alternatively, some respondents seemed to enjoy sarcasm as a form of humor and openly discussed that they would use sarcasm and appreciated sarcasm used by leaders. One landscape architect mentioned that sarcasm was a common and acceptable form of humor at work that decreased the social distance created by hierarchy in his organization, "We're all really sarcastic with each other. I throw jokes at the owner of the company. He throws them back at me. It's a really loose, light, young, vibrant sort of atmosphere." (22)

Stated simply, humor type was not a clear determinant of the appreciation of humor expressed by leaders. As illustrated by the previous examples, leaders could express any kind of humor, even deprecating or sarcastic humor, and elicit a positive reaction in certain circumstances. This insight is consistent with research on humor in groups which observed that a group of Canadian police officers used putdown humor to become a more cohesive unit (Terrion & Ashforth, 2002). Although the putdown humor might be perceived as aggressive by outsiders, to the officers this humor signaled growing trust and solidarity. In summary, perceived hedonic tone, rather than humor type, appears to be a key moderating factor.

Humor and LMX

Respondents described many different ways in which leader humor could influence exchange quality. Although some scholars view LMX as unidimensional (Graen,

Novak, & Sommerkamp, 1982), others conceptualize LMX as being multidimensional (Dienesch & Liden, 1986), including the dimensions of affect, loyalty, contribution, and professional respect (Liden & Maslyn, 1998). The diverse range of comments from the interviews seemed to be consistent with the multidimensional perspective and closely mapped onto the four dimensions proposed by Liden and Maslyn (1998). Thus, this four-dimensional framework was adopted for analysis as I iteratively shifted between data and extant theory. Next, I describe each of the four exchange dimensions and offer examples of humor varying in hedonic tone influencing these dimensions.

Affect and loyalty

Respondents most frequently mentioned the impact of leader humor in terms of its influence on the affective component of the relationship. The affect dimension is defined as "the mutual affection members of the dyad have for each other based primarily on interpersonal attraction rather than work or professional values" (Dienesch & Liden, 1986, p. 625). As mentioned previously, respondents discussed a total of 18 managers in the "good humor" category and 15 managers in the "bad humor" category. For each of these 33 examples, respondents noted some sort of affective reaction to that person (i.e. that they liked/disliked them, enjoyed being around them or not, found them to be offensive, etc.). This suggests that if the subordinates enjoy the humor, then it can increase their liking for the leader and extend the relationship beyond a working relationship to a more personal level. However, to the extent that a subordinate finds a leader's humor hurtful or unpleasant, even if the humor in question is not focused towards that particular subordinate, it can destroy or prevent the creation of any personal bonds between the two.

Individuals who appreciated their leader's humor discussed how the leader's use of humor made them feel they had a relationship that extended beyond a simple working relationship. An account manager for an entertainment management firm described her experience:

> When my boss jokes around with me, it makes me feel more comfortable around him . . . It makes me feel like it's not all serious and not all business all the time [and] that we've got a relationship beyond the factual day to day business . . . that we have to do. I definitely think it's beneficial. (12)

Respondents felt that humor could bring "the professional level of communication to a personal level of communication." Leaders show the "human" side of themselves when they express humor, enabling subordinates to relate to them more readily. One human resources manager related her experience:

> If the general manager, which is the highest position you can have here, is goofing off and wears funny looking clothes and he's doing that to be humorous, it makes him seem more like a person – more like me . . . more

> like us and not on a pedestal. So I think [humor] definitely plays a very important role. (20)

Similarly, a former vice-president of a large textile manufacturing company believed that by using humor leaders could prevent their subordinates from "fearing" or being intimidated by them because of their position in the organization's hierarchy. He lamented, "If you have humor in the workplace, there's less fear – less fear of the things you do [your work] not being accepted by the organization or the boss. And if there's less fear, there's more productivity." (5)

Conversely, if the leader used humor in a way that was negative or unpleasant, then personal bonds were injured. A high-level civilian employee in the United States military described some problems he saw occur because one of his reports consistently used very negative humor with his subordinates:

> He's one of those people that is very rye in his humor and so it doesn't come across well. And he uses it, I think, as a crutch when being very aggressive doesn't work. He's not being effective, so he resorts to humor as a way to alleviate the situation. But it's beyond salvage and the humor doesn't come across at all . . . [His subordinates] absolutely detest him. (28)

Moreover, negative humor by leaders also affected third-party bystanders. If a leader used humor that was hurtful towards a specific subordinate, this tended to elicit negative feelings from other subordinates who observed the interaction. A former political campaign staff member described his experience:

> If a [campaign] supervisor or a candidate rips you a new one and not just calls you on whatever misdeed you did, but starts to attack your personality or who you are with some bad humor or a side crack, I think that can affect a lot of people – not just the person involved and the supervisor, but probably anyone who witnessed it. (13)

Leader humor also affected the exchange relationship by influencing the amount of loyalty the subordinate felt for the leader. In the LMX literature, loyalty is described as "the expression of public support for the goals and the personal character of the other member of the LMX dyad" (Dienesch & Liden, 1986, p. 625). A leader in a large aerospace company described another leader he worked with who was very effective at using humor and noted that her subordinates were so loyal they followed her whenever she changed departments. The company had placed this leader in a fast-track program in which she had to rotate departments every year and a half. At the end of each position term, her staff would voluntarily follow her to her next appointment. (36)

Leader humor, however, is detrimental to subordinate loyalty if the humor is perceived as negative in tone. A leader in a professional printing company offered a comparative example when he described the loyalty he and his co-workers felt towards two higher level leaders in his organization, one who tended to use humor negatively and the other who used it more positively. The respondent began by describing the humor of the first leader as "very rough . . . almost to the point of abusive . . . so that kind of pushes people away." By contrast, the respondent described the second leader as "more approachable and the humor part of it plays into [him being more approachable]." These leaders oversaw the same set of subordinates, however, the respondent noted that his co-workers felt "much more loyalty" towards the leader who used positive humor. (32)

A business school administrator described problems that arose in one student service department that stemmed from that department head's negative use of humor. He described her humor as "sarcastic . . . and always at someone else's expense" and believed that her use of this humor was a barrier to creating a positive work environment within that department. He believed that positive humor in the workplace was essential to creating a sense of "sharedness" and commented on the lack of loyalty in that particular department compared to others, "There is no loyalty, because there is no real sharing." (27) Another respondent who worked for a small Internet start-up also contended that negative leader humor could affect the loyalty of multiple members: "If a manager, and I'm thinking of multiple organizations I've been involved with, uses humor as a way of belittling an employee or another member of the staff in front of others, I think that's a dangerous loyalty-crusher." (13)

As the previous examples illustrate, a leader's humor drives members' liking of, and loyalty towards, that leader, positively or negatively, thus affecting the quality of the exchange relationship. Upon this discovery, I made the connection between the themes from the interviews and the multidimensional conceptualization of LMX that includes contribution and professional respect in addition to affect and loyalty (Dienesch & Liden, 1986; Liden & Maslyn, 1998). I will continue with a discussion of interview themes related to these final two dimensions.

Professional respect and contribution

Some of the original work on LMX (Dienesch & Liden, 1986) identified the dimension of contribution, which is the perception of each of the exchange members of the amount of work-oriented activity put forth by the other. More recent work on LMX discovered the fourth dimension, professional respect, which is the perception of the degree to which each member of the dyad has built a reputation within and/or outside the organization of excelling at his or her line of work (Liden & Maslyn, 1998). I relied on these definitions as I analyzed the interviews from the perspective of the subordinate and how they perceived the leader's work activity and professional reputation.

In total, 13 respondents were asked to explicitly compare the contributions of leaders who differed in their ability to use humor. Of these respondents, ten stated that each type of individual was very capable of fulfilling the requirements of their own job (i.e. as engineer, architect, lawyer, etc.). In fact, most of the leaders being compared were characterized as "high-achievers" or "excellent performers" regardless of their ability to use humor, implying that these leaders were all valued contributors. The following two quotes are representative:

> Both of them are efficient at what they do. Both of them are very effective at getting work done. (29)

> They're both stellar in everything that they do. They go about things in different ways but they get the job done very effectively. They are probably two of the better hires the company has done. (22)

Only two of these 13 respondents thought that the leader who was more effective at using humor was also more effective in their job, overall. Differences in performance between the two types of leader arose, however, when respondents reflected upon their ability to manage people. Leaders who were skillful at using humor were always categorized as better leaders than those not skillful in this area. Eight respondents commented as such. These two quotes are representative:

> The individual performance [of these two leaders] is the same, but when you look at their departments all of a sudden you see that one person's department is happier than the other. (29)

> They're both good performers. But [the leader who is effective at using humor] is better, [because] he's a better manager. He's better with people. He's got better leadership skills and things like that. (35)

As for comparisons regarding professional respect, since respondents tended to believe that both types of leaders were as effective in the non-managerial aspects of their jobs, they believed that those leaders' subordinates respected them on a professional basis. Only one respondent believed that the leader who was ineffective at using humor was not as respected by his subordinates, because his humor was offensive.

My ability to infer themes related to contribution and professional respect was somewhat limited because of fewer comments on these issues. However, I tentatively conclude that leader humor, when perceived as positive in tone, may be able to benefit perceptions of the leader's work-related contributions and the degree to which they are respected professionally. Moreover, these inferences are consistent with previous discussions of humor as an important leadership tool (Bass, 1990; Crawford, 1994) and empirical findings that leaders who use humor receive higher performance ratings (Avolio et al., 1999).

Discussion

The interviews offered two critical insights into leader humor. First, each subordinate might interpret and appreciate a given leader's humor differently, thus leading to varying effects of humor. In other words, leader humor appeared to be more accurately portrayed by a dyadic rather than an average leadership style perspective, leading me to the LMX literature (Graen & Uhl-Bien, 1995). Further support for the utility of the LMX paradigm was apparent when respondents spoke explicitly about issues related to the four LMX dimensions as a response to open-ended (rather than leading) questions. In generating this observation, the interviews also implied that humor represents an important, yet unacknowledged, antecedent of LMX quality (Gerstner & Day, 1997).

Second, the stories describing positive versus negative humor were useful for identifying a key contingency of leader humor, hedonic tone. Hedonic tone, whether the subordinate finds the humor to be pleasant or unpleasant, was the factor driving subordinates to have divergent reactions to the humor of a particular leader, and influencing the quality of dyadic exchanges. Hedonic tone was determined by three aspects of leader humor: level of preparedness, focus, and general tone, with general tone exhibiting the most variability. For preparedness, spontaneous (e.g. good-natured teasing, spontaneous joking, etc.) rather than canned humor, was viewed more positively for leaders in work environments. Subordinates had a greater appreciation for spontaneous humor at work, because they perceived it to be more relevant to the immediate work situation. When interviewees discussed canned jokes at work, they deemed this type of humor as more distracting or frivolous. It seemed that even if canned humor was work-related, spontaneous work-related humor was still more effective.

Regarding focus, interviews indicated that subordinates had a greater appreciation for their leader's humor if that humor was work-related rather than unrelated to the work situation. The reasons offered were similar to those for humor preparedness: humor that was unrelated to the work situation was, generally, less functional. On the whole, respondents perceived much of the humor occurring at work and much of the humor produced by their leaders to be functional for their work in some way or another, by relieving stress, helping to build relationships, and the like. The final aspect of hedonic tone, general tone, exhibited the most variability and served as the primary factor determining subordinate perceptions of hedonic tone. Even if the leader expressed humor which was negative or degrading in some way, if the subordinate found this amusing, then *for them* the general tone was positive.

These two insights, which are summarized in Figure 2.1 as a testable model, are useful for advancing research on leader humor. In particular, linking leader humor to the LMX paradigm: 1) provides humor scholars with a valid and widely-accepted theoretical framework to inform their research on leader humor; and 2) offers guidance regarding how levels of analysis should be treated in research design and data analysis. The concept of hedonic tone is also quite useful, in that it directs attention away from efforts to identify and measure specific types of humor (e.g. sarcasm, teasing), which are likely to lead to inconsistent or misleading results, and towards measuring more general attributes of and reactions to humor.

Future research and key challenges

I was inspired to research humor after reading the article by Avolio and colleagues (1999) that found humor moderated the effects of different leadership styles on workgroup performance and ratings of leader effectiveness. Notably, this article by Avolio and colleagues (1999) as well as other empirical and theoretical work on leader humor (Dubinsky, Yammarino, & Jolson, 1995; Holmes & Marra, 2006; Malone, 1980) adopts an 'average leadership style' approach in researching humor. In other words, these scholars implicitly treat humor as an aspect of the leader that is relatively constant in its influence across members of the workgroup. Conceptualizing leader humor as a primarily dyadic phenomenon, as I have done here, stands in contrast to this approach. Attending to levels of analysis issues will be critical to the advancement of humor research (Sosik, 2012). Empirical research will need to compare the relative utility of these two approaches or identify conditions in which one is a more accurate description than the other.

Additionally, if support is found for the viability of the dyadic perspective, then characteristics of both dyad members will need to be considered by scholars studying leader humor. In other words, since the LMX approach emphasizes that subordinates influence relationship quality, this will imply the need to focus on the role of both parties, not just the leader, in generating the humor relationship and its effects. Investigating the role subordinates play in determining leader humor's effectiveness will necessitate collecting leader ratings of subordinates in terms of how often the subordinates use humor and whether it is appreciated by the leader. Assessing both leader and subordinate humor will allow researchers to empirically test which seems to be a more robust predictor of LMX quality as rated by either member of the dyad. If results clearly indicate that some leader-subordinate dyads develop better joking relationships, other studies can try to discern what facilitates this development. For example, personality similarity on certain dimensions such as extraversion or agreeableness might allow two people to share humor more readily and easily in a relationship. Similar capacities for self-monitoring and emotional intelligence might also play a role (Robert & Wilbanks, 2012).

Aside from addressing the levels of analysis question mentioned above, research on leader humor could benefit from many more empirical studies on any of a variety of topics, including linking humor to outcomes, developing humor measures, and investigating contingencies of humor's effectiveness. Currently, the literature on humor in organizations related to leadership appears to contain a high ratio of theoretical and conceptual writings (e.g. Cooper 2005, 2008; Cooper & Sosik, 2012; Robert & Wilbanks, 2012) compared to empirical ones (e.g. Avolio et al., 1999; Priest & Swain, 2002; Robert, Dunne, & Iun, 2015). An attempt to summarize only the existing empirical studies, perhaps in a meta-analysis if enough studies are available, would certainly be a valuable contribution. This type of summary would help scholars identify where there are voids of empirical research. Though Mesmer-Magnus and Glew (2012) offer a meta-analysis of 'positive humor in the workplace,' this review was not focused on leader humor and also confounded humor as a behavior (i.e. the focus of this chapter) with "sense of humor" in the analysis.

Scholars could also test some of the ideas put forth in the myriad of conceptual papers which have yet to be tested. Cooper (2008), for example, proposed a number of underlying processes (i.e. mediators) through which humor can transmit effects, but these ideas have not been empirically verified. The lack of attention given to testing theoretical ideas is unfortunate, particularly since, to date, very little is still known about what processes transmit the effects of leader humor. Of course, in this case I must assume some responsibility for not following through to test my own ideas – but it would also be disingenuous not to acknowledge this shortcoming! One exception is a study by Robert and colleagues (2015) that empirically tested whether LMX mediates the relationship between leader humor and employee job satisfaction. Though they did not find support for mediation, which contrasts with what I propose in this chapter, this study offers a good starting point to examine relevant contingencies. For example, Robert and colleagues (2015) used a self-report humor scale for leaders but asked leaders about their humor style, in general, rather than with each specific subordinate. Future research might need to collect each measure as a dyad-specific measure (e.g. the leader reports how they use humor with each subordinate).

One key challenge in conducting empirical research is the lack of a widely-accepted validated measure of leader humor. Clearly, careful scale development initiatives to create a measure that can be used in the study of leader humor would be a worthy contribution. Alternatively, I encourage researchers who are not interested in scale development to use a scale already existing in the literature. For example, scholars can refer to the scale used by Avolio and colleagues (1999) for a measure of leader positive humor, or research by Cooper (2002; Cooper & Kong, 2014) for a more general leader humor scale. Since there is no commonly accepted "theory of humor" which may be used across contexts, another hurdle is framing humor research so that it may be published in our theory-driven management journals. One approach would be to guide and frame research on leader humor using an existing leadership theory. Though Bass's full-range leadership model has been used previously (Avolio et al., 1999), the current study implies that LMX theory might be very useful as well for the study of leader humor.

Conclusion

In conclusion, the goal of this chapter was to share insights gained from an interview study I conducted when first embarking into humor research. These insights led me to recognize that leader humor might be most appropriately viewed as a dyadic phenomenon and, if so, the potential that LMX theory has to serve as a theoretical foundation for this topic. The interviews also caused me to develop a healthy skepticism of the value of considering humor types (e.g. sarcasm, self-deprecation, puns) for research on humor in organizations. This skepticism was further encouraged by reading Terrion and Ashforth's (2002) description of Canadian police officers valuing putdown humor and using putdowns to become a more cohesive unit. I encourage scholars to proceed with research on leader humor but with these two caveats in mind. In general, though scholars and practitioners seem to be interested in the topic of leader humor, academic research in this area has been published only intermittently and empirical studies are scant. Building a base of empirical research on leader humor, particularly linking leader humor to key organizational outcomes, is the most important area to initially emphasize. Demonstrating relationships between leader humor and objective outcomes will address the "so what?" question with academics and concurrently bolster the business case for humor with practicing managers.

References

Avolio, B. J., Howell, J. M., & Sosik, J. J. (1999). A funny thing happened on the way to the bottom line: Humor as a moderator of leadership style effects. *Academy of Management Journal*, 42, 219–227.

Bass, B. M. (1990). From transactional to transformational leadership: Learning to share the vision. *Organizational Dynamics*, 18, 19–31.

Bauer, T. N., & Green, S. G. (1996). Development of leader-member exchange: A longitudinal test. *Academy of Management Journal*, 39, 1538–1567.

Berger, A. A. (1976). Anatomy of a joke. *Journal of Communication*, 26, 113–115.

Cooper, C. D. (2002). *No laughing matter: The impact of supervisor humor on leader-member exchange (LMX) quality*. Doctoral dissertation, University of Southern California, Los Angeles.

Cooper, C. D. (2005). Just joking around? Employee humor expression as an ingratiatory behavior. *Academy of Management Review*, 30, 765–776.

Cooper, C. D. (2008). Elucidating the bonds of workplace humor: A relational process model. *Human Relations*, 61, 1087–1115.

Cooper, C. D., & Kong, D. J. (2014). *A field study of leader humor and leader-member exchange quality*. Paper presented at the annual meeting of the Society for Industrial-Organizational Psychology, Honolulu.

Cooper, C. D., & Sosik, J. J. (2012). The laughter advantage: Cultivating high quality connections and workplace outcomes through humor. In G. M. Spreitzer, & K. Cameron (Eds.), *The handbook of positive organizational scholarship* (pp. 474–489). New York: Oxford University Press.

Coser, R. L. (1960). Laughter among colleagues: A study of the social functions of humor among the staff of a mental hospital. *Psychiatry*, 23, 81–95.

Crawford, C. B. (1994). Theory and implications regarding the utilization of strategic humor by leaders. *The Journal of Leadership Studies*, 1, 53–68.

Creswell, J. W. (1998). *Qualitative inquiry and research design: Choosing among five traditions.* Thousand Oaks, CA: Sage Publications.

Day, D. V., & Crain, E. C. (1992). The role of affect and ability in initial exchange quality perceptions. *Group and Organization Management*, 17, 380–397.

Dienesch, R. M., & Liden, R. C. (1986). Leader-member exchange model of leadership: A critique and further development. *Academy of Management Review*, 11, 618–634.

Dubinsky, A. J., Yammarino, F. J., & Jolson, M. A. (1995). An examination of linkages between personality characteristics and dimensions of transformational leadership. *Journal of Business and Psychology*, 9, 315–335.

Duncan, W. J., Smeltzer, L. R., & Leap, T. L. (1990). Humor and work: Applications of joking behavior to management. *Journal of Management*, 16, 255–278.

Gerstner, C. R., & Day, D. V. (1997). Meta-analytic review of leader-member exchange theory: Correlates and construct issues. *Journal of Applied Psychology*, 82, 827–844.

Glaser, B. G., & Strauss, A. L. (1967). *Discovery of grounded theory: Strategies for qualitative research*. Chicago, IL: Aldine.

Graen, G. B. (1976). Role-making processes within complex organizations. In M. D. Dunnette (Ed.), *Handbook of industrial and organizational psychology* (pp. 1201–1245). Chicago, IL: Rand McNally.

Graen, G. B., & Uhl-Bien, M. (1995). Relationship-based approach to leadership: Development of leader-member exchange (LMX) theory of leadership over 25 years: Applying a multi-level multi-domain perspective. *The Leadership Quarterly*, 6, 219–247.

Graen, G. B., Novak, M., & Sommerkamp, P. (1982). The effects of leader-member exchange and job design on productivity and job satisfaction: Testing a dual attachment model. *Organizational Behavior and Human Performance*, 30, 109–131.

Holmes, J., & Marra, M. (2006). Humor and leadership style. *Humor: International Journal of Humor Research*, 19, 119–138.

Liden, R. C., & Maslyn, J. M. (1998). Multidimensionality of leader-member exchange: An empirical assessment through scale development. *Journal of Management*, 24, 43–72.

Liden, R. C., Sparrowe, R. T., & Wayne, S. J. (1997). Leader-member exchange theory: The past and potential for the future. In G. R. Ferris (Ed.), *Research in personnel and human resources management*, vol. 15 (pp. 47–119). Greenwich, CT: JAI Press.

Lundberg, C. C. (1969). Person-focused joking: Pattern and function. *Human Organization*, 28, 22–28.

Malone, P. B. (1980). Humor: A double-edged tool for today's managers? *Academy of Management Review*, 5, 357–360.

Martin, R. A., & Lefcourt, H. M. (1984). Situational humor response questionnaire: Quantitative measure of sense of humor. *Journal of Personality and Social Psychology*, 47, 145–155.

Mesmer-Magnus, J., Glew, D. J., & Viswesvaran, C. (2012). A meta-analysis of positive humor in the workplace. *Journal of Managerial Psychology*, 27(2), 155–190.

O'Quin, K., & Derks, P. (1997). Humor and creativity: A review of the empirical literature. In M. A. Runco (Ed.), *The creativity research handbook* (pp. 227–256). Cresskill, NJ: Hampton Press.

Priest, R. F., & Swain, J. E. (2002). Humor and its implications for leadership effectiveness. *Humor: International Journal of Humor Research*, 15, 169–189.

Robert, C., & Wilbanks, J. E. (2012). The wheel model of humor: Humor events and affect in organizations. *Human Relations*, 65, 1071–1099.

Robert, C., Dunne, T. C., & Iun, J. (2015). The impact of leader humor on subordinate job satisfaction: The crucial role of leader-subordinate relationship quality. *Group and Organization Management*. Advance online publication. doi:10.1177/1059601115598719.

Romero, E. J., & Cruthirds, K. W. (2006). The use of humor in the workplace. *Academy of Management Perspectives*, 20, 58–69.

Sosik, J. J. (2012). Taking levels of analysis in humor more seriously: Comment on Romero and Arendt. *Psychological Reports*, 110, 527–534.

Strauss, A., & Corbin, J. (1990). *Basics of qualitative research: Grounded theory procedures and techniques*. Newbury Park, CA: Sage Publications.

Terrion, J. L., & Ashforth, B. E. (2002). From 'I' to 'we': The role of putdown humor and identity in the development of a temporary group. *Human Relations*, 55, 55–88.

3

HUMOR AND PERSON PERCEPTION

Lisa M. Finkelstein, Cynthia A. Cerrentano, and Elora C. Voyles

Think about the last time you met someone who was really funny. Chances are you had fun during that encounter, and probably would say you liked that person – but what else did you think of her? What role did labeling her as *humorous* play in determining the other qualities that you think she has, as well as how you expect her to behave in the future? If you met her at work, will this quality of funniness also impact your work-relevant impressions? In other words, is there a "halo of humor" whereby the characteristic of being "funny" becomes associated with a network of work-related characteristics (Cerrentano & Finkelstein, 2009)?

In this chapter, we explore these questions through the lens of social psychological person-perception research. We focus specifically on how we perceive those who are funny, as well as those who are not. Initial impressions have the potential to shape our workplace judgments of and subsequent relationships with others. After all, Uleman and Kressel (2013) observe that "impression formation is about everything in social psychology," (p. 63), and we argue that this logic could be extended to "everything" at work, including judging new applicants, clients, bosses, and teammates. Our goal here is not to focus on the processes by which humor itself impacts the workplace, but rather to shed light on how applying the label of *funny* or *humorous* to the people we encounter in the workplace colors our judgment of them and, importantly, why.

The ability to form quick impressions and to store person-relevant information are both essential tools, and had the human brain not developed these fundamental processes, our abilities to function in the social sphere would be severely hampered. The drive to understand those around us, though universal, is likely to increase in circumstances when those people may impact us in some way, making person-perception of particular importance in the workplace.

We begin with a description of some classic impression formation work and present some of our own humor research that was inspired by that approach.

We expand the focus to a host of other approaches to person perception, and consider how *humorous* as a person descriptor could function in the workplace through those lenses. Although we hope you actually read the whole chapter, we'll give you the punchline now: it is likely that perceptions of someone as "humorous" (or not) are associated with a host of other perceptions, yet little humor research has considered these perspectives. If you are looking for some solid grounding for some new humor research, you are in luck – we discuss several new avenues for research on humor and person perception in a workplace context.

Impression formation and the halo of humor

Asch's (1946) work on impression formation explained that certain halo traits (*warm* and *cold*) were central to our understanding of people, so much so that those two traits cast a halo around a separate set of traits. Cerrentano and Finkelstein (2009) suggested that humor may function in a similar fashion, and use the phrase "the halo of humor" to describe the phenomenon that once we perceive a target to be humorous, it colors our view of that person's traits and behaviors.

In a four-part study replicating and extending Asch's original work, Cerrentano and Finkelstein (2009) asked participants to rate targets on a favorability index who were said to be *intelligent, skillful, industrious,* ________, *determined, practical, cautious* (Asch's original words) and either *humorous, serious,* or *humorless* as the key missing descriptor. The authors' second study embedded the key words in series of leadership traits. Both studies found that humorous targets were viewed more favorably than humorless ones. Humorous leaders may be given the benefit of the doubt due to the halo of humor whereas humorless leaders are likely to be judged more harshly – even when all other factors remain equal.

Cerrentano and Finkelstein's third study moved further into the work realm with a consideration of the moderating impact of job performance. In a 2 (humor style: humorous or serious) x 3 (performance: good, ambiguous, poor) between-subjects design, participants rated fictional supervisors on liking and respect. Humorous supervisors were liked and respected at significantly higher rates than their serious counterparts. Additionally, good performers were given the most respect, followed by ambiguous and then poor performers. Even poor performing humorous leaders were liked more than good performing serious leaders.

In their final study, Cerrentano and Finkelstein (2009) examined how the halo of humor might impact memory about traits and behaviors through schema theory. Schema theory asserts that individuals have generic mental frameworks that allow people to understand concepts similarly. In the same way that people are likely to conjure up a similar mental image if we say "librarian," so too are we likely to share a sense of what it means to be "funny," "serious," and "humorless." Schemas can work in two different ways. First, they might allow a person to forget information that is not congruent with their mental framework (e.g. forget the time when your humorous co-worker snapped at you for spilling coffee on him). In contrast, the *schema copy plus tag model* (Graesser & Nakamura, 1982) asserts that we might pay special attention to schema *incongruent* information (e.g. remember that your co-worker is generally funny *and* recall that he snapped when you spilled coffee).

To test these two competing theories, participants were given a short description about a target who was either humorous or serious and told three things about that target individual – one of which was schema congruent (e.g. he watches Comedy Central), one which was schema incongruent (e.g. he rarely tells jokes), and one of which was unrelated (e.g. he likes the color yellow). Participants were given a surprise recall task to see what they remembered about the target. For humorous targets, humorous actions were recalled significantly more often than both serious and unrelated actions supporting a schema-based model for recalling information about humorous individuals. For serious targets, a different pattern emerged where participants were equally likely to recall serious and humorous actions.

The cognitive assertions we make about an individual may depend on whether or not he or she is humorous or serious. Serious and humorous employees who exhibit similar patterns of performance may be judged differently in a variety of contexts – performance appraisals, promotion, downsizing, selection, team interactions, etc. – based on their sense of humor (or lack thereof) rather than the quality of their work. Due to the halo of humor, we may ascribe a host of positive traits to employees (and even supervisors) as humor casts a halo around that individual's other traits.

Theoretical perspectives on person perception applied to humor

Our initial investigation described above inspired us to dive into the social perception literature to explore other explanations for this apparent halo, and to consider moderators of its occurrence. In this section, we present a host of person perception theories, provide a synopsis of each theoretical framework, and describe how each has been/could be applied to help us better understand how we view funny people at work.

Implicit personality theories and spontaneous trait inferences

The essence of the implicit personality theories (IPT) (Schneider, 1973) is that people develop their own idiosyncratic theories of what qualities go together in people, but because these theories develop over time and experiences within shared contexts (e.g. co-workers have similar experiences with leaders), this gives rise to the typical commonalities that exist across perceivers' theories. Decades of research have been devoted to examining what traits are connected, how they are connected, and how amenable they are to change in the light of inconsistent information. This literature is extensive, and we highlight just a few components that may prove relevant for our focus on *humorous* as a key person descriptor in the workplace.

First, debate has focused on whether people make connections among traits based on their descriptive similarity or on evaluative similarity. Descriptive similarity means that trait words have similar meanings (e.g. kind and nice). Evaluative similarity means that trait words elicit similar evaluative reactions (e.g. they are both good or both bad traits), even if the words have distinctive meanings (e.g. kind and interesting). There is some support for both sources of trait interrelations rather than the sheer predominance of one over the other (Van Der Pligt & Taylor, 1984).

Other investigations have aimed to sort out whether trait connections just covary or if they are causally related (Sedikedes & Anderson, 1994). Using cluster analysis, for example, Sedikedes and Anderson have shown that people include some traits that differ substantially in meaning and linguistic similarity from others within the same cluster. They found evidence that in these cases the non-similar traits appearing in the same prototype might be strongly connected through causal links. This is important, because if our implicit theories of personality include causal explanations (e.g. being mean causes you to be selfish) as opposed to mere covariance explanations (e.g. people who are mean are often also selfish), the connection is likely to be more lasting and salient.

Some newer research has also suggested that even if trait connections are not causal, they may be unidirectional (e.g. selfish people tend to be mean; mean people are not necessarily selfish) (Orehek, Dechesne, Fishback, Kruglanski, & Chun, 2010). The particular direction may differ depending on a person's beliefs about the meaning of those traits. Or, if trait associations are activated early in the relationship, they may impact what characteristics we subsequently notice, store, and retrieve. If some traits are thought to be causally related we might struggle more with evidence that one exists without the other within a person. Tendencies toward confirmation bias may lead us to even try to seek out a third factor that allows us to create conjunctions between newly discovered information (Siebler, 2008) to create a more coherent image.

A related body of work has focused specifically on the spontaneous nature of the inferences we make about the traits of a target when we learn information about that target's behavior. Skowronski, Carlston, and Hartnett (2008) recount that there had been a strong belief in social psychology that impressions were formed about people when there was motivation to exert cognitive effort. However, Carlston and Skowronski (1994) demonstrated consistently that even under conditions with no impression-formation goals, traits are spontaneously inferred from behaviors, and often without the conscious recognition of the perceiver; these are referred to as spontaneous trait inferences (STIs).

From this brief overview it becomes clear that IPT-based explanations for person-perception are more complex than they may first appear and provide some interesting perspectives for examining how *humorous* as a trait descriptor may factor into impressions of people at work. Below we provide examples of the small body of work that have either directly considered an IPT approach using *humor* as a descriptor or have implicated such a connection.

IPT and humor research

Some humor research has directly examined how the trait *humorous* connects with ratings of other personality characteristics, in essence taking an IPT approach. For example, Thorson, Powell, Sarmany-Schuller, and Hampes (1997) review a series of studies that have looked at how personality correlates with their self-report *multidimensional sense of humor* scale, finding that one's self-perception as *funny* correlates positively with extraversion, assertiveness, gregariousness, and dominance, and negatively with such things as neuroticism, order, deference, and pessimism. Similarly, Beins and O'Toole (2010) found that people with a high or medium self-reported sense of humor perceived themselves to be higher on extraversion and openness than their low sense of humor counterparts. Turning from self to other ratings, Cann and Calhoun (2001) had participants rate targets who were "below average," "typical," or "well above average" in sense of humor on a series of traits. Those deemed to have a "well above average" sense of humor were rated higher on desirable terms (friendly, pleasant, perceptive, extraverted, agreeable) and lower on undesirable terms (complaining, cold, spiteful). Below average targets were rated as being higher on neuroticism and conscientiousness. Beins and O'Toole (2010) asserted that "people hold implicit theories of the link between humor and personality and apply it reliably to both themselves and to others" (p. 267).

Based on this research, one might assume that the halo of humor, driven by IPT, only involves positively-valenced attributes. To the contrary, three studies, similar in nature (Cann & Matson, 2014; Kuiper & Leite, 2010; Zeigler-Hill, Besser, & Jett, 2013), addressed perceptions of humorous targets who varied in their humor styles. Targets who used adaptive (affiliative/self-enhancing) humor were seen as friendlier, more pleasant, considerate, interesting, and creative, while those targets who used maladaptive (aggressive/self-defeating) humor were rated as more introverted, cold, spiteful, and likely to complain. This aligns with previous research that suggests that self-defeating and aggressive humor is associated with neuroticism, disagreeableness (Vernon, Martin, Schermer, & Mackie, 2008), psychopathy, and Machiavellianism (Veselka, Schermer, Martin, & Vernon, 2010) and lower levels of social competence (Yip & Martin, 2006). Kuiper and Leite (2010) suggest that:

> a lack of [adaptive] humor in a person signals the absence of a highly valued attribute. In turn, this leads to further perceptions of low levels of other positive traits and high levels of negative traits, resulting in a more negative overall impression of the person (p. 121).

In summary, humor styles impact personality impressions differently. We return to this important recognition of humor styles shortly.

How might this affect workplace behavior specifically? Individuals' use of humor, and different humor types, could color our broader judgments of them, potentially impacting ratings of job fit, evaluations, and even promotion, tenure, or dismissal decisions through automatized connections to other more job-relevant characteristics.

However, the potential complexities of *humorous* in our IPTs have not yet been fully explored. For example, it could be quite informative to see whether humorous is connected bidirectionally, unidirectionally, or even causally to some of these other traits, and how resistant impressions of humorous others in our workplace are to contrary information.

Further, although STI research has largely ignored the trait *funny* (see Callozo, McCarthy, & Skowronski, 2013, for an exception), we appear to be making spontaneous trait inferences when we view others' behavior, even if we don't have a particular motivation to understand another person, and even when we don't realize we are doing it. Moreover, a fascinating offshoot of the work on STI, termed spontaneous trait *transference* (STT) (see Skowronski et al., 2008) has discovered that not only do we spontaneously make trait inferences from the description of a target's own behavior, but we also make inferences about a target when they are reporting on the behavior of a third party. This would imply that even if you yourself are not particularly funny, if you are describing the humorous acts of others, you might later be remembered as being funny.

The centrality of warmth in perceiving others

As discussed earlier, Asch's classic work was a precursor to a line of exploration suggesting that warmth may be a primary and central characteristic on which we judge others. Fiske, Cuddy, and Glick (2007) describe the dimensions of warmth and competence as a universal framework for organizing social cognition, and evidence has accumulated pointing toward a "primacy-of-warmth" effect, such that warmth information may have a stronger and more lasting effect on our impressions than other qualities. For example, Wojciszke, Bazinska, and Jaworski (1998) demonstrated a more consistent accessibility for warmth information, whereby participants paid more attention to and recalled information regarding a person's goodness as compared to competence. Ames and Biachi (2008), in a related investigation of agreeableness (a warmth-loaded big five trait), showed that people are most apt to look for evidence of agreeableness in others, though they are not always accurate in their judgments of others' agreeableness.

Why would warmth-related traits matter so much? In addition to a simple approach-avoidance drive (i.e. warm may indicate lack of potential harm), Scholer and Higgins (2008) explain in their *people as resources model* that we are driven to judge others in terms of the resources they have and how likely they are to use them to benefit us. Thus, competence may be one important indicator of resources, but information on competence is useful to us only in the context of warmth. In other words, competence is of value as a useful resource in a person with whom we have some sort of (work or non-work) relationship to the degree it is likely to be used in a way that benefits us. Casciaro and Lobo (2008) found similar support for this idea in three social network studies, concluding that "people appear to need active liking to seek out the task resources of potential work partners and fully tap into the knowledge that resides in organizations" (p. 655).

Warmth and humor

The potential centrality of warmth may be important for understanding the role of humor at work because funniness may be seen as a trigger for warmth ratings. Although we found recent studies of warmth based on sense of humor, they have been in the context of dating. For example, Wilbur and Campbell (2011) found that women's ratings of humor in dating profiles were related to perceptions of target warmth. Thus, there is evidence for the use of humor information to infer warmth in others, and no reason to believe this would not generalize from dating partners to co-workers. Scholer and Higgins' (2008) model seems potentially pertinent in a work setting. If humor indicates warmth, those who show humor may be utilized as resources, whereas those who do not (or use mean-spirited humor, signaling a lack of warmth) may not have their competence and other resource contributions valued. Such an exploration would have implications for realms such as high-potential designation, team selection, and social capital.

Role of affect in person perception

The theoretical perspectives outlined thus far are cognitively laden and have not explicitly considered the role of affect. Although affect and cognition have a synergistic interplay, we focus here on how affect impacts cognitions about other people. Forgas' affect infusion model (1995) suggests that mood can color our judgments when we process both heuristically and systematically. When we process heuristically (as we may do in many impression formation situations), our current mood serves as a cue to be used in the judgment (e.g. I feel great so this person I'm interacting with must have great qualities). Substantive processing may happen when we are more motivated to form an impression. Research on mood congruence effects, for example, suggests that we are more likely to notice and store positive information when we are in a good mood (Isen, Shalker, Clark, & Karp, 1978).

Recent work-relevant research by Damen, van Knippenberg, and van Knippenberg (2008) looking at attributions of charisma following leaders' display of high-arousal positive affect (e.g. enthusiasm) speaks to an additional place to consider affect. Their results demonstrated that a target's positive affect display was contagious, and a partial mediating mechanism in the attribution of the charisma trait. More specifically, when a leader exhibited displays of enthusiasm, followers "caught" this enthusiasm and became positively aroused, which was related to rating the leader as more charismatic. Thus, the mood we experience that may go on to impact our cognition of others may be "caught from" that target him/herself, or may be present for other reasons and have an indirect effect on target perception.

Perceptions of humorous people at work: Role of affect

Affective approaches to person perception may be especially relevant to humor, because the most immediate and prominent reactions to displays of humor in a target are laughter, joy, and mirth – generally high-arousal positive affect. Please note, however, that we are focusing not on how humor plays out as an affective event, as is the focus of Robert and Wilbanks' (2012) wheel model of humor. Rather, we consider how positive affect produced by a humorous target might infuse a person-perception situation with affect that is utilized as information in the process of forming an impression of that target – or perhaps, even, of others in the environment.

We found no studies that measured this particular process we are outlining in its entirety; to our knowledge, no one has manipulated exposure to a humorous target, measured affective responses to the humor, and looked specifically at subsequent trait impressions of the target and/or others in the environment. However, we have evidence that speaks to the second link in that process among the many studies looking at affect infusion in impressions, and we also have evidence for the first part link in that process, with the well-known finding across many circumstances that truly funny people make us happy (Captain Obvious, 2016). That said, empirically examining the process would allow us to appreciate the degree to which our impressions of funny people are built on the affect they produce as opposed to our prototypes and implicit personality theories described earlier. Moreover, such research could be expanded to compare affect resulting from humor versus affect resulting from other behaviors, such as organizational citizenship behaviors, which may be lower-arousal but perhaps more meaningful positive affect.

The role of attractiveness in person perception

Broadly, there have been two main findings in the realm of physical attractiveness and person perception. The first is that physically attractive people are thought to have greater social power than do less attractive people (Anderson, John, Keltner, & Kring, 2001). The second is that physically attractive people are perceived more positively and liked better than less attractive people (Eagly, Ashmore, Makhijani, & Longo, 1991). There are several perspectives on why physical attractiveness is associated with positive qualities. For example, the evolutionary perspective suggests that people have evolved a preference for physically attractive mates because physical attractiveness may indicate health and fertility (Kenrick, Sadalla, Groth, & Trost, 1990). Alternatively, the strong sociocultural physical attractiveness stereotype that people who are beautiful on the outside are also beautiful on the inside leads to the associations of positive traits onto physically attractive people – another type of halo effect (Eagly et al., 1991). Regardless of the origin, decades of study have demonstrated a positive bias toward those who look good to us, including within the workplace.

Humor, physical attractiveness, and person perception: Chicken or egg?

According to McGee and Shevlin (2009), researchers have overlooked the potential role of humor in interpersonal attraction. However, studies examining desirable qualities in potential mates have consistently found that humor is among the top desired qualities (Kenrick et al., 1990), while others have found that physical attractiveness is a strong predictor of attraction and interest in potential mates (Smith, Waldorf, & Trembath, 1990). Yet, there is a paucity of research investigating the direction of influence between humor and perceptions of physical attractiveness.

According to the social transformation model (STM), humor interacts with a person's characteristics to influence person perception (Lundy, Tan, & Cunningham, 1998). The STM functions by first transforming a perceiver's views on a humor object and then by influencing the perceiver's perceptions of humorous person. For example, Lundy et al., suggested that self-deprecating humor would be a successful humor style in the dating context because self-deprecation indicates receptivity to others. Results showed that participants rated a male target to be more attractive as a potential dating/marriage partner if they were humorous, but only if they were also physically attractive. According to the STM, it seems that humor may interact with physical attractiveness to change how others perceive a humorous person.

A big question still remains: does attractiveness influence perceptions of an individual's humorousness? Or, do perceptions of humor influence perceptions of an individual's attractiveness? Many of us likely have had the experience of finding an acquaintance more attractive after being around his or her funny personality. Might humor get connected to positive qualities partially through perceptions of attractiveness? Li, Griskevicius, Durante, Jonason, Pasisz, and Aumer (2009) sought to determine the temporal order of perceptions of humor and attraction by using two competing theories: sexual selection (humor is attractive) or the interest indication model (IIM) (attractiveness may lead one to be seen as funnier).

The sexual selection theory suggests that a humorous person may be perceived as more attractive because they appear more socially adaptive and more evolutionarily fit. Therefore, humor has been examined as an indicator of mate fitness. Specifically, Miller (1998) suggested that humor could be an indicator of general intelligence and quality genes. In contrast, the IIM theory posits that initial physical attraction may increase perceptions of a good-looking persons' funniness. Specifically, this suggests that people use humor to indicate interest in attractive people. According to this model, jokes told by an attractive person may be viewed as funny whereas the same jokes told by an unattractive person would fall flat. Evidence supporting the IIM (i.e. physical attraction begets perceptions of humor) seems to be accumulating. Li and colleagues (2009) found that both sexes were more likely to use humor and respond positively to humor when interacting with an attractive person. This is supported by Lundy et al. (1998) who found that women found men who used humor more attractive, but only if they were physically attractive. For now, it is safe to say that the jury is still out on whether physical attractiveness influences perceptions of humor, or perceptions of humor increase perceptions of physical attractiveness, and more research is needed to sort out the interplay of these factors on how we perceive others in a workplace context.

Integration, future research ideas, and implications: What next?

We began this investigation to gain a better understanding what we think of funny people at work and why, and turned to the person perception literature in social psychology to assist. Do we have a better understanding? Yes and no. We found out how much we do not yet know, but we have a better roadmap to get there.

Being labeled humorous at work is often correlated with other positive traits, many of which are thought to have direct workplace relevance. But we know very little about the details of the implicit theories that connect humor to these traits. For example, we do not know to what degree these connections are causal, which would lead them to be stronger and resistant to change. We do not yet know if there is a funny person prototype that is shared and lasting and generalizes across workplace contexts, or if there are subtypes based on the particular industry or style of humor used, and thus packed with differing associated traits. We also do not know how relatively important affect is in the process, or even if the oft-cited role of attractiveness in shaping our view of others comes into play with humor and at what stage. We have good research models in social psychology to follow, and yet we may call into question the controlled laboratory settings from which many of these research programs derive.

Beyond the guidance provided by these approaches, we also found ourselves thinking "yes, but what about . . ." as we thought of workplace applications, and below we provide additional ideas for further exploration.

Moderators in impression formation: Situations and individual differences

From the STI research tradition, we know that motivation to form an impression is not *necessary* for trait formation to occur. However, there could be a variety of circumstances that lead to more purposeful, goal-driven impressions (Skowronski et al., 2008). For example, if a person is acting according to our expectations of that person's social group, we may engage in more automatic, categorical impression formation, ascribing traits typical of the group. But, if our expectations are violated seriously enough, we may use resources to engage in individuated processing (Fiske & Neuberg, 1990). Perhaps if a target person's humorous behavior is inconsistent with the expectations perceivers have for members of that target group, more effortful, individuated processing may be activated, helping to lessen the impact of category-based stereotypes.

Further, if a person is someone upon whom we are outcome dependent – he or she is of particular importance to us as a resource (Scholer & Higgins, 2008) or a potential threat to something we value – our drive to know what makes them tick is understandably enhanced (Erber & Fiske, 1984). In a workplace context, a supervisor will be such a target, as may a co-worker with whom our work is particularly interdependent. A person about whom we are making a high-stakes decision, such as hiring, would likely be included here as well.

There are also some individual differences that influence the process of person perception. For example, Dweck, Chiu, and Hong (1995) have demonstrated that some of us operate with an underlying belief that characteristics are based on fixed traits (entity theorists) while others believe our characteristics are more malleable (incremental theorists). Entity theorists are more likely to make trait judgments and put confidence in their stability across contexts and over time. Moreover, Poon and Koehler (2008) found that entity theorists also form stronger intertrait relations within the context of IPT. So, the personal theory of the perceiver could affect how much instances of humor and any associated trait connections go on to impact decisions and behavior toward that person in the future.

The specific content of the traits that are connected with humor and how we connect them might also vary cross-culturally. Uleman and Kressel (2013) observed that person perception is not a reflection of objective reality, and "what we 'see' has been wondrously diverse across time, culture, and subculture" (p. 54). Some cultures, for example, have words to describe combinations of traits that do not have a parallel in other cultures. The importance of a cross-cultural examination of humor at work has been previously explicated (Robert & Yan, 2007); this idea adds another dimension to that need. Even when jokes translate and humor is contextually appropriate across cultures (two big hurdles), trait associations that accompany *humorous* could still differ.

Humor styles

As a starting point, we geared the chapter toward a better understanding of the label *humorous* or *funny* and its role in how we view people at work. Yet, the reader is likely as aware as we are that this is a simplification, and we know from work on humor styles (and our own observation of funny people) that there are many ways to be funny, and they are not created equally when it comes to how we perceive people (Martin, Puhlik-Doris, Larsen, Gray, & Weir, 2003). Even using just the simple dichotomy of positive (self and other enhancing) versus negative (self and other derogating) humor, we are unlikely to use humor as a warmth cue when that humor is used in a derogatory way. But, sometimes even negative humor makes us laugh – could positive affect still color our judgment positively in this case? Will the positive affect produced by laughing at not-so-nice humor about a co-worker impact our judgment about the humor producer in the same way that positive affect derived from gentler humor might? How does self-directed humor impact associated trait judgments of competence – will being self-derogating always point toward lower competence ratings than being self-enhancing? Perhaps the work context (e.g. morgue versus daycare) sets a normative stage for the style that fits best. Humor styles add a layer of complexity that requires more systematic examination.

Dyadic interactions

Person perception research has largely focused on static one-way impressions, examining what happens when a perceiver forms an impression of a target. Although this framework is methodologically straightforward, much impression formation happens in a more dynamic and dyadic (or group) context. When I am judging your traits based on my perception of your funniness, you may well be doing the same with me, and both of our judgments affect our subsequent choice of words or behaviors, humorous or otherwise, in a dynamic cycle. Research methods that can capture such interactions in real time and use techniques such as the social relations model (Santuzzi, 2007) to look at the effects of actors, partners, and their interdependence on impressions could result in a richer, more ecologically valid understanding of humor's role at work. It also allows for a better way to assess accuracy (often ignored in social cognition research; Uleman & Kressell, 2013), as does the introduction of metaperceptions, described below.

Metaperceptions of humor

There is another side of the social perception coin that is bound to impact social interactions – whether or not the target person *thinks you think* he/she is funny. The term metaperceptions encompasses the cognitions individuals have about how they are perceived by others (Laing, Phillipson, & Lee, 1966). Our metaperceptions can be general (what we think most people think of us), based on group membership (i.e. metastereotypes, or what we think other groups think of members of the group we belong to; Finkelstein, King, & Voyles, 2015), or very specific to a dyadic or group interaction (what I think this person thinks of me now as we interact; Santuzzi, 2007). Each party is sizing up the other, but some cognitive resources are also tied up in gauging what the other party is thinking of them, and modifying the interaction based on the combination of these social judgments.

To our knowledge, metaperceptions have not yet been a focus of workplace humor research, and we think they should be. Clearly you can (happily) think of a time when you made a witty observation and had your interaction partner burst into laughter. Conversely, we have likely (sadly) all been in a situation where a joke fell flat and thought "uh oh, they all think I'm an idiot now." Whether they did or not, the perception that you are being judged to have negative traits is bound to impact your behavior. There is developing clinical psychology evidence for a condition called gelotophobia (Ruch & Proyer, 2008), the fear of being laughed at. This condition often leads people to avoid mirthful situations and to come across as quite humorless.

Although much research on metaperceptions focuses on reactions we have when we think others view us negatively, thinking that people ascribe positive traits to you can also impact your interactions and behaviors. Moreover, it has been proposed that positive and negative metaperceptions could both have positive or negative outcomes. For example, if we think someone found us funny and were thus ascribing other characteristics to us that we know are inaccurate, this could lead to anxiety around unrealistic expectations (Finkelstein et al., 2015).

Researchers have suggested that our metaperceptions have the potential to play a larger role in social interactions than our other perceptions (Sheldon & Johnson,

1993); we may be more worried about what people think of us than what we think of them. Given this possibility, humor research in this area should be a priority.

Serious, humorless, or attempting and failing at humor – what's the difference?

We would be remiss to omit a discussion surrounding how seriousness, humorlessness, and failed humor shape impressions. Cerrentano and Finkelstein (2009) discovered that people have different ideas about what the opposite of *humorous* is. Responses varied greatly with some participants referring to these non-humorous targets as *serious* (most frequent response), *boring, humorless, oafish, lame*, or *blah*. In two of their studies participants consistently provided the lowest favorability ratings for humorless targets as compared to humorous or serious targets. This may be because being serious can be a good thing, with other meanings and associations aside from being "not funny," but being humorless has no redeeming qualities associated with it. Arguably seriousness may be necessary in the workplace from time to time (although the authors of this chapter beg to differ), therefore seriousness may not always bear a negative connotation. In the workplace, individuals described as humorless may rarely be given the benefit of the doubt in hiring, retention, and promotion, while serious individuals may bear fewer negative connotations with other traits and possibly even some positive ones.

What about those who attempt humor but fail at it? Although failed humor has rarely been studied, it has the potential to greatly impact person perception, perhaps in a way different than just being serious. For example, Bell (2009) explored how participants reacted to hearing a variation of this bad joke, "What did the big chimney say to the little chimney? Nothing. Chimneys can't talk." She found that among the participants who responded to the bad joke with a comment ("you're a dork") or evaluation ("is that supposed to be funny?"), 23.5 percent of her sample evaluated the joke teller/experimenter negatively as opposed to just the joke (49 percent reacted negatively) or both the joke and its teller (15 percent reacted negatively). The responses to the teller ranged from he/she being described as *silly, dumb, nerd, dork*, and *douchebag*. These varied responses imply that negative impressions stem from a bad joke being told. Bell also found that the most negative reactions came from those close to the joke teller (friends and family) while strangers and acquaintances responded neutrally; how much of an impact failed humor has on our trait perceptions may then depend on when this occurs in the timeline of acquiring trait information. Uleman and Kressel (2013) noted that negative traits are given more attention and weight in the formation of impressions. It could be that being perceived as having a dorky (to quote Bell's participants) sense of humor could do more harm than being perceived as humorous could do good. We suggest that researchers should be careful about how they conceptualize the opposite end of the humorous continuum, and consider exploring differences in both cognitive associations and affective reactions to those who are humorless, serious, and those who give it the old college try but hear crickets.

Practical implications

Though we have focused our efforts on sparking much-needed research on how humor influences our perceptions of others in the workplace, some tentative practical implications are worth mentioning. First, as an employee making impressions in the work environment, you should recognize that others are likely making inferences based on your humorous behavior. Based on spontaneous trait inferences and spontaneous trait transference, how others describe you to their co-workers, or perhaps even how you describe others' humor can alter people's perceptions of your qualities and traits. These inferences could come back to affect you in the future if the perceivers must make a decision about you based on qualities they believe you have – particularly if they go with their gut rather than structured assessments of work-relevant traits. Others may be looking for indicators of warmth (or lack thereof) when they get to know you, and judicious use of humor could be a way to signal this quality. This could offer benefits including gaining idiosyncrasy credit to get away with more workplace violations, or solidifying a more central place in the social network of the organization. Wise people can utilize their humor skills to produce humor at crucial times in early impression formation. If you are not confident in your skills in this arena, or uncertain of the norms for humor style, it may be safer to attempt to ignite positive affect in others through other means.

What if you are the perceiver and not the perceived? Decision makers may not have awareness that a halo of humor could affect how they judge others over whom they have power. Similar to how attractiveness may sometimes color our perceptions of others without our awareness, humor may likewise operate – and as we saw, operate in tandem with attractiveness. It is always good practice to have the self-awareness to know we are not above natural cognitive processes and biases, and to question the veracity of our beliefs about others – what are our sources, and are they valid? Recognize that in addition to the other factors we are taught to recognize as sources of potentially biased information (e.g. demographics, cultural differences), humor can cast a halo around other traits, and often unexpectedly, have the potential to alter the course of a career, a team composition, an organizational chart, and more.

References

Ames, D. R., & Biachi, E. C. (2008). The agreeableness asymmetry in first impressions: Perceivers' impulse to (mis)judge agreeableness and how it is moderated by power. *Personality and Social Psychology Bulletin*, 34, 1719–1736.

Anderson, C., John, O. P., Keltner, D., & Kring, A. M. (2001). Who attains social status? Effects of personality and physical attractiveness in social groups. *Journal of Personality and Social Psychology*, 81(1), 116.

Asch, S. E. (1946). Forming impressions of personality. *Journal of Abnormal and Social Psychology*, 41, 258–290.

Beins, C. B., & O'Toole, S. M. (2010). Searching for the sense of humor: Stereotypes of ourselves and others. *Europe's Journal of Psychology*, 6, 267–287.

Bell, N. (2009). Responses to failed humor. *Journal of Pragmatics*, 41, 1825–1836.

Callozo, R., McCarthy, R., & Skowronski, J. J. (2013). Using Facebook to elicit spontaneous trait references. *The New School Psychology Bulletin*, 10, 14–24.

Cann, A., & Calhoun, L. G. (2001). Perceived personality associations with differences in sense of humor: Stereotypes of hypothetical others with high or low senses of humor. *Humor*, 14(2), 117–130.

Cann, A., & Matson, C. (2014). Sense of humor and social desirability: Understanding how humor styles are perceived. *Personality and Individual Differences*, 66, 176–180.

Carlston, D. E., & Skowronski, J. J. (1994). Savings in the relearning of trait information as evidence for spontaneous inference generation. *Journal of Personality and Social Psychology*, 66, 840–856.

Casciaro, T., & Lobo, M. S. (2008). When competence is irrelevant: The role of interpersonal affect in task related ties. *Administrative Science Quarterly*, 53, 655–684.

Cerrentano, C., & Finkelstein, L. (2009, April). *The halo of humor: How humor affects leadership perceptions*. Paper presented at the 24th Annual Meeting of the Society for Industrial and Organizational Psychology, New Orleans, LA.

Damen, F., Van Knippenberg, D., & Van Knippenberg, B. (2008). Leader affective displays and attributions of charisma: The role of arousal. *Journal of Applied Social Psychology*, 38, 2594–2614.

Dweck, C. S., Chiu, C., & Hong, Y. (1995). Implicit theories and their role in judgments and reactions: A world from two perspectives. *Psychological Inquiry*, 6, 267–285.

Eagly, A. H., Ashmore, R. D., Makhijani, M. G., & Longo, L. C. (1991). What is beautiful is good, but. . .: A meta-analytic review of research on the physical attractiveness stereotype. *Psychological Bulletin*, 110(1), 109.

Erber, R., & Fiske, S. T. (1984). Outcome dependency and attention to inconsistent information. *Journal of Personality and Social Psychology*, 47, 709–726.

Finkelstein, L. M., King, E. B., & Voyles, E. C. (2015). Age metastereotyping and cross-age interactions: A meta view of age stereotypes at work. *Work, aging and retirement*, 1, 26–40.

Fiske, S. T., & Neuberg, S. L. (1990). A continuum model of impression formation, from category-based to individuating processes: Influences of information and motivation on attention and interpretation. *Advances in Experimental Social Psychology*, 23, 1–74.

Fiske, S. T., Cuddy, A. J., & Glick, P. (2007). Universal dimensions of social cognition: Warmth and competence. *Trends in Cognitive Sciences*, 11, 77–83.

Forgas, J. P. (1995). Mood and judgment: The affect infusion model. *Psychological Bulletin*, 117, 39–66.

Graesser, A. C., & Nakamura, G. V. (1982). The impact of schema on comprehension and memory. *The Psychology of Learning and Motivation*, 16, 59–109.

Isen, A. M., Shalker, T. E., Clark, M., & Karp, L. (1978). Affect, accessibility of material in memory, and behavior: A cognitive loop? *Journal of Personality and Social Psychology*, 36, 1–12.

Kenrick, D. T., Sadalla, E. K., Groth, G., & Trost, M. R. (1990). Evolution, traits, and the stages of human courtship: Qualifying the parental investment model. *Journal of Personality*, 58(1), 97–116.

Kuiper, N. A., & Leite, C. (2010). Personality impressions associated with four distinct humor styles. *Scandinavian Journal of Psychology*, 51, 115–122.

Laing, R. D., Phillipson, H., & Lee, A. R. (1966). *Interpersonal perception: A theory and a method of research*. London: Tavistock.

Li, N. P., Griskevicius, V., Durante, K. M., Jonason, P. K., Pasisz, D. J., & Aumer, K. (2009). An evolutionary perspective on humor: Sexual selection or interest indication? *Personality and Social Psychology Bulletin*, 35, 923–936.

Lundy, D. E., Tan, J., & Cunningham, M. R. (1998). Heterosexual romantic preferences: The importance of humor and physical attractiveness for different types of relationships. *Personal Relationships*, 5(3), 311–325.

Martin, R. A., Puhlik-Doris, P., Larsen, G., Gray, J., & Weir, K. (2003). Individual differences in uses of humor and their relation to psychological well-being: Development of the Humor Styles Questionnaire. *Journal of Research in Personality*, 37(1), 48–75.

McGee, E., & Shevlin, M. (2009). Effect of humor on interpersonal attraction and mate selection. *The Journal of Psychology*, 143(1), 67–77.

Miller, G. F. (1998). How mate choice shaped human nature: A review of sexual selection and human evolution. *Handbook of Evolutionary Psychology: Ideas, issues, and applications*, 87–129.

Orehek, E., Dechesne, M., Fishbach, A., Kruglanski, A. W., & Chun, W. Y. (2010). On the inferential epistemics of trait centrality in impression formation. *European Journal of Social Psychology*, 40, 1120–1135.

Poon, C. S. K., & Koehler, D. J. (2008). Person theories: Their temporal stability and relation to intertrait inferences. *Personality and Social Psychology Bulletin*, 34, 965–977.

Robert, C., & Wilbanks, J. E. (2012). The wheel model of humor: Humor events and affect in organizations. *Human Relations*, 65, 1071–1099.

Robert, C., & Yan, W. (2007). The case for developing new research on humor and culture in organizations: Toward a higher grade of manure. *Research in Personnel and Human Resource Management*, 26, 205–267.

Ruch, W., & Proyer, R. T. (2008). The fear of being laughed at: Individual and group differences in gelotophobia. *Humor*, 21, 47–67.

Santuzzi, A. M. (2007). Perceptions and metaperceptions of negative evaluation: Group composition and meta-accuracy in a social relations model. *Group Processes and Intergroup Relations*, 10, 383–398.

Schneider, D. J. (1973). Implicit personality theory: A review. *Psychological Bulletin*, 79, 294–309.

Scholer, A. A., & Higgins, E. T. (2008). People as resources: Exploring the functionality of *warm* and *cold*. *European Journal of Social Psychology*, 38, 1111–1120.

Sedikides, C., & Anderson, C. A. (1994). Causal perceptions of intertrait relations: The glue that holds person types together. *Personality and Social Psychology Bulletin*, 20, 294–302.

Sheldon, K., & Johnson, J. (1993). Forms of social awareness: Their frequency and correlates. *Personality and Social Psychology Bulletin*, 19, 320–330.

Siebler, F. (2008). Emergent attributes in person perception: A comparative test of response time predictions. *Social Psychology*, 32, 83–89.

Skowronski, J. J., Carlston, D. E., & Hartnett, J. (2008). Spontaneous impressions derived from observations of behavior. In J. Skowronski, & N. Ambady (Eds.), *First impressions* (pp. 313–333). New York: The Guilford Press.

Smith, J. E., Waldorf, V. A., & Trembath, D. L. (1990). Single white male looking for thin, very attractive. . . *Sex Roles*, 23(11–12), 675–685.

Thorson, J. A., Powell, F. C., Sarmany-Schuller, I., & Hampes, W. P. (1997). Psychological health and sense of humor. *Journal of Clinical Psychology*, 53, 605–619.

Uleman, J. S., & Kressel, L. M. (2013). A brief history of theory and research on impression formation. In D. Carlston (Ed.), *Oxford handbook of social cognition* (pp. 53–73). Oxford: Oxford University Press.

Van Der Pligt, J., & Taylor, C. (1984). Trait attribution: Evaluation, description and attitude extremity. *European Journal of Social Psychology*, 14, 211–221.

Vernon, P. A., Martin, R. A., Schermer, J. A., & Mackie, A. (2008). A behavioral genetic investigation of humor styles and their correlations with the Big-5 personality dimensions. *Personality and Individual Differences*, 44, 116–1125.

Veselka, L., Schermer, J. A., Martin, R. A., & Vernon, P. A. (2010). Relations between humor styles and the dark triad traits of personality. *Personality and Individual Differences*, 48, 772–774.

Wilbur, C. J., & Campbell, L. (2011). Humor in romantic contexts: Do men participate and women evaluate? *Personality and Social Psychology Bulletin*, 37(7), 918–929.

Wojciszke, B., Bazinska, R., & Jaworski, M. (1998). On the dominance of moral categories in impression formation. *Personality and Social Psychology Bulletin*, 24, 1245–1257.

Yip, J. A., & Martin, R. A. (2006). Sense of humor, emotional intelligence, and social competence. *Journal of Research in Personality*, 40, 1202–1208.

Zeigler-Hill, V., Besser, A., & Jett, S. E. (2013). Laughing at the looking glass: Does humor style serve as an interpersonal signal? *Evolutionary Psychology*, 11, 201–226.

4

HUMOR AND ORGANIZATIONAL NETWORKS

Functions and dysfunctions

James D. Westaby and B. Alan Echtenkamp

This chapter examines some of the diverse ways that humor operates and functions in organizational networks. While traditional network frameworks can provide a helpful perspective on how entities are interconnected, such as examining positive and negative linkages as illustrated on the left side of Figure 4.1, or examining the density and centrality of network structures (Borgatti, Mehra, Brass, & Labianca, 2009), traditional social network frameworks have not been leveraged to provide a deeper theoretical treatment about how humor functions and operates in organizational networks. Likewise, even though research has examined psychological aspects of humor, such as it being triggered by violations that are seen as benign (McGraw, 2010; McGraw, Warren, Williams, & Leonard, 2012), much of the research has focused exclusively at the individual level (Mesmer-Magnus, Glew, & Viswesvaran, 2012) and not on how humor operates in networks. Taken together, very little theoretically-based research has examined how both psychological and network factors are involved in humor processes. Fortunately, with the recent development of dynamic network theory (Westaby, 2012), which combines psychological and network science, a novel platform is now available to attempt to portray some of the complex motivational and emotional ways in which humor operates in such settings.

Thus, the purpose of this chapter is to use concepts and processes from dynamic network theory to explore the processes, functions, and potential concerns regarding humor in organizational networks. This framing goes beyond past work that articulated select mechanisms of humor in organizational settings (Duncan, 1982) by discussing both psychological and network mechanisms. Furthermore, this chapter goes beyond past treatments of humor as social influence (O'Quin & Aronoff, 1981) by providing specificity about the way in which humor functions in the context of underlying goals and network roles. This chapter also responds to Westaby, Pfaff, and Redding's (2014) recent call for research that examines psychologically-based motivational and emotional issues in social networks. That is, we attempt to portray how such mechanisms operate in the context of humor, which often occurs in socially rich and highly nuanced contexts.

Overview of dynamic network theory

Dynamic network theory indicates that implicit or explicit judgment and decision-making processes trigger the activation of eight different types of social network roles (or their combinations), which in turn impact behavior, feedback processes, and the network rippling of emotions. These roles include goal striving, system supporting, goal preventing, supportive resisting, system negating, system reacting, interacting, and observing. What's very unique about the theory is that only these eight network roles are needed to explain many of the critical social complexities associated with any behavioral or goal pursuit. While goals can fluidly change for any context, the eight social network roles or their combinations stay the same. In the context of this chapter, "using humor" can be conceptualized as a focal behavior (or goal) around which the network roles can be described. For example, some entities in a network may support another's humor striving, while others may react negatively to it. The eight roles are presented next, which allows us to understand how social networks form and react to humor events. See Table 4.1 for a summary.

TABLE 4.1 The eight social network roles in dynamic network theory

Social Network Role	*Label*	*Illustration*
1 Goal striving	G	Person trying to tell a humorous story, joke, anecdote, or simply trying to be funny.
2 System supporting	S	Person supporting another's attempt at humor in the social network.
3 Goal preventing	P	Person working against another's humor attempt or disagreeing with it.
4 Supportive resisting	V	Third party supporting another that is working against someone trying to be funny.
5 System negating	N	Negative affect or emotion toward another who is trying to be humorous.
6 System reacting	R	Negative affect or emotion toward those trying to resist the humorist's efforts.
7 Interacting	I	Someone in the vicinity of humor attempts, but not paying close attention.
8 Observing	O	Bystanders, observers, or curious entities that are processing another's act of humor, but not forming a judgment of support or resistance about it. They're neutral.

The eight social network roles

Given the focus of this chapter, we illustrate the eight network roles in the context of an attempted humor event. In this case, imagine that Pat activates a *goal striving* role (G) of trying to tell a funny story. Pat presumes that enacting this goal will trigger a derivative response, such as laughter among others in the immediate network listening to the story. This behavior is technically shown on the right side of Figure 4.1 in a dynamic network chart, which is based on methods articulated in the theory. Squares represent entities and ovals represent the psychological goal construct(s). Paths indicate social network role behaviors, the key mechanisms of influence. In this case, Pat (a network entity) has a G path to the humor goal (the psychological goal construct). The Work Buddy in this example is a *system supporter* (S), who often supports Pat's humorous attempts out of loyalty. An S path shows this support from the Work Buddy to Pat. In contrast, Pat's joking effort is being attempted in a work environment where some other network members don't like joking around. In this case, an initial wave of resistance is shown by a New Co-Worker who tells Pat not to joke around at work. Such obstruction behavior is referred to as *goal prevention* (P) in the theory and is shown with a P dashed path to the goal, illustrating that the Co-Worker is directly trying to thwart Pat's humor goal. Furthermore, this New Co-Worker is rather upset emotionally by Pat's joking behavior, which theoretically represents *system negation* behavior (N) toward those

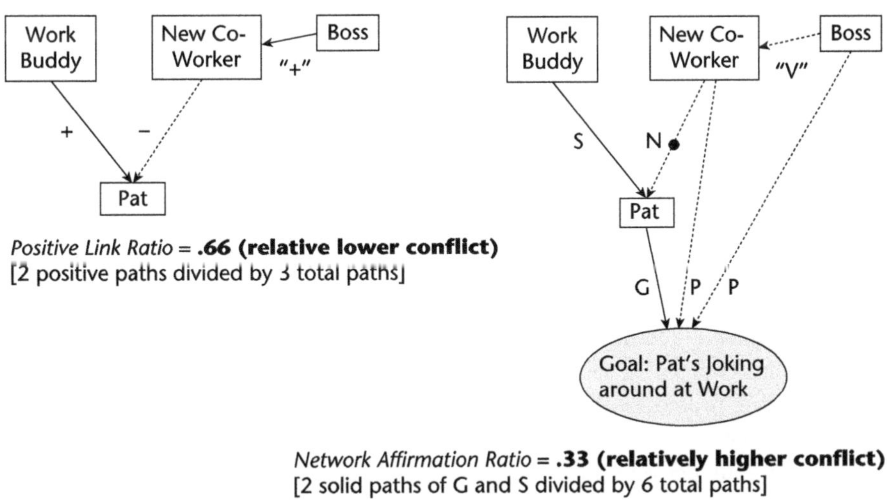

FIGURE 4.1 Chart comparisons: (left) Traditional social network; (right) Dynamic network chart.

Note: + indicates positive link. – indicates negative link. Quotation marks illustrate links that significantly differ between the approaches (i.e. the positive, "+" link in Part A between Boss and New Co-Worker is a supportive resistance link working against Pat's goal of joking around at work in Part B, thereby not being positive for the focal goal). G = goal striving; S = system supporting; P = goal preventing; V = supportive resisting; N = system negating. System reacting (R), interacting (I), and observing (O) are not illustrated for simplicity.

pursuing or supporting the goal. This role is displayed in dynamic network charts with dashed lines with a small black embedded circle to denote how it's a conflict emotion motivationally oriented against the goal (and the circle differentiates the path from supportive resistance).

Because Pat is not emotionally bothered by the New Co-Worker's prevention or negation, there is no reciprocal negativity shown. If so, such negative emotions toward those showing resistance or negativity is represented by *system reactance* role behavior (R).[1] To continue the example, a Boss exists in Pat's network, who is also trying to reduce Pat's humorist efforts by telling Pat to spend less time joking around at work (P). This Boss also supports the New Co-Worker's resistance against Pat's joking around. This represents *supportive resistance* in the network and is denoted in the chart with a dashed V path. However, the Boss is not showing system negation toward Pat, meaning that the Boss is fairly unemotional about the whole thing and is just trying to get Pat to tone it down some, perhaps out of respect for the New Co-Worker's feelings.[2]

The above six roles illustrate key motivational and emotional functions a network can have for and against a given goal and behavioral pursuit. The last two roles in dynamic network theory illustrate important peripheral forces that can have more indirect motivational effects (see Westaby, 2012, for a fuller treatment). The first is the *observer role* (O), such as if another person, or bystander, is observing Pat's joking behavior, but does not have a motivational orientation toward it, good or bad. In contrast, the *interactant role* (I) illustrates individuals that are often in the immediate physical surroundings of the given goal pursuit but are not necessarily paying attention to, or observing, what's going on. In Pat's case, it may be another employee at the organization that is literally in hearing-range of the joking behavior, but is not paying close attention to it, given his or her focus on another task. The above paths could be shown in dynamic network charts, such as with simple gray lines and labelled O and I, respectively. We did not illustrate them in Figure 4.1 for simplicity and focus. Alternatively, an all-black-line method is possible too, where single black paths are entirely used and social network role labels are placed next to the basic paths.

To capture real world complexities, it is important to note that the above roles are often implemented in *multiplex* combinations. For example, an SIO role combination illustrates a link where a system supporter is observing another's pursuit and is in close proximity. In contrast, a pure S role illustrates a person who may morally support someone, but is not near the person nor is he or she keeping-up on observing the person's pursuits.

How traditional network analysis and dynamic network theory differ

The discussion thus far has illustrated the ways in which dynamic network theory provides insight into motivational and interpersonal mechanisms underlying humor in network structures. But how does it differ from traditional social network analysis? Are there differences? Yes. We now turn to some of the most critical aspects.

Different views about motivated linkages

Westaby et al. (2014) discussed how traditional network analyses may not sufficiently capture how positive and negative links theoretically operate in the context of a person's goal or behavioral pursuit. We can see this contrast in Figure 4.1 in regards to the linkage between the Boss and New Co-Worker. Here, a traditional network analysis could, quite intuitively, show a positive linkage between the Boss and New Co-Worker. This is because the two are sharing a positive connection and similar motivation and orientation with each other. However, this positive linkage is not entirely positive when viewed in the context of the goal pursuit under study, which is Pat's behavior of trying to tell a funny story. In this context, the Boss's positive link to the New Co-Worker (via traditional analysis) is actually a behavior that supports resistance against Pat's humorist striving. Thus, in dynamic network theory, this is a resistance linkage and not a positive link that is helping Pat's goal striving. It's hurting it. Experimentally, from a dynamic network theory perspective, one would expect that if the link between the Boss and New Co-Worker was eliminated, it would result in a more positive system for Pat's joking behavior. In contrast, the traditional approach would suggest that removing a presumed positive link would result in more negativity in the system. Such experiments are ripe for future study to advance our understanding about how networks are causally involved in social and organizational systems.

Different interpretations about overall positivity in a system

Figure 4.1 illustrates a wider and more systemic difference between the approaches when examining the presumed positivity of the whole system. A traditional network approach may illustrate in this example that the overall positivity of the interpersonal social network is moderately strong. That is, the positivity ratio of the network linkages is 0.66. This simply illustrates that 2 out of the 3 interpersonal linkages are positive (66 percent). In other words, this suggests that a moderately positive interpersonal system exists among the entities from a traditional network lens that uses positive and negative indicators.

In contrast, dynamic network theory provides a much different perspective, suggesting a more negative situation for Pat's overall goal striving network. That is, only 2 out of the 6 social network role linkages are positively orientated in the goal network (33 percent). The two positively oriented roles (referred to as network affirmation) in this context are G and S.[3] The negatively oriented roles (referred to as network de-affirmation) are the two P paths, the N path, and the V path. Thus, 33 percent of the motivated linkages in the system are positive and 66 percent are more negative in orientation. Dynamic network theory demonstrates this unique explanation because it examines individuals' connections to goal nodes (G and P) and it provides a different interpretation of V in this example (i.e. it's a negative force for Pat's goal, not a positive force). Hence, a dynamic network theory approach illustrates that there is much more negativity in this example than a traditional approach.

More generally, these contrasts illustrate that the theoretical and methodological approach taken can influence how we make meaning out of positive and negative linkages, social influence forces, and systems overall. This analysis is consistent with Westaby et al. (2014) and Westaby and Redding's (2014) arguments that traditional network analyses that use positive and negative linkages may underestimate negativity in goal pursuit systems that have conflict, which might be particularly relevant in the context of humor events that are generally assumed to be positive and socially supported phenomena.

Other important processes in dynamic network theory

There are other unique mechanisms in dynamic network theory that can explain humor behavior in organizational networks. We highlight two important issues concerning the network rippling of emotions and dynamic network intelligence next.

Network rippling of emotions

Emotions are critical elements of humor. Fortunately, the way in which emotional outcomes flow across networks is also predicted in dynamic network theory, which is contingent on perceived goal completion. According to the network rippling of emotions process (Westaby et al., 2014), positive emotions often spread to the goal strivers and system supporters upon perceived goal success or progress, while negative emotions can ripple to those in network de-affirmation roles (i.e. P, V, and N) during these same times. In Pat's example, let's assume that the humor attempt or joke was viewed as successful by Pat and the Work Buddy. Since they held goal striving and system supporting roles, respectively, one would predict that they would experience positive emotions, that manifest through laughter or smiling. In contrast, the New Co-Worker was enacting goal prevention and system negation toward Pat's behavioral attempt and thus would be expected to experience negative emotional reactions when seeing Pat and the Work Buddy laughing, which implies that they view the humor attempt as successful. The Boss would be expected to have relatively less intense negative emotional reactions because only one network de-affirmation force was generated (i.e. P only, not N and P). However, one would expect that more negative emotional reactions may emerge over time for the Boss, if the joking behavior continues in light of the Boss continually trying to thwart it (i.e. NP may eventually emerge after continued P failure (Westaby, Woods, & Pfaff, 2016).

As for broader dynamics, the positive and/or negative network rippling of emotions could become widespread and highly contagious in a network when the behavior becomes very salient and other people start to discuss the humor behavior, as knowledge of the event spreads. The degree to which it spreads in positive and/ or negative ways depends on the level of system support versus goal prevention, system negation, and supportive resistance occurring in relation to the focal goal or behavior. An important area for future research is to use computational modeling to make more complex projections of network behavior during such goal pursuits and emotional reactions (Westaby & Shon, forthcoming).

Dynamic network intelligence (DNI)

Another important concept involved in network systems is *dynamic network intelligence,* which generally represents how accurately an individual knows other people's social network role behaviors (Westaby et al., 2014). This extends work on cognitive accuracy in social networks (Krackhardt & Kilduff, 1999) by looking at accuracy in the context of the networks involved in goal and behavioral pursuits. To illustrate, a goal striver's ability to generate a humor response from a network and the predicted positive network rippling of emotions would depend on how well the humorist striver is able to accurately determine that others in the network are going to support the attempt. When accuracy is off, a goal striver may surprisingly discover, for example, that another person finds a joking behavior offensive, likely because the joke teller did not know important things about the listening audience.

Thus, it is assumed that having high DNI about humor striving will greatly increase the likelihood that the humor events will be met with positive reactions and not with resistance or network de-affirmation. This requires that humorist strivers are capable of knowing considerable detail about other network members' internal states, either directly through personal closeness and intimacy (Clark & Lemay, 2010), or indirectly through making inferences about the network audience through assumptions (e.g. my audience is all professional, therefore, it may be safe to make a joke about people that are poor). If assumptions are wrong or not supported, unexpected reactions would occur (e.g. some of those observing a joke may boo or grimace because the humorist striver did not know that some of them are currently unemployed and financially struggling, therefore showing N and P reactions). We now turn to more of the complexities associated with humor; some good, some bad.

Positive and negative aspects

With some of the basic processes articulated above, we now examine some of the positive and negative issues associated with humor in organizational networks. This discussion presents a sampling of possibilities and is not presumed to be exhaustive.

Positive aspects

Improving Moods

When humor efforts are effective, it can break up monotony and boredom and stimulate positive moods at work, even if only temporarily. This conceptualizing is related to Cooper's (2008) notion of affect reinforcement and Robert and Wilbanks' (2012) notion of humor and affect cycles, although we extend it to more nuanced processes in social networks. For example, an effective humor event could generate a positive network rippling of emotions to partner goal strivers and system supporters in the network. This may be especially useful in environments that are "intense, high-pressure, and passionate," which could have an inoculating effect on workers who are repeatedly exposed to trauma, such as emergency workers (Nelson, 1992). Scogin and Pollio (1980) have also noted the importance of support mechanisms in the context of humor exchange, albeit not comprehensively tied to networks and emotional contagion. More broadly, we would expect greater spread and contagion of humor when there's high interconnectivity (I), such as when employees have close proximity or are in highly centralized positions, which allows them to more easily transfer information across network entities.

Building positive climates

When humor triggers the network rippling of positive emotions, it also has the potential to facilitate positive climates. In other words, it is likely that positive climates would emerge when employees expect humorous events to occur at a reasonable rate and without serious resistance or network de-affirmation. These arguments are somewhat related to Martin, Puhlik-Doris, Larsen, Gray, and Weir's (2003) affiliative dimension of humor, and, at the group level, the notion of joking cultures (Fine & De Soucey, 2005) and humor-supportive culture (Robert & Wilbanks, 2012). Robert (2014) also notes how different types of humor can further build relationships, such as how self-deprecating humor from a higher-status individual can make others feel more comfortable around the high status individual. In dynamic network theory, the high status individual is likely intentionally engaging in self-deprecation to reduce defenses and resistance (P, N, or V), which could ease the generation of greater system support (S) in the system.

This type of humor may also fit Martin et al.'s (2003) dimension of self-defeating humor, although we would argue that it is often less self-defeating than it is meant to help build-up others in comparison. From a network perspective, this suggests that individuals may choose various types of humor to impact social network roles. While self-deprecating humor may attempt to reduce defenses and resistance in efforts to generate system support, other types of humor, such as aggressive forms, may be intentional efforts to show resistance or negation to others, likely with underlying hostility motives. Such conceptualizing goes beyond the idea that "humor stimulates affect" to imply that humor occurs "because of" or "reflective of" network relationships, or perhaps in an attempt to establish certain types of network role relationships.

Bolstering self-worth during poor performance

When a highly and mutually supportive climate exists at work, one may also find that employees will use humor to boost the morale and the self-worth of others experiencing poor performance or unfortunate events. For example, imagine that an employee states something inaccurately during a meeting, which could generate some embarrassment. In such cases, other employees that are deeply supportive (S) of the employee may provide assistance in a socially sensitive way along with a warm-hearted laugh or giggle. This laugh or giggle, albeit perhaps subtle, can be very meaningful and symbolic because it helps show the person making the mistake that he or she is still supported (Westaby et al., 2016). The giggle implies that it's not a big deal and can be laughed off. Of course, if poor or objectionable performance were to become commonplace for the individual, it is likely that other network members' support would wither and so too the use of humor in the future to repair the social situation. Otherwise, employees that make understandable mistakes would feel supported by the network and would not fear exclusion. This is psychologically important given the maladaptive effects that exclusion can have on motivational and cognitive processes (Baumeister, DeWall, Ciarocco, & Twenge, 2005).

Once again, the above conceptualizing implies that acts of humor can often occur *because of* the types of network relations that exist between parties and vice versa. Thus, certain humor may be more easily generated because of the established social network role relationships between entities. Supportive ones may be more amenable to kind-hearted humor attempts whereas competitive ones may be more susceptible to aggressive or mean-spirited humor attempts, the latter of which may implicate more sinister or subconsciously prejudiced orientations toward the given party. Thus, the enactment of humor may be closely connected to the social network role expectations in the given context.

Promoting intrinsic motivation

Work environments that have predictable instances of humor may also lead employees to expect satisfaction and enjoyment in the work itself, one of the classically important facets of job satisfaction (Kinicki, McKee-Ryan, Schriesheim, & Carson, 2002). That is, even dry tasks could be bolstered with intrinsic motivation when employees share in humor and the concomitant positive network rippling of emotions. Such positive outcomes of humor would be particularly expected in jobs (or portions of jobs) that are highly automated or relatively simple to execute, therefore not sacrificing cognitive and behavioral resources from the job at hand (Kanfer, Ackerman, Murtha, Dugdale, & Nelson, 1994). In other words, it will not distract them from performing their important work. Given that intrinsic factors are important in subjective well-being (Diener, Ng, Harter, & Arora, 2010), rightly balanced humor may provide great dividends motivationally and emotionally at work in the right jobs and right contexts. Future research needs to examine such balance and in the contexts that it varies.

Mitigating conflict in networks

Many individuals experience conflict, including conflicts at work (Coleman, Deutsch, & Marcus, 2014). In some of these settings, other network members may try a humorous behavior, mannerism, or story to break up tensions arising from P, V, N, or R. Theoretically, these members are implicitly or explicitly trying to enact system support (S) for those involved in the conflict to help reduce tension. If those interjecting humor have high dynamic network intelligence (i.e. accurately anticipating that parties will respond with laughter from their tension-reduction humor attempt), the humor could help change the trajectory of conflict or provide individuals with a brief psychological break in which they would see, or be reminded consciously or subconsciously, that system support exists in the network, despite the conflict. The timing and content of such humor efforts often needs to be masterful, since even good content without proper timing can fall flat, especially in tense settings.

In general, we anticipate that network systems with highly stable patterns of system support and previous norms for humorist goal striving will be more likely to implement such humorist striving when conflicts occur, again, reminding the network that shared system support undergirds the network. Robert (2014) also notes how humor can help individuals communicate about difficult matters as well as reduce defensiveness and save face. All of these mechanisms would be expected to keep network de-affirmation roles (P, V, and N) at bay or help keep them from escalating to more serious levels. However, we also recognize that there can be functionality in some types of conflict, especially when it represents *constructive resistance* that aims to provide better long-term outcomes to the parties, despite short-term conflict (Westaby et al., 2014).

Negative aspects

When thinking about humor behavior or events, the natural tendency is to think about their positive effects, given the presumed positive emotions that occur through humor. However, as we illustrate below, humor efforts can go awry and have dysfunctional effects in organizational settings that are either caused by existing network relationships, or that drive the change or formation of relationships.

Awkwardness

One way in which humor behavior can be socially ineffective is when humorist goals simply fail. For example, a person may attempt to tell a funny story, but it does not connect with the observers in the network or even presumed system supporters. This can result in a network rippling of negative emotions and the humorist feeling awkward, embarrassed, or incompetent in his or her efforts, especially when the network is not motivated to show any reparative system support, as discussed in the previous sections. Much greater dysfunction would be expected when a goal striver's attempts at humor are consistently flat, ineffective, or inappropriate. In such cases, if continued, the person will likely lose all system support for the behavior and possibly be ignored, shunned, or be the recipient of intense goal prevention, supportive resistance, and/or system negation. Such behaviors would also likely trigger the emergence of higher-order cognitive evaluations, such as the person being perceived as untrustworthy or incompetent at work.

Potential distraction

Another situation in which humor or joking behavior can be dysfunctional is when it distracts employees from important work. The type of task and goal striving is likely a critical moderator. For example, in highly complex work that is not automated, even moderate levels of humor could be potentially damaging. A rather unexperienced surgeon joking around during a complex new procedure under immense time pressure with a patient's life-signs quickly deteriorating would likely be met with tremendous goal prevention and negation, given the presumption that all energy should be focused on saving the patient's life. Any distraction from the focal task would likely be considered catastrophic in this network context. In other less complex tasks, humor may pose little distraction. In these cases, it could provide intrinsic value for the employees.

Lowered productivity when humor becomes the focus

If a group becomes more pre-occupied with humor striving than the work at hand, it makes logical sense that such humor would be dysfunctional for achieving organizational performance goals. In such cases, a goal conflict (Westaby, 2012) emerges and the employees are prioritizing humor goals over work goals. Many of us have seen this when a group of employees are "goofing off" and not paying attention to the customers. In such cases, one would expect system negation and goal prevention directed at the employees (i.e. the customers are upset about the employee behavior and want it to stop). Moreover, at the individual level, a person that is continuously focused on humor may not demonstrate competence at achieving work goals and hence not be treated seriously. This in turn could weaken the employee's potential future opportunities at work. On the other hand, an employee that is never willing or able to participate in a laugh or two may be perceived by his or her co-workers as not being very supportive of the group.

Outgroup derogation

Some acts of humor can implicitly or explicitly target outgroup members and trigger network resistance and de-affirmation toward the striver. In some unintentional cases, the humorist striver may have low dynamic network intelligence, since she or he is not aware of how the striving behavior is triggering network de-affirmation among implicated outgroup members. For example, one executive may try to make a funny remark to another executive about a working class employee who did not understand a technical word during a presentation the previous day. However, the effort may fall flat and generate overt or covert system negation from the other executive if the humorist does not know that the other executive has friends with working class backgrounds and is sympathetic to how education levels can limit advanced vocabulary levels. This example also illustrates how the behavior of a humorist goal striver can implicitly reveal potential bias, discrimination, or microaggression in social contexts (Sue, Capodilupo, Torino, Bucceri, Holder, Nadal, & Esquilin, 2007). In the above example, it seems implicit that the executive humorist feels superior to working class individuals.

In more aggressive forms of humor (Martin et al., 2003), one may intentionally target outgroups within the safety of his or her ingroup. Although such efforts may temporarily result in an ingroup network rippling of positive emotions (e.g. contagious laughing within the ingroup at the outgroup's expense), it can result in negative organizational outcomes when healthy, supportive, and respectful interactions are expected among everyone in a highly interconnected, diverse, and inter-dependent firm. Such derogatory motives may also be symbolic of deeper stereotypical beliefs or bias, which can detract from interpersonal cohesion (Fiske & Tablante, 2015) or create environments that are susceptible to dysfunctional stereotype threat (Steele & Aronson, 1995).

Acidic attacks

Westaby et al. (2016) have recently used dynamic network theory parameters to code social interactions in real time, which may have implications for understanding humor behavior in networks as well. For example, some *acidic* forms of conflict occur when individuals laugh at others at their expense (pure N). Many forms of bullying reflect this behavior, including those in work contexts. To illustrate, a "bully" may experience delight, joy, or amusement by putting co-workers down or belittling them for their mistakes or poor performance. Obviously, this can have serious psychological consequences for the recipients, especially when the recipients fear reporting the behavior to superiors if there are power and political issues involved. This also reflects some notions about subversive humor where humorists may ridicule and mock others (Robert, 2014), although we extend such thinking into the network sphere.

However, it is important to note there is often a fine line between pure system negation (where one takes delight in seeing others put down) and fake/covert system negation (where one is seemingly putting others down, but doesn't really mean it). We propose that fake system negation in conjunction with true system support is another common way individuals generate humor. For example, a very close friend may intensely tease or make fun of you for a simple mistake you made, but the close friend is not really wanting to experience joy through your being hurt. He or she is likely doing it knowing that you're going to laugh at the silliness of the event yourself and then the friend will start laughing with you as well in an authentically supportive way, implying no big deal. The person is laughing with you, not at you. From a dynamic network intelligence perspective, the person making the mistake likely knows that the friend is faking the acidic negation and is just trying to have fun with you. However, when deep support does not exist (or if it is not perceived to exist), using system negation in humor can be tricky and can sometimes backfire, resulting in very hurt feelings, anger, and potential retaliation.

Legal trouble

Another serious way in which an act of humor takes a wrong turn is when the recipients of unwanted humor respond with litigation against the company, such as claims of hostile work environments. In today's highly digitized world, it is also much easier for employees to document such behavior, which increases the odds of plaintiff success. The cost of legal defense and resulting monetary damages can be extreme. Consider the case in Florida where a waitress participated in a beer-selling contest at work that advertised a "free Toyota" as the prize. When she won, the prize was actually a toy Yoda doll – "April Fools!" She sued and the restaurant had to buy her the car (USATODAY, 2002). Sometimes the stakes are even higher, as when the city of Los Angeles was sued by a firefighter after being fed dog food as a prank. The victim sued and won $2.7 million in a racial discrimination lawsuit. Then, the fire captains also sued and won $2.5 million in a lawsuit claiming that because they were labeled "racists," they were overlooked for promotions (Tennie Pierce versus City of Los Angeles, 2006). In these cases, a rich and complicated set of network links emerge, often where the humorist goal striving (G) was intended to be funny, hoping for supportive reactions from others in the network (S), but dynamic network intelligence was low and others reacted with harsh resistance (P) and strong negative emotional reactions (N) to those who attempted the misplaced humor. Thus, trying to sensitize employees about the appropriateness of humor and the types of humor that can be damaging may be useful in future practice, such as during employee orientations or continuing education and training against hostile or harassing climates.

Conclusion

This chapter illustrated how humor may operate in network structures. Dynamic network theory was used as an integrative platform given its ability to synthesize both psychological and network mechanisms involved in motivation, emotion, and behavior. This not only provided a perspective to understand how humor operates and flows in networks, but also a perspective to understand how it may work in functional or dysfunctional ways. The theory also demonstrated unique conceptual insight into motivational issues in comparison to traditional network analyses, which have not sufficiently integrated the importance of goal pursuit linkages in complex network systems. Including goal nodes into networks was critical to understand much more of the complexities associated with humor acts in social and organizational systems.

Notes

1 This role is technically shown in dynamic network charts with a solid line with a small embedded black circle to denote how it's a conflict emotion but motivationally oriented for the goal, not against it. It is thus part of network affirmation (e.g. motivational defending the goal, not working against it). Ironically, this illustrates that negative links can serve positive goal functions.
2 Additional research could examine the implications and meaning of loosening these restrictions and examining other social network role links to goal nodes.
3 System reactance (R) is also part of network affirmation, because it suggests an interpersonal force in the network defending or reacting negatively to other negative or resistance forces. Thus, albeit fueled with negative affect and emotion, the purpose of system reactance often is in defense of a goal, thereby providing motivation for it.

References

Baumeister, R. F., DeWall, C. N., Ciarocco, N. J., & Twenge, J. M. (2005). Social exclusion impairs self-regulation. *Journal of Personality and Social Psychology*, 88, 589–604.

Borgatti, S. P., Mehra, A., Brass, D. J., & Labianca, G. (2009). Network analysis in the social sciences. *Science*, 323, 892–895.

Clark, M. S., & Lemay, E. P. Jr., (2010). Close relationships. In S. T. Fiske, D. T. Gilbert, & G. Lindzey (Eds.), *Handbook of social psychology*, vol. 2 (pp. 898–940). Hoboken, NJ: Wiley.

Coleman, P. T., Deutsch, M., & Marcus, E. C. (2014). *The handbook of conflict resolution: Theory and practice* (3rd edition). San Francisco, CA: Jossey-Bass.

Cooper, C. (2008). Elucidating the bonds of workplace humor: A relational process model. *Human Relations*, 61, 1087–1115.

Diener, E. Ng, W, Harter, J., & Arora, R. (2010). Wealth and happiness across the world: Material prosperity predicts life evaluation, whereas psychosocial prosperity predicts positive feeling. *Journal of Personality and Social Psychology*, 99, 52–61.

Duncan, W. J. (1982). Humor in management: Prospects for administrative practice and research. *Academy of Management Review*, 7, 136–142.

Fine G. A., & De Soucey, M. (2005). Joking cultures: Humor themes as social regulation in group life. *Humor*, 18, 1–22.

Fiske, S. T., & Tablante. C. B. (2015). Stereotyping: Processes and content. In M. Mikulincer, P. R. Shaver, E. Borgida, & J. A. Bargh (Eds.), *APA handbook of personality and social psychology*, vol. 1 (pp. 457–507). Washington, DC: American Psychological Association.

Kanfer, R., Ackerman, P. L., Murtha, T. C., Dugdale, B., & Nelson, L. (1994). Goal-setting, conditions of practice, and task-performance: A resource-allocation perspective. *Journal of Applied Psychology*, 79, 826–835.

Kinicki, A. J., McKee-Ryan, F. M., Schriesheim, C. A. & Carson, K. P. (2002). Assessing the construct validity of the job descriptive index: A review and meta-analysis. *Journal of Applied Psychology*, 87, 14–32.

Krackhardt, D., & Kilduff, M. (1999). Whether close or far: Social distance effects on perceived balance in friendship networks. *Journal of Personality and Social Psychology*, 76, 770–782.

Martin, R. A., Puhlik-Doris, P., Larsen, G., Gray, J., & Weir, K. (2003). Individual differences in uses of humor and their relation to psychological well-being: Development of the Humor Styles Questionnaire. *Journal of Research in Personality*, 37(1), 48–75.

McGraw, A. P. (2010). Benign violations: Making immoral behavior funny. *Psychological Science*, 21, 1141–1149.

McGraw, A. P., Warren, C., Williams, L. E., & Leonard, B. (2012). Too close for comfort, or too far to care? Finding humor in distant tragedies and close mishaps. *Psychological Science*, 23, 1215–1223.

Mesmer-Magnus, J., Glew, D. J., & Viswesvaran, C. (2012). A meta-analysis of positive humor in the workplace. *Journal of Managerial Psychology*, 27(2), 155–190.

Nelson, D. S. (1992). Humor in the pediatric emergency department: A 20 year retrospective. *Pediatrics*, 89, 1089–1090.

O'Quin, K., & Aronoff, J. (1981). Humor as a technique of social influence. *Social Psychology Quarterly*, 44, 349–357.

Robert, C. (2014). Social networks and sociometrics. In S. Attardo (Ed.), *Encyclopedia of humor studies* (pp. 708–710). Thousand Oaks, CA: Sage.

Robert, C., & Wilbanks, J. E. (2012). The wheel model of humor: Humor events and affect in organizations. *Human Relations*, 65, 1071–1099.

Scogin, F. R., & Pollio, H. R. (1980). Targeting and the humorous episode in group process. *Human Relations*, 33, 831–852.

Steele, C. M., & Aronson, J. (1995). Stereotype threat and the intellectual test-performance of African Americans. *Journal of Personality and Social Psychology*, 69, 797–811.

Sue, D. W., Capodilupo, C. M., Torino, G. C., Bucceri, J. M., Holder, A. M. B., Nadal, K. L., & Esquilin, M. (2007). Racial microaggressions in everyday life. *American Psychologist*, 62, 271–286.

Tennie Pierce versus City of Los Angeles (2006). Los Angeles Superior Court Case No. BC 345845. Claim File No. C05-4714.

Westaby, J. D. (2012). *Dynamic network theory: How social networks influence goal pursuit.* Washington, DC: American Psychological Association.

Westaby, J. D., & Redding, N. (2014). Social networks, social media, and conflict resolution. In P. T. Coleman, M. Deutsch, & E. C. Marcus (Eds.), *The handbook of conflict resolution: Theory and practice*, 3rd edition (pp. 998–1022). San Francisco, CA: Jossey-Bass.

Westaby, J. D. & Shon, D. (forthcoming). Simulating the social networks involved in human goal striving. In R. R. Vallacher, S. J. Read, & A. Nowak (Eds.), *Computational models in social psychology*. New York: Psychology Press.

Westaby, J. D., Pfaff, D. L., & Redding, N. (2014). Psychology and social networks: A dynamic network theory perspective. *American Psychologist*, 69, 269–284.

Westaby, J. D., Woods, N., & Pfaff, D. L. (2016). Extending dynamic network theory to group and social interaction analysis: Uncovering key behavioral elements, cycles, and emergent states. *Organizational Psychology Review*, 6, 34–62.

USATODAY.com (2002). Former Hooters waitress settles toy Yoda suit. (2002, May 9). Retrieved January 14, 2016, from http://usatoday30.usatoday.com/news/nation/2002/05/09/toy-yoda.htm

5

HUMOR AND CREATIVITY

Emuna Eliav, Ella Miron-Spektor, and Julia B. Bear

> *Laughter is an expression of freedom – freedom from the strict laws of rational thinking and freedom to play with new ideas.*
>
> *(Penjon, 1891, p. 121)*

Introduction

In modern work environments, employees and managers are increasingly required to solve problems creatively and to promote innovation (Amabile, 1996). Scholars and practitioners share a strong interest in identifying factors and conditions that promote creativity (Grant & Berry, 2011). Humor has long been seen as a catalyst for creativity. Early theorists revealed the liberating and energizing power of humor as fuel for creative thinking (Freud, 1960; Koestler, 1964). Humor is also considered a creative act that entails sudden shifts in cognitive perspectives and thinking patterns (Dixon, 1980; Koestler, 1964; Martin & Lefcourt, 1983; O'Connell, 1976). The positive association between the ability to express humor (or sense of humor) and creativity has been well documented (O'Quin & Derks, 1997). However, despite the existence of few studies that established a causal link between engaging in humor and creative outcomes (Ziv, 1976, 1983, 1988) and the humor–creativity link in organizations (Lang & Lee, 2010; Slåtten, Svensson, & Sværi, 2011), there is still much to learn about the interplay between humor and creativity in organizations. In this chapter, we review extant research on humor and creativity and conjecture on psychological processes that explain the effect of humor on creativity, as well as conditions that shape the humor–creativity relationship.

Creativity refers to an idea, product, or process that is both novel and appropriate (Amabile, 1983). Creativity was initially viewed as a characteristic of exceptional individuals, such as artists, inventors, and scientists (Simonton, 1997). More recently, creativity has been characterized as a way to find new and useful solutions to problems (Amabile & Pillemer, 2012), and is seen as a skill that can be improved with training (Stevenson, Kleibeuker, De Dreu, & Crone, 2014). Creativity is a multi-level phenomenon that involves individuals, teams, and organizations (Woodman, Sawyer, & Griffin, 1993), and entails a multi-stage process of problem presentation, preparation, response generation, and idea validation (Amabile, 1996).

Humor in organizations is considered a discrete communication that is intended to be amusing and to produce a positive affective response (Robert & Wilbanks, 2012). Humor can be manifested as a behavior (e.g. humor expression), as a reaction to another person's humor expression (e.g. humor appreciation), or as a trait (e.g. sense of humor) (Cooper, 2005). The expression and appreciation of humor is a basic element of human communication and frequently occurs in interpersonal interactions at work, both among friends and colleagues, and across hierarchical levels (Duncan, Smeltzer, & Leap, 1990; Smeltzer & Leap, 1988).

Most research on humor and creativity has focused on how an individual's expression of, or reaction to, humor influences creativity (O'Quin & Derks, 1999). Theorists suggest that humor evokes cognitive, affective, and social processes that are conducive to creative thinking (Koestler, 1964; Romero & Pescosolido, 2008; Wood, Beckman, & Rossiter, 2011). Empirical research, however, has lagged behind in this regard, providing little insight about mediating processes and boundary conditions under which humor is more or less beneficial to creativity.

This chapter advances knowledge on the interplay between humor and creativity in organizations. It is divided into three sections: First, we review prior research on humor and creativity. Second, we propose emotional, cognitive and social mechanisms through which humor may affect creativity. Third, we conjecture concerning moderating factors and conditions that shape the humor–creativity link, including characteristics of the humor expresser, the humor expression and the context. We summarize the proposed mechanisms and moderators in a theoretical model, depicted in Figure 5.1. The model is derived from the integration of various literatures, and we hope that it will be useful for helping researchers identify aspects of the humor–creativity relationship that can be fruitfully explored in future research. Throughout the chapter, we identify specific questions and directions for future research, particularly in terms of organizations.

The interplay between humor and creativity

Although humor and creativity are distinct constructs, at their essence, they share fundamental properties. Both humor and creativity involve making non-obvious connections between two seemingly unrelated and incongruous elements (Murdock & Ganim, 1992). Creativity occurs by combining remote elements into new ideas (Mednick, 1962), and benefits from the ability to juxtapose opposing frameworks and contradictory perspectives (Miron-Spektor, Gino, & Argote, 2011b; Rothenberg, 1979). For example, Einstein invented the Theory of Relativity when he imagined an object that is in motion and at rest at the same time (Rothenberg, 1979). In a similar vein, humor results from switching the frame of reference

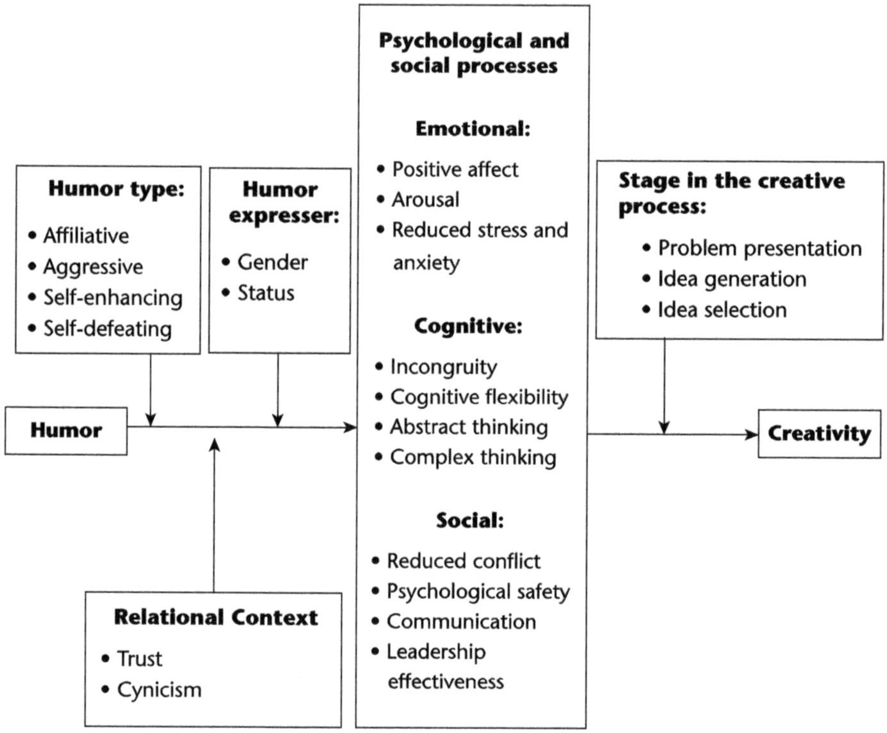

FIGURE 5.1 Theoretical model.

(O'Connel, 1976) and bisociation, or the connection of incompatible frames (Koestler, 1964). For example, Woody Allen's saying "I failed to make the chess team because of my height" is humorous because of the incongruity between two unrelated frameworks (i.e. "chess and intelligence" and "basketball and height").

Furthermore, both humor and creativity elicit a sense of surprise (Filipowicz, 2006), but, at the same time, should be appropriate. To be considered creative, a novel idea should also be useful (Amabile, 1996). Likewise, in order to amuse, a humor expression should be appropriate for the situation (McGraw & Warren, 2010). Put differently, both humor and creativity entail breaking some frameworks while adhering to others. These similarities have inspired researchers to investigate the relationship between humor and creativity in terms of traits (Lieberman, 1965), behaviors (Lang & Lee, 2010; Slåtten, Svensson, & Sværi, 2011), and outcomes (Ziv, 1976, 1983).

Humor as a catalyst of creativity

Initial empirical work on the relationship between humor and creativity identified sense of humor as a characteristic of creative individuals (Getzels & Jackson, 1962).

These studies suggested that individuals with a better sense of humor (measured as a trait, propensity, or ability) are more likely to generate creative ideas (Goodchilds, 1972). Specifically, the positive relationship between sense of humor and creativity was documented among young children (Lieberman, 1965), teenagers (Fabrizi & Pollio, 1987), and adults (Goodchilds & Smith, 1964) using different creativity tasks (e.g. Treadwell, 1970). A meta-analysis of these studies revealed a correlation of 0.34 between humor expression and creative behavior (O'Quin & Derks, 1997).

Research also examined whether engaging in humor expression can improve creative performance. For example, individuals who engaged in training in improvisational comedy experienced significant improvement in their creativity in a subsequent product generation task, compared to individuals who did not engage in this type of training (Kudrowitz, 2010). Another study found that framing a task as fun and silly resulted in better creative performance compared to framing the task as serious (Friedman, Förster, & Denzler, 2007). Similarly, instructing participants to use humor when completing the Torrance creativity test improved their creativity relative to standard instructions (Ziv, 1983). Together, these findings suggest that engaging in humor, before or while performing a creativity task, has a positive effect on creativity.

Research also suggests that mere exposure to humor can fuel creativity. For instance, in an experimental study, listening to humorous expressions increased adolescents' scores on the Torrance creativity test compared to a control group (Ziv, 1976). Similarly, watching a comedy film increased performance on insight creativity tasks (Isen, Daubman, & Nowicki, 1987). Recent studies on sarcasm revealed that observing sarcastic remarks likewise improved creative thinking (Huang, Gino, Galinski, 2015; Miron-Spektor, Efrat-Treister, Rafaeli, & Schwarz-Cohen, 2011a).

In organizational contexts, research on humor and creativity is relatively scarce. Several studies have demonstrated a positive relationship between self-reported humor expressions at work and creativity (Lang & Lee, 2010; Slåtten, Svensson & Sværi, 2011). Research on groups suggests that the presence of just one member who uses humor deliberately and frequently is enough to improve group performance in problem solving tasks (Smith & Goodchilds, 1963). Relatedly, leaders who use humor with their subordinates improve communication and knowledge sharing (Wood et al., 2011) which enhances creativity (Pan, Sun, & Chow, 2012; Volmer, Spurk, & Niessen, 2012). Research suggests that leaders who express humor effectively inspire their subordinates to find creative and innovative solutions to complex problems (Lee, 2015). In this way, humor contributes to transformational leadership (Avolio, Howell, & Sosik, 1999), which subsequently enhances creativity (Jaussi & Dionne, 2003). Finally, several studies suggested that employees working in organizations with a humor climate, meaning a climate in which humor expressions are legitimate and frequent, tend to be more creative (Ekvall, 1996; Isaksen & Lauer, 2002; Slåtten, Svensson & Sværi, 2011).

Underlying emotional, cognitive and social mechanisms of humor

The creative benefits of humor have been attributed to various interwoven emotional, cognitive, and social processes (O'Quin & Derks, 1999; Wood et al., 2011). In the following sections, we theorize about emotional, cognitive, and social routes through which humor may enhance creativity.

Humor and creativity: The emotional route

According to the wheel model of humor (Robert & Wilbanks, 2012), humor events consist of amusing communications that elicit positive affect in organizations. Amusing communication creates emotional contagion (Barsade, 2002) and positive emotional cycles, in which the positive affect produced by the humor expresser is then transferred to other organizational members who did not necessarily directly participate in the humor event (Hareli & Rafaeli, 2008; Miron-Spektor & Rafaeli, 2009; Miron Spektor et al., 2011a; Robert & Wilbanks, 2012). Empirical support for the effect of humor on positive affect mainly comes from experimental work on creativity. For example, Isen and colleagues (1987) used clips from comedies to elicit positive affect that, in turn, increased creativity. Similarly, according to the broaden-and-build theory of positive emotions (Fredrickson, 1998), positive emotions such as joy broaden individuals' momentary thought–action repertoires, thereby building mental, psychological, and social resources. Specifically, widening the array of thought–action repertoires enables greater exploration and cognitive flexibility that enhances creative outcomes (Fredrickson, 2001). A recent meta-analysis on emotions and creativity (Baas, De Dreu, & Nijstad, 2008) suggests that joy, amusement, and happiness are high arousal, promotion-focused emotions that broaden the focus of attention and thus the responsiveness to peripheral and less accessible elements and cues that contribute to the generation of new solutions. This effect is stronger when creativity tasks are constructed as fun and silly rather than serious and important (Friedman et al., 2007).

Affective reactions also vary in terms of activation and arousal (Baas et al., 2008; Russell, 1980; Watson & Tellegen, 1985). Several studies found that watching comedies and cartoons increases arousal relative to watching other types of films (Averill, 1969; Langevin & Day, 1972). Similarly, the more humorous the joke, the more individuals experienced increased skin conductance and heart rate both during the body of the joke and the punchline (Godkewitsch, 1976). A recent meta-analysis suggests that increased arousal of emotions such as joy and happiness is conducive to creativity (Baas et al., 2008). Indeed, watching humorous videotapes was shown to increase creativity only among participants who reported feeling pleasantness and surprise coupled with high arousal (Filipowicz, 2006).

Humor can also create relief from stress (Berlyne, 1972; Meyer, 2000), which has been shown to impede creativity (Amabile, Hadley, & Kramer, 2002). Humor can be an antidote to stress, or at least buffer its deleterious effect, not only by increasing positive affect in general, but also by neutralizing the negative emotions that stressors produce (Freud, 1960). Humor distracts attention from and attenuates the negative impact of stressful (Abel, 2002; Martin & Lefcourt, 1983) and embarrassing situations (Fink & Walker, 1977). For example, adding humorous items to an exam was shown to reduce anxiety and improve performance (Smith, Ascough, Ettinger, & Nelson, 1971).

More research is needed to establish the effect of humor on creativity through positive affect in organizations. Specifically, future research could examine the extent to which positive affect accounts for the humor–creativity relationship at work. Future research can also challenge the assumption that humor necessarily leads to positive affect, and examine additional affective reactions (such as embarrassment, discomfort, and insult) that may be associated with humor. As per appraisal theories of emotions (e.g. Frijda, 1986; Lazarus, 1991; Smith & Ellsworth, 1985), emotional responses occur based on the way individuals evaluate, or appraise, events. Thus, depending upon the nature of the humor expression, and, in turn, the appraisal, individuals may have a negative affective response, thereby dampening creativity. To be sure, the effects of humor on emotional and cognitive processes are likely to be complex and interwoven, consistent with extant research on the interplay between emotion and cognition (e.g. Barrett, Mesquita, Ochsner, & Gross, 2007).

Humor and creativity: The cognitive route

Humor also affects cognitive processes, as it entails awareness of an incongruity between two elements, thoughts, or meanings (Wyer & Collins, 1992). As Suls (1972, 1983) explains, the initial information presented during a humor expression activates a set of schema or bodies of knowledge that are used to subsequently interpret the humor expression. These schemas set expectations concerning the information to follow. The incongruity occurs when people face new information (that creates the punchline), which cannot be interpreted using the initial schemas, thus deviating from expectations.

The ability to shift between incongruent frameworks has long been identified as a cognitive process that enhances creativity (Rothenberg, 1971). Creative problem-solving requires bisociative thinking, or the ability to think simultaneously about more than one matrix and to combine unrelated and often conflicting elements in a new way (Dubitzky, Kötter, Schmidt, & Berthold, 2012; Koesteler, 1964). Likewise, experimental work suggests that adopting paradoxical frames that encourage the juxtaposition and integration of conflicting elements enhances creative problem-solving (Miron-Spektor et al., 2011b). Future research will benefit from integrating research on paradoxical frames and integrative thinking to establish the mediation of the effect of humor on creativity by incongruity.

Cognitive flexibility is another potential mechanism explaining humor's relationship with creativity (Ziv, 1988). Cognitive flexibility refers to the breadth and number of distinct knowledge domains and semantic categories that a person accesses and integrates, and it also reflects the ability to switch approaches, frameworks, and goals (Baas et al., 2008). Future research can examine to what extent the expression of humor versus exposure to humor increases cognitive flexibility. In other words, future research could examine whether mere exposure to humor is enough to increase cognitive flexibility, or whether it is necessary to actually express humor oneself in order to reap the cognitive benefits.

Research on sarcasm has also suggested two possible mediating processes: Cognitive complexity and abstract thinking. Interpreting sarcasm requires complex thinking in order to simultaneously decode the literal meaning and interpret the nuances of the message by relying on contextual and situational cues (Gibbs, 1986). One study found that listening to sarcastic remarks increased complex thinking and creative problem-solving (Miron-Spektor et al., 2011a), whereas a follow-up study suggested abstract thinking, which is a cognitive processing style that focuses on the superordinate and general features of events (versus incidental and contextualized; Trope & Liberman, 2010), as an alternative mediating process (Huang et al., 2015).

Future research could also examine the effect of humor on the novelty and usefulness dimensions of creativity. A recent experiment revealed that cognitive flexibility leads to novel ideas, whereas cognitive closure increases idea usefulness (Miron-Spektor & Beenen, 2015). In line with these findings, we conjecture that humor will mainly enhance the novelty dimension of creativity but will have weaker or even negative effects on the usefulness dimension. Finally, given that humor events may serve as refreshing interruptions from work, future research can draw from findings from the incubation literature showing that cognitive breaks enhance creativity (Eliav & Miron-Spektor, 2015; Sio & Ormerod, 2009).

Humor and creativity: The social route

Research has emphasized the effect of the social context on creative achievements (Amabile & Pillemer, 2012). Humor in organizations occurs in social situations among co-workers and managers. People are often reluctant to raise creative ideas that may seem weird and uncertain, and thus be ridiculed and rejected (Mainemelis, 2010; Miron-Spektor, Paletz, & Lin, 2015; Torrance, 1995). Humor in social settings helps to construct and maintain positive and psychologically safe work environments (Edmondson, 1999) that are conducive to creativity (Romero & Pescosolido, 2008). Indeed, an analysis of humor use in work groups revealed that humor expressions help to establish effective workplace relationships that, in turn, foster creativity (Holmes, 2007). Humor also reduces social distance between people (e.g. Kane, Suls, & Tedeschi, 1977; Sherman, 1988), and promotes team cohesion and trust (Hampes, 1999), as well as harmony and collegiality (Holmes, 2006; Stogdill, 1972). Humor enables the communication of disagreements and criticism, as well as the effective management of conflicts, which may contribute to creativity (De Dreu, 2006; Holmes, 2000; Jehn, 1995). In this way, the positive effects of humor on interpersonal relationships may indirectly benefit the creative process.

Exploring the social effects of humor on creativity is an important research avenue. Future research can examine how humor increases trust, knowledge sharing and prosocial behavior among team members, thereby aiding collective creativity (Hargadon & Bechky, 2006). It also may be interesting to examine whether humor expression reduces psychological distance, particularly when there is a status differential, thereby making high status individuals seem more approachable (Hoption, Barling, & Turner, 2013). Lastly, future research should examine nonlinear effects, since too much emphasis on humor can focus individuals on social relationships rather than the work itself (Fleming, 2005; Westwood & Johnston, 2013) and ultimately backfire in terms of creative performance.

Boundary conditions and moderating factors

To be sure, humor is not always beneficial. Research on humor and creativity assumes that humor expressions are necessarily amusing, overlooking humor expressions that fail to amuse, or even worse, have negative effects. What may be amusing to the humor expresser may be offensive to the humor receiver. In the sections below, and in Figure 5.1, we suggest factors that will moderate the effects of humor, including humor type, as well as gender and status of the humor expresser and receiver.

Humor type

Research on humor in organizations has focused on positive humor, within which there are two sub-types: self-enhancing, used intrapsychically especially to cope with adversity; and affiliative, used interpersonally to develop social bonds with others (Martin, Puhlik-Doris, Larsen, Gray, & Weir, 2003; Mesmer-Magnus, Glew, & Viswesvaran, 2012). Yet organizational life is rife with examples of negative humor, namely, aggressive and self-defeating (Morreall, 2008; Plester & Sayers, 2007). *Aggressive* humor is targeted at another person, either present (i.e. denigrating the recipient) or absent (i.e. laughing at an individual behind his or her back). *Self-defeating* humor is targeted at oneself, and is used to ridicule oneself in order to amuse and seek acceptance and approval from others. Negative humor, in particular aggressive humor, may suppress creativity, not only by narrowing the cognitive processing style, but also by demotivating employees to generate original ideas and take the risk of sharing them (Kuiper, Martin, & Olinger, 1993). Few studies have empirically studied how these different humor types affect creativity. One study found that only self-enhancing humor used by managers was positively and significantly associated with subordinates' creativity, as compared to affiliative and aggressive humor (Lee, 2015). Another study examining different functions of workplace humor (i.e. to control others versus to relieve stress) likewise found differential effects of humor type on creative outcomes (Lang & Lee, 2010). In summary, the humor–creativity relationship is not uniformly positive, but rather, the humor type being expressed is an important moderator of the interplay between humor and creativity.

Effects of gender and status

Humor research has been paying growing attention to the role of gender and has demonstrated gender differences in humor appreciation and expression (Kottohoff, 2006). Regarding the former, gender has been found to moderate the effect of humor on creative performance. Specifically, after watching humorous videotapes, men's performance increased on a creativity task whereas women's performance did not change. Furthermore, the humor manipulation increased both positive affect and arousal in men, but only increased positive affect in women (Filipowicz, 2006). Another study found similar effects, such that exposure to humor increased men's (but not women's) performance on a mental rotation task (Belanger, Kirkpatrick, & Derks, 1998). These findings demonstrate that gender of the humor receiver appears to moderate the effects of exposure to humor on creativity.

Regarding the effect of gender on humor expression, studies have shown minor or no gender differences in humor expression ability (Mickes, Walker, Parris Mankoff, & Christenfeld, 2012). However, men tend to express humor more frequently than women (McGhee, 1979). Relatedly, women's humor expressions are less frequently perceived as amusing and successful compared to expressions by men (Robinson & Smith-Lovin, 2001), perhaps because humor expression is considered to be a stereotypically masculine behavior. When women express humor, the reaction is less predictable and tends to be more extreme (both positively and negatively depending on the effectiveness of the humor expression), compared to humor used by men (Decker & Rotondo, 2001). These findings suggest that gender of the humor expresser may moderate the effect of the humor expression on creativity, but further research is required to examine this hypothesis.

Gender differences in the effectiveness of humor expression may arise from differences in socio-structural status, with men typically occupying higher status roles compared to women (Ridgeway, 1997). In fact, humor is usually expressed among members of the same status level (Bradney, 1957), but when humor occurs between status levels, it is typically aimed downward (Duncan et al., 1990). Moreover, lower-ranking group members tend not to express humor to higher status members (Lundberg, 1969). We suggest that the status of the expresser may moderate the effectiveness of humor, but the nature of the effect will also depend upon the authenticity of the encounter. On the one hand, humor expressed by a higher status individual, such as a manager, may be less likely to evoke true amusement in that subordinates may feel forced to express amusement, and thus the beneficial effects of humor are unlikely. On the other hand, if the humor expression of a high status individual elicits authentic amusement, then it should have a positive impact on creativity.

Relational context: Trust

The effectiveness of humor also depends on the relational and organizational context within which the humor expression occurs. Since humor expresses a message in a non-literal way, its proper understanding relies on shared values, beliefs, and associations and, therefore, it can easily be misinterpreted. In this way, the degree of trust between the humor expresser and receiver should influence the way in which the humor expression is interpreted, particularly when the expression is ambiguous (Huang et al., 2015; Lee, 2015). One study examined the moderating role of followers' trust in their leader on the humor–creativity relationship. Under high levels of trust, both the positive effect of the leader's positive humor and the negative effect of the leader's aggressive humor on followers' creativity were stronger (Lee, 2015). Another study found that sarcasm increased both creativity and conflict with low levels of trust, but with high levels of trust sarcasm led to greater creativity without increasing conflict (Huang et al., 2015).

When employees do not trust their supervisor, or management in general, they tend to interpret management's actions cynically (Anderson & Bateman, 1997). If an employee doubts the authenticity of the humor expresser's intentions, the humor expression might be interpreted as disingenuous and increase cynicism, which, in turn, may hinder creativity. Similarly, some organizations intentionally try to create "fun cultures," in which humor plays an important role (Barsoux, 1993; Bolman & Deal, 2000), but these explicit attempts to induce humor and make work fun may result in increased employee cynicism (Fleming, 2005), which most likely dampens creativity.

Stages of the creative process

Creativity research distinguishes among different stages of the creative process (Lubart, 2001). We propose that humor may have different effects on creative outcomes depending upon the phase in the creative process. In the first stage of the creative process – problem presentation – humor may help to frame the task as enjoyable, thereby generating positive affect, which has been shown to enhance creativity (Baas et al., 2008). In the next stage – idea generation – humor is also likely to facilitate creativity by the promotion of divergent thinking (Morreall, 1991; Ziv, 1976). However, in the later stages of the creative process, namely idea selection and validation, convergent thinking is required, necessitating a focused style of information processing (Cropley, 2006). Humor is less likely to be beneficial for this type of activity. Future research should examine the effect of humor throughout the different stages of the creative process, and whether the positive effects of humor during the initial stages have lingering, negative effects in the later stages of the creative process.

Conclusion

Humor clearly facilitates creativity in organizations. Expressing, receiving and, above all, exchanging humor has beneficial effects on emotion, cognition, and social relationships, all of which are crucial for creativity. Furthermore, the creative process not only requires the generation of novel and useful ideas, but also that these ideas will be accepted by others. Accordingly, humor not only facilitates divergent thinking and idea creation, but may also mitigate criticism and resistance to new ideas. We hope that our integration of the literature and theoretical model will stimulate future endeavors that can further our understanding of how and when humor engenders creativity in organizations.

References

Abel, M. H. (2002). Humor, stress, and coping strategies. *Humor: International Journal of Humor Research*, 15(4), 365–381.

Amabile, T. M. (1983). The social psychology of creativity: A componential conceptualization. *Journal of Personality and Social Psychology*, 45(2), 357–376.

Amabile, T. M. (1996). *Creativity in the context*. Boulder, CO: Westview Press.

Amabile, T. M., & Pillemer, J. (2012). Perspectives on the social psychology of creativity. *The Journal of Creative Behavior*, 46(1), 3–15.

Amabile, T. M., Hadley, C. N., & Kramer, S. J. (2002). Creativity under the gun. *Harvard Business Review*, 80(8), 52–61.

Andersson, L. M., & Bateman, T. S. (1997). Cynicism in the workplace: Some causes and effects. *Journal of Organizational Behavior*, 18(5), 449–469.

Averill, J. R. (1969). Autonomic response patterns during sadness and mirth. *Psychophysiology*, 5(4), 399–414.

Avolio, B. J., Howell, J. M., & Sosik, J. J. (1999). A funny thing happened on the way to the bottom line: Humor as a moderator of leadership style effects. *Academy of Management Journal*, 42(2), 219–227.

Baas, M., De Dreu, C. K., & Nijstad, B. A. (2008). A meta-analysis of 25 years of mood-creativity research: Hedonic tone, activation, or regulatory focus? *Psychological Bulletin*, 134(6), 779–806.

Barrett, L. F., Mesquita, B., Ochsner, K. N., & Gross, J. J. (2007). The experience of emotion. *Annual Review of Psychology*, 58, 373–403.

Barsade, S. G. (2002). The ripple effect: Emotional contagion and its influence on group behavior. *Administrative Science Quarterly*, 47(4), 644–675.

Barsoux, J. L. (1993). *Funny business: Humor management and business culture*. New York: Cassell.

Belanger, H. G., Kirkpatrick, L. A., & Derks, P. (1998). The effects of humor on verbal and imaginal problem solving. *Humor*, 11, 21–31.

Berlyne, D. E. (1972). Humor and its kin. In J. H. Goldstein, & P. E. McGhee (Eds.), *The psychology of humor: Theoretical perspectives and empirical issues* (pp. 43–60). New York: Academic Press.

Bolman, L. G., & Deal, T. E. (2000). *Escape from cluelessness*. New York: AMACOM.

Bradney, P. (1957). The joking relationship in industry. *Human Relationship*, 10, 179–187.

Cooper, C. D. (2005). Just joking around? Employee humor expression as an ingratiatory behavior. *Academy of Management Review*, 30(4), 765–776.

Cropley, A. (2006). In praise of convergent thinking. *Creativity Research Journal*, 18(3), 391–404.

Decker, W. H., & Rotondo, D. M. (2001). Relationships among gender, type of humor, and perceived leader effectiveness. *Journal of Managerial Issues*, 13(4), 450–465.

De Dreu, C. K. (2006). When too little or too much hurts: Evidence for a curvilinear relationship between task conflict and innovation in teams. *Journal of Management*, 32(1), 83–107.

Dixon, N. F. (1980). Humor: Cognitive alternative to stress. *Bulletin of the British Psychological Society*, 33, 18–18.
Dubitzky, W., Kötter, T., Schmidt, O., & Berthold, M. R. (2012). *Towards creative information exploration based on Koestler's concept of bisociation*. Berlin: Springer.
Duncan, W. J., Smeltzer, L. R., & Leap, T. L. (1990). Humor and work: Applications of joking behavior to management. *Journal of Management*, 16(2), 255–278.
Edmondson, A. (1999). Psychological safety and learning behavior in work teams. *Administrative Science Quarterly*, 44(2), 350–383.
Ekvall, G. (1996). Organizational climate for creativity and innovation. *European Journal of Work and Organizational Psychology*, 5(1), 105–123.
Eliav, E., & Miron-Spektor, E. (2015). The recovery effect: The creative potential of frequent interruptions. Academy of Management Proceedings, USA, January 2015, 18083.
Fabrizi, M. S., & Pollio, H. R. (1987). Are funny teenagers creative? *Psychological Reports*, 61(3), 751–761.
Filipowicz, A. (2006). From positive affect to creativity: The surprising role of surprise. *Creativity Research Journal*, 18(2), 141–152.
Fink, E. L., & Walker, B. A. (1977). Humorous responses to embarrassment. *Psychological Reports*, 40(2), 475–485.
Fleming, P. (2005). Workers' playtime? Boundaries and cynicism in a "culture of fun" program. *The Journal of Applied Behavioral Science*, 41(3), 285–303.
Fredrickson, B. L. (1998). What good are positive emotions? *Review of General Psychology*, 2(3), 300–319.
Fredrickson, B. L. (2001). The role of positive emotions in positive psychology: The broaden-and-build theory of positive emotions. *American Psychologist*, 56(3), 218–226.
Freud, S. (1960). *Jokes and their relation to the unconscious*. New York: Norton (1st German edition, 1905).
Friedman, R. S., Förster, J., & Denzler, M. (2007). Interactive effects of mood and task framing on creative generation. *Creativity Research Journal*, 19(2–3), 141–162.
Frijda, N. H. (1986). *The emotions*. New York: Cambridge University Press.
Getzels, J., & Jackson, P. (1962). *Creativity and intelligence*. New York: John Wiley & Sons.
Gibbs, R. W. (1986). On the psycholinguistics of sarcasm. *Journal of Experimental Psychology: General*, 115(1), 3–15.
Godkewitsch, M. (1976). Physiological and verbal indices of arousal in rated humour. In A. J. Chapman, & H. C. Foot (Eds.), *Humor and laughter: Theory, research and applications* (pp. 117–138). London: John Wiley & Sons.
Goodchilds, J. D. (1972). On being witty: Causes, correlates, and consequences. In J. H. Goldstein, & P. E. McGhee (Eds.), *The psychology of humor: Theoretical perspectives and empirical issues* (pp. 173–193). New York: Academic Press.
Goodchilds, J. D., & Smith, E. E. (1964). The wit and his group. *Human Relations*, 17(1), 23–31.
Grant, A. M., & Berry, J. W. (2011). The necessity of others is the mother of invention: Intrinsic and prosocial motivations, perspective taking, and creativity. *Academy of Management Journal*, 54(1), 73–96.
Hampes, W. P. (1999). The relationship between humor and trust. *Humor*, 12(3), 253–260.
Hareli, S., & Rafaeli, A. (2008). Emotion cycles: On the social influence of emotion in organizations. *Research in Organizational Behavior*, 28, 35–59.
Hargadon, A. B., & Bechky, B. A. (2006). When collections of creatives become creative collectives: A field study of problem solving at work. *Organization Science*, 17(4), 484–500.

Holmes, J. (2000). Politeness, power and provocation: How humour functions in the workplace. *Discourse Studies*, 2(2), 159–185.

Holmes, J. (2006). Sharing a laugh: Pragmatic aspects of humor and gender in the workplace. *Journal of Pragmatics*, 38(1), 26–50.

Holmes, J. (2007). Making humour work: Creativity on the job. *Applied Linguistics*, 28(4), 518–537.

Hoption, C., Barling, J., & Turner, N. (2013). "It's not you, it's me": Transformational leadership and self-deprecating humor. *Leadership & Organization Development Journal*, 34(1), 4–19.

Huang, L., Gino, F., & Galinsky, A. D. (2015). The highest form of intelligence: Sarcasm increases creativity for both expressers and recipients. *Organizational Behavior and Human Decision Processes*, 131, 162–177.

Isaksen, S. G., & Lauer, K. J. (2002). The climate for creativity and change in teams. *Creativity and Innovation Management*, 11, 74–86.

Isen, A. M., Daubman, K. A., & Nowicki, G. P. (1987). Positive affect facilitates creative problem solving. *Journal of Personality and Social Psychology*, 52(6), 1122–1131.

Jaussi, K. S., & Dionne, S. D. (2003). Leading for creativity: The role of unconventional leader behavior. *The Leadership Quarterly*, 14, 475–498.

Jehn, K. A. (1995). A multimethod examination of the benefits and detriments of intragroup conflict. *Administrative Science Quarterly*, 40(2), 256–282.

Kane, T. R., Suls, J., & Tedeschi, J. T. (1977). Humor as a tool of social interaction. In A. J. Chapman, & H. C. Foot (Eds.), *It's a funny thing, humor* (pp. 13–16). Elmsford, NY: Pergamon Press.

Koestler, A. (1964). *The act of creation: A study of conscious and unconscious processes of humor, scientific discovery and art.* New York: The Macmillan Company.

Kotthoff, H. (2006). Gender and humor: The state of the art. *Journal of Pragmatics*, 38(1), 4–25.

Kudrowitz, B. M. (2010). *Haha and aha!: Creativity, idea generation, improvisational humor, and product design* (Doctoral dissertation). Retrieved from MIT Theses Collection: http://hdl.handle.net/1721.1/61610 (accessed August 16, 2016).

Kuiper, N. A., Martin, R. A., & Olinger, L. J. (1993). Coping humor, stress and cognitive appraisals. *Canadian Journal of Behavioral Science*, 25(1), 81–96.

Lang, J. C., & Lee, C. H. (2010). Workplace humor and organizational creativity. *The International Journal of Human Resource Management*, 21(1), 46–60.

Langevin, R., & Day, H. I. (1972). Physiological correlates of humor. In J. H. Goldstein, & P. E. McGhee (Eds.), *The psychology of humor: Theoretical perspectives and empirical issues* (pp. 129–142). New York: Academic Press.

Lazarus, R. S. (1991). *Emotions and adaptation*. New York: Oxford University Press.

Lee, D. R. (2015). The impact of leader's humor on employees' creativity: The moderating role of trust in leader. *Seoul Journal of Business*, 21(1), 59.

Lieberman, J. N. (1965). Playfulness and divergent thinking: An investigation of their relationship at the kindergarten level. *The Journal of Genetic Psychology*, 107(2), 219–224.

Lubart, T. I. (2001). Models of the creative process: Past, present and future. *Creativity Research Journal*, 13(3–4), 295–308.

Lundberg, C. (1969). Person-focused joking: Pattern and function. *Human Organization*, 28(1), 22–28.

Mainemelis, C. (2010). Stealing fire: Creative deviance in the evolution of new ideas. *Academy of Management Review*, 35(4), 558–578.

Martin, R. A., & Lefcourt, H. M. (1983). Sense of humor as a moderator of the relation between stressors and moods. *Journal of Personality and Social Psychology*, 45(6), 1313.

Martin, R. A., Puhlik-Doris, P., Larsen, G., Gray, J., & Weir, K. (2003). Individual differences in uses of humor and their relation to psychological well-being: Development of the Humor Styles Questionnaire. *Journal of Research in Personality*, 37(1), 48–75.

McGhee, P. E. (1979). The role of laughter and humor in growing up female. In C. B. Kopp (Ed.), *Becoming female* (pp. 183–206). New York: Springer.

McGraw, A. P., & Warren, C. (2010). Benign violations: Making immoral behavior funny. *Psychological Science*, 21(8), 1141–1149.

Mednick, S. (1962). The associative basis of the creative process. *Psychological Review*, 69(3), 220.

Mesmer-Magnus, J., Glew, D. J., & Viswesvaran, C. (2012). A meta-analysis of positive humor in the workplace. *Journal of Managerial Psychology*, 27(2), 155–190.

Meyer, J. C. (2000). Humor as a double-edged sword: Four functions of humor in communication. *Communication Theory*, 10(3), 310–331.

Mickes, L., Walker, D. E., Parris, J. L., Mankoff, R., & Christenfeld, N. J. (2012). Who's funny: Gender stereotypes, humor production, and memory bias. *Psychonomic Bulletin & Review*, 19(1), 108–112.

Miron-Spektor, E., & Beenen, G. (2015). Motivating creativity: The effects of sequential and simultaneous learning and performance achievement goals on product novelty and usefulness. *Organizational Behavior and Human Decision Processes*, 127, 53–65.

Miron-Spektor, E., & Rafaeli, A. (2009). The effects of anger in the workplace: When, where, and why observing anger enhances or hinders performance. *Research in Personnel and Human Resources Management*, 28, 153–178.

Miron-Spektor, E., Efrat-Treister, D., Rafaeli, A., & Schwarz-Cohen, O. (2011a). Others' anger makes people work harder not smarter: The effect of observing anger and sarcasm on creative and analytic thinking. *Journal of Applied Psychology*, 96(5), 1065.

Miron-Spektor, E., Gino, F., & Argote, L. (2011b). Paradoxical frames and creative sparks: Enhancing individual creativity through conflict and integration. *Organizational Behavior and Human Decision Processes*, 116(2), 229–240.

Miron-Spektor, E., Paletz, S. B. F., & Lin, C. C. (2015). To create without losing face: The effects of face cultural logic and social-image affirmation on creativity. *Journal of Organizational Behavior*, 36, 919–943.

Morreall, J. (1991). Humor and work. *Humor*, 4, 359–373.

Morreall, J. (2008). Applications of humor: Health, the workplace, and education. In V. Raskin (Ed.), *The primer of humour research* (pp. 449–478). Berlin: Mouton de Gruyter.

Murdock, M. C., & Ganim, R. M. (1992). Creativity and humor: Integration and incongruity. *Journal of Creative Behavior*, 27, 57–70.

O'Connell, W. E. (1976). Freudian humour: The eupsychia of everyday life. In A. J. Chapman, & H. C. Foot (Eds.), *Humor and laughter: Theory, research, and applications* (pp. 313–329). Piscataway, NJ: Transaction Publishers.

O'Quin, K. & Derks, P. (1997). Humor and creativity: A review of the empirical literature. In M. A. Runco (Ed.), *Creativity research handbook*, vol. 1 (pp. 223–252). Cresskill, NJ: Hampton Press.

O'Quin, K. & Derks, P. (1999). Humor. In M. Runco, & S. Printzker (Eds.), *Encyclopedia of creativity*, vol. 1 (pp. 845–853). San Diego, CA: Academic Press.

Pan, W., Sun, L. Y., & Chow, I. H. S. (2012). Leader-member exchange and employee creativity: Test of a multilevel moderated mediation model. *Human Performance*, 25(5), 432–451.

Penjon, R. (1891). Le rire at la liberte. *Revue Phylosophique*, 2, 113–125.

Plester, B. A., & Sayers, J. (2007). "Taking the piss": Functions of banter in the IT industry. *Humor*, 20(2), 157–187.

Ridgeway, C. L. (1997). Interaction and the conservation of gender inequality: Considering employment. *American Sociological Review*, 62, 218–235.

Robert, C., & Wilbanks, J. E. (2012). The wheel model of humor: Humor events and affect in organizations. *Human Relations*, 65(9), 1071–1099.

Robinson, D. T., & Smith-Lovin, L. (2001). Getting a laugh: Gender, status, and humor in task discussions. *Social Forces*, 80(1), 123–158.

Romero, E., & Pescosolido, A. (2008). Humor and group effectiveness. *Human Relations*, 61(3), 395–418.

Rothenberg, A. (1971). The process of Janusian thinking in creativity. *Archives of General Psychiatry*, 24(3), 195–205.

Rothenberg, A. (1979). Einstein's creative thinking and the general theory of relativity: A documented report. *The American Journal of Psychiatry*, 136, 38–43.

Russell, J. A. (1980). A circumplex model of affect. *Journal of Personality and Social Psychology*, 39, 161–178.

Sherman, L. W. (1988). Humor and social distance in elementary school children. *Humor*, 1(4), 389–404.

Simonton, D. K. (1997). *Genius and creativity: Selected papers*. Greenwich, CO: Ablex Publishing Corporation.

Sio, U. N., & Ormerod, T. C. (2009). Does incubation enhance problem solving? A meta-analytic review. *Psychological bulletin*, 135(1), 94.

Slåtten, T., Svensson, G., & Sværi, S. (2011). Empowering leadership and the influence of a humorous work climate on service employees' creativity and innovative behaviour in frontline service jobs. *International Journal of Quality and Service Sciences*, 3(3), 267–284.

Smeltzer, L. R., & Leap, T. L. (1988). An analysis of individual reactions to potentially offensive jokes in work settings. *Human Relations*, 41(4), 295–304.

Smith, C. A., & Ellsworth, P. C. (1985). Patterns of cognitive appraisal in emotion. *Journal of Personality and Social Psychology*, 48, 813–838.

Smith, E. E., & Goodchilds, J. D. (1963). The wit in large and small established groups. *Psychological Reports*, 13(1), 273–274.

Smith, R. E., Ascough, J. C., Ettinger, R. F., & Nelson, D. A. (1971). Humor, anxiety, and task performance. *Journal of Personality and Social Psychology*, 19(2), 243.

Stevenson, C. E., Kleibeuker, S. W., De Dreu, C. K., & Crone, E. A. (2014). Training creative cognition: Adolescence as a flexible period for improving creativity. *Frontiers in Human Neuroscience*, 8, 827.

Stogdill, R. M. (1972). Group productivity, drive, and cohesiveness. *Organizational Behavior and Human Performance*, 8(1), 26–43.

Suls, J. M. (1972). A two-stage model for the appreciation of jokes and cartoons: An information-processing analysis. In J. H. Goldstein, & P. E. McGhee (Eds.), *The psychology of humor: Theoretical perspectives and empirical issues* (pp. 81–100). New York: Academic Press.

Suls, J. M. (1983). Cognitive processes in humor appreciation. In P. E. McGhee, & J. H. Goldstein (Eds.), *Handbook of humor research* (pp. 39–57). New York: Springer.

Torrance, E. P. (1995). Insights about creativity: Questioned, rejected, ridiculed, ignored. *Educational Psychology Review*, 7(3), 313–322.

Treadwell, Y. (1970). Humor and creativity. *Psychological Reports*, 26(1), 55–58.

Trope, Y., & Liberman, N. (2010). Construal-level theory of psychological distance. *Psychological Review*, 117(2), 440.

Volmer, J., Spurk, D., & Niessen, C. (2012). Leader–member exchange (LMX), job autonomy, and creative work involvement. *The Leadership Quarterly*, 23(3), 456–465.

Watson, D., & Tellegen, A. (1985). Toward a consensual structure of mood. *Psychological Bulletin*, 98, 219–235.
Westwood, R. I., & Johnston, A. (2013). Humor in organization: From function to resistance. *Humor*, 26(2), 219–247.
Wood, R. E., Beckmann, N., & Rossiter, J. R. (2011). Management humor Asset or liability? *Organizational Psychology Review*, 1(4), 316–338.
Woodman, R. W., Sawyer, J. E., & Griffin, R. W. (1993). Toward a theory of organizational creativity. *Academy of Management Review*, 18(2), 293–321.
Wyer, R. S., & Collins, J. E. (1992). A theory of humor elicitation. *Psychological Review*, 99(4), 663–688.
Ziv, A. (1976). Facilitating effects of humor on creativity. *Journal of Educational Psychology*, 68(3), 318.
Ziv, A. (1983). The influence of humorous atmosphere on divergent thinking. *Contemporary Educational Psychology*, 8(1), 68–75.
Ziv, A. (1988). Teaching and learning with humor: Experiment and replication. *The Journal of Experimental Education*, 57(1), 4–15.

6

HUMOR, STRESS, AND COPING

Melanie Booth-Butterfield and
Melissa Bekelja Wanzer

We would all like to find a way to effectively cope with our fast-paced lives. An important, and yet often stressful part of our lives is our work. Indeed, employment is necessary, and often very fulfilling. But work situations create pressure and stress which may negatively affect job satisfaction, as well as other aspects of our lives such as health. Using humor at work is one way to alleviate stress and enhance employment satisfaction. But communicating with humor may be fraught with problems, and the decision and encoding processes are complex. Hence, in this chapter, we will investigate the humor enactment link to stress responses.

The basic premise of this chapter is that work pressures create stress which negatively impacts physiological functioning, psychological well-being, and productivity in one's career. We may not be able to avoid stressful situations altogether, but we can learn to change how we, and others around us, handle the situations, ultimately to cope more effectively. One way of accomplishing this re-direction of stress response is through humorous communication. Creating and enacting entertaining, humorous messages can re-route both cognitive and emotional processes, and has been proven to alleviate negative outcomes for the source of the communication, as well as the more-often studied receivers of the humor (e.g. Bonnanno, 2004; Booth-Butterfield, Wanzer, Weil, & Krezmien, 2014; Horan, Bochantin, & Booth-Butterfield, 2012; Lazarus & Folkman, 1987).

Appropriate humorous interactions can lighten the mood, help people laugh at themselves, heighten liking, build group cohesion, and even break the tension in workplace interactions. But being funny can also exacerbate tension and stress if it is not enacted appropriately. We will examine both the benefits and the potential pitfalls of humor enactment to alleviate stress. To begin this discussion of humor's role in reducing stress in the workplace, we offer three basic parameters for the chapter: *definitions of humor, source orientation*, and *presentational versus conversational humor.*

Definitions of humor communication

First, humorous communication is primarily defined here as the "intentional use of verbal and nonverbal messages which elicit laughter, chuckling, and other spontaneous behaviors taken to mean pleasure, delight or surprise in the targeted receiver" (Booth-Butterfield & Booth-Butterfield, 1991, p. 206). This definition represents a pro-social, positive approach to humor enactment, one that will be more acceptable in workplace interactions (see also McIlheran, 2006). Another broad way to define humor is that it is an "event shared by an agent with a target that is intended to be amusing to the agent and/or the target, and that the target thinks of as an intentional act" (Geunter, Schreurs, Emmerik, Gijsbers, & Van Iterson, 2013, p. 575). Both definitions emphasize the intentional nature of humor; however, the first recognizes the communicative nature of humor, which is a central component of our approach. Of course, we recognize that *all* humor might not be positive and light hearted. Researchers such as Martin, Puhlik-Doris, Larsen, Gray, and Weir (2003) have extended the study of humor enactment to focus on both positive and negative types of humor. Comparisons of negative or maladaptive enactment dimensions of humor (e.g. aggressive or self-defeating), with adaptive styles of humor, result in quite different effects (Kuiper & McHale, 2009). While such negative patterns are clearly observable in real life and the workplace, they are less likely to alleviate stress in either the source or receiver. For example, a recent study by Guenter et al. (2013) using diary methods to track employees' use of adaptive and maladaptive humor at work found that employees were more engaged when they expressed adaptive humor, and more emotionally exhausted on days when they expressed maladaptive humor. Examining the effects of employees' use of adaptive and maladaptive forms of humor in the workplace helps us understand the differential effects of humor on employee stress and, "calls into question the use of one-dimensional measures of humor expression" (Guenter et al., 2013, p. 587).

Expanding the way that humor is operationalized in empirical research has helped us understand both positive and negative effects of humor. However, there is significantly more scholarship on positive/successful humor in the workplace compared to negative styles. More work is certainly needed to understand how and why employees enact maladaptive or "dark" humor at work and the implications of such communication (Mesmer-Magnus, Glew, & Viswesvaran, 2012).

Source/enactment perspective

One way to organize the extensive body of humor research conducted in fields such as communication and social psychology is to delineate between studies that use a source versus receiver approach. Receiver approaches to humor typically examine the effects of humor exposure on study participants, their sense of humor, response to specific stimuli, and humor appreciation (Wanzer, Booth-Butterfield, & Booth-Butterfield, 1995). Although receivers may benefit from humor in work settings, what individuals perceive as "funny" tends to be highly idiosyncratic. Receivers also are responders rather than controllers of the humor encoding. Here, we focus on the more active, strategic communication role of the source. The source is the person who originates and enacts the humor to gain some type of outcome or benefit in the interaction, e.g. relieving stress, increasing life satisfaction, eliciting positive reactions from others or increasing one's social attractiveness (Wanzer, Booth-Butterfield, & Booth-Butterfield, 1996; Wanzer, Booth-Butterfield, & Booth-Butterfield, 2005; Wanzer, Sparks, & Frymier, 2009). Therefore, while receivers benefit from their laughter, relief, or amusement, it is the source who strategically and consciously communicates such humorous messages.

Presentational versus conversational humor

Third, humorous communication entails both *presentational and conversational perspectives*. When people envision humorous communicators, they often think of comedians, those entertainers who make their living by consecutively telling jokes, relating amusing anecdotes, or acting out funny sketches in front of a receptive audience. This perspective is "presentational" and one in which the focus is quite one-sided – watching/listening to the funny person. In real life, and especially in work contexts, this is rarely the form humor enactment takes. Instead of a presentational perspective, most people engage in humor within ongoing, informal, interactive contexts; i.e. the "conversational" perspective. In a conversational perspective, the process and message seems spontaneous rather than rehearsed, and often emerges out of the immediate situation as communicators play off of each other (see also Miczo, 2012, and Motley, 1997, for further explanation of such distinctions). In this chapter we will focus primarily on conversational or interactive forms of humor enactment.

Clearly there is a great array of information about humor enactment and its role in stress. In this chapter we will consider: a) how work settings differ from social or family settings in using humor; b) what types of stressors tend to be confronted in organizations; c) why/how humor enactment works to alleviate stress; d) description of benefits found to be associated with humor use; and not surprisingly, e) some limitations to humor enactment. We end with suggestions for effectively communicating humor in the workplace.

Work settings and interactions differ from social or family communicative interactions

In spite of positive outcomes associated with humor enactment, the workplace involves restrictions on humorous communication. The goals, structures, and expectations of the work context versus social contexts drive communication, and those differences impact humor enactment. As obvious as it may seem, you typically cannot be humorous in the same forms across social compared to work contexts. Humor encoding may need to be "sanitized," and made more appropriate, i.e. safe for everyone's consumption, rather than the authentic, sometimes raunchy, irreverent, or politically incorrect humor which you may otherwise find entertaining. Let's examine why this is true.

First, work relationships are different from non-work relationships because they are typically characterized by clear status or power differences between individuals. When there are real or perceived power differences between communicators, this can affect both the quality and quantity of communication exchanges. Lower status employees may experience more restrictions when it comes to expressing discontent. A recent study by Graner, Chandler, and Wallace (2015) illustrated how powerless/low status employees use humorous messages in the workplace to express dissatisfaction. College interns provided descriptive accounts of how and why they used humor to express workplace dissatisfaction. The researchers focused on interns because they are historically the most powerless individuals in organizational settings. As politeness theory would predict, college interns often used different types of humorous messages to express their job dissatisfaction. Rather than express their dissatisfaction explicitly and outwardly to higher status individuals, interns used humor to achieve goals at work such as making changes, venting problems, or protecting themselves from getting in trouble.

Clearly humor enactment between supervisors and subordinates can also be risky for supervisors. For example, a sexual harassment lawsuit was filed when a male supervisor recounted a joke from a *Seinfeld* episode to a female employee (Rabinowitz, 1998, May 11). While the supervisor claimed that he was attempting to be funny, the employee perceived her supervisor's humor attempt differently. The status gap cannot be ignored in such interactions, no matter how friendly they may appear. Bosses may overestimate their entertainment quotient, and their employees aren't fully able to provide honest feedback (Keltner, Gruenfeld, & Anderson, 2003). The more powerful position held by supervisors and managerial employees tends to desensitize them to subordinates' concerns, overlooking their own threat value, as well as disinhibiting their communicative behavior (e.g. Galinsky, Magee, Inesi, & Gruenfeld, 2006). In contrast, employees may feel more constrained, pressured to laugh along, and find that teasing their supervisor backfires if the jab isn't taken in stride (Gillen & Booth-Butterfield, 2013).

Another aspect of the organizational humor "risk" is financial. In social relationships if humor goes "wrong," or is misinterpreted, you may be able to remediate and recoup. But poorly enacted humor in the workplace holds risk for work benefits, potential promotion, and even continued employment. Humor enactment among equal-status colleagues is less risky, but whenever the interaction is among people of differing organizational status, there are subtle, and often not openly stated, rules and risks.

Second, the bottom line of a working organization is task-oriented. That means that unlike social contacts who participate in an interaction for positive affect, commitment, and an entertaining time, organizations must make money, or at least they cannot lose money. For example, if humorous enactments lead to customer complaints, unfinished tasks, or other employees' dissatisfaction and even grievances, the humor is counter to the organization's objectives. Such a task-orientation must remain the primary goal of organizations, and employees need to adhere to that norm. Humor could at times be inconsistent with those task goals.

Third, in our social relationships we make up our own rules; they are developed and negotiated among the individuals as a relationship progresses. In contrast, workplace rules are more formalized and legally binding. Humor falls within those rules. In organizations, despite diversity in specific group norms, a larger set of laws and rules cover the full array of employee and client interactions, so they are more restrictive and legally stated. Humor which is perceived as offensive, insensitive, or politically incorrect will likely be sanctioned (see, for example, Kauffman, 2009). Thus, any enacted humor needs to fall within the organizational boundaries if it is to be helpful in reducing stressful situations.

Finally, the workplace is filled with relationships with other people whom we did not select. Social relationships tend to be relationships of choice. That is, in social relationships we choose to interact, or not interact with those individuals. Sometimes our friendships are based substantially on similarities in taste and values, which can be reflected in humor enactment. Working organizations do not afford that full freedom. We spend a great many of our waking hours at work – often without the relief of simply being able to leave the room if activities become tense, tiring, or stressful. Consequently, if our, or others', humor is distasteful, we do not have the freedom to immediately leave the situation, avoid communication, or improve the interactional context. So we must be aware when enacting humor in our meetings, conversations, or presentations, that others with whom we work may not share our appreciation of what is "funny."

Overall, in order to be successful in communicating humor to cope with stress in the workplace, we need to recognize these restrictions on our humorous messages, and adapt our humor enactment accordingly. To do otherwise may actually elevate potential stress in work settings (e.g. McGraw, Williams, & Warren, 2014; Williams & Emich, 2014).

Stress in the workplace

Within the work context, Ganster and Rosen (2013) labeled stress as "the process by which workplace psychological experiences and demands (stressors) produce both short-term (strains) and long-term changes in mental and physical health" (p. 1088). Weinberg and Cooper (2011) discuss the difficulty of coming up with a single definition of stress, but emphasize that all contemporary definitions of stress portray it as negative. Stress often involves intrusive thoughts that you can't eliminate, and which maintain an activated state in your body. It is this activation with the accompanying chemical and physiological changes that cause negative bodily symptoms.

Many researchers conceive of stress occurring when individuals perceive they do not have "resources" to deal with some threat. This might include inadequate personnel focused on a task, impending time deadlines, financial support, or lack of decision-making experience. Note that stress reactions are not whether you *actually* have the resources (ability, money, time), but whether you perceive that you don't, and hence feel pressured (Pham, Taylor, & Seeham, 2001). People may experience stress reactions over a myriad of different causes: family troubles, health problems, financial difficulties, conflict, time pressures. The list of stressors may be endless. Stressors can include both negative and positive situational factors, "second-hand stress" from those around us, and then personality differences in contending with stress (see, for example, Kanner, Coyne, Schafer, & Lazarus, 1981). *Negative situational factors* that increase our arousal and cause us to feel "stressed out" might include work deadlines, role strain between family and work life, conflict with co-workers, physically dangerous work activities, financial difficulties, and negative feedback. For example, nurses in intensive care units are particularly vulnerable to the high pressure of the workplace. But they also enact humor to alleviate stress and increase job satisfaction (Wanzer et al., 2005).

We may feel at a loss to contend with a stressor, especially when it's a negative occurrence, but *positive situations* can also cause stress. While we may be eagerly anticipating new jobs and projects, these situations can also be quite stressful; some may even label weddings, new offices, babies, and even vacations as stressful! Any situation, even smaller "hassles", that increases pressure to adapt, deal with change, increase cognitive effort, and heighten workload may cause stress (Kanner et al., 1981).

Next, we must recognize a phenomenon called "second-hand stress" which is quite common in the workplace. Second-hand stress occurs when someone around you is strained, angry, and/or experiences pressure (Buchanan, Bagley, Stansfield, & Preston, 2012; Miron-Spektor & Rafaeli, 2009; Selye, 1976). Your awareness of their tension creates anticipation of negative interactions for you. In this case you may not have direct stress in your own life, but the spillover from others, especially those closest to you, causes you to feel the stressful symptoms (Bakker, Westman, & Van Emmerik, 2009). In addition, some work environments have a climate of barely-controlled panic (e.g. news rooms), or there may be periods of extreme pressure (hospitals, competitions, seasonal challenges). Haggard, Robert, and Rose (2011) found that a pattern of co-rumination and excessive discussion about negative workplace factors exacerbated stress conditions, especially for women. Thus stress may exhibit a contagion effect, exacerbated by tense interactions, and may be mitigated through humor enactments, and sense of humor (Abel, 2002; Bonnano, 2004).

However, all feelings of stress do not originate with situational factors. *Personality traits and attitudes* also influence how we label events and respond to stressors (Kobasa, 1979). Some people are more adaptable, flexible, and have more personal resources to face stressors. Employees who view their job as important and are committed to the task tend to be hardier. Others, because of how they react to confrontation, may feel stressed at very low levels of situational demand. For example, anxious people don't tend to cope as well as non-anxious people. Trait anxiety has primary effects because the individual is less able to handle conflicting demands, higher workload, and other pressures. People who tend to be nervous, highly reactive, or who possess an external locus of control have a more immediate response to even low-level stressors (e.g. Kobasa, 1979; Kohn, Lafreniere, &

Gurevich, 1991). These are just a few examples of how individuals may differentially experience stress, but they are important for the potential humor source to understand.

Importantly, enacting humor might also alleviate stress in different ways depending on the *source of stress*. Humorous messages shared with one's supervisor might be different than humor after hours with colleagues, and the type of humor may differ depending on job type as well. But ultimately, appropriate humorous communication should heighten coping if communicated skillfully.

Why humor enactment reduces stress: The mechanisms

Certainly the physiological changes and psychological benefits that accrue to people who respond to humor with laughter and amusement are well accepted, although perhaps not always empirically supported (e.g. Avtgis, 2012; Eisend, 2009; Martin, 2001; Pollack, 2012). There do appear to be physiological changes that improve functioning when people laugh, for example respiration changes, immune-functioning, and even exercise benefits (Dillon, Minchoff, & Baker, 1985; Fry, 1994). But psychological and physiological changes are less extensively studied for humor *enactment*. How does the encoding and communication of humor alleviate stress reactions in the source of the humor?

There are several different mechanisms which may explain how humor helps coping with life's challenges, and in all probability these mechanisms work in conjunction with each other. First, very simply, humor enactment requires an external orientation. When you encode entertaining messages and gauge your intended receivers' reactions, you are less likely to be inwardly focused, and more likely to be socially oriented. In other words, the humor construction and enactment refocuses one's attention. Although Galinsky et al. (2006) found that the external attention may not always be entirely accurate in perspective-taking, the very crafting of humor for intended receivers requires thinking about them and not as extensively about one's own tensions. For example, Alston (2007) used qualitative data from 30 interviews to investigate how humor may work in high-stress life conditions and health-related jobs. Her conclusions included that humor was often employed as a diversion, as well as a means of opening up topic areas that might otherwise be unapproachable by employees. Hence, humorous messages may be communicated to re-focus, re-orient, and direct employees' attention in more productive directions. A second widely employed model explaining how humorous communication works to alleviate negative emotions and cope with stress is the Transactional Model of Stress and Coping.

Basic model of coping: Folkman and Lazarus' Transactional Model

The Transactional Model of Stress and Coping is a well-established framework used to understand the process of coping with difficult or stressful life events (Lazarus &

Folkman, 1987). This model has two main elements: cognitive appraisal and subsequent coping. The first part of the model, labeled cognitive appraisal, addresses our basic human tendency to evaluate situations and events based on their self-relevance. According to Lazarus and Folkman, individuals engage in primary and secondary appraisal processes when they confront emotional problems. Primary appraisal refers to our need to question the relevance of an event or occurrence and whether it is germane to us or not (harm, threat, challenges).

A second way we evaluate occurrences is by questioning whether there are specific actions that can be taken to improve or alter the situation, a process labeled secondary appraisal. When deciding how to best manage the situation, individuals typically consider their internal and external coping options, and any resources they might have to manage the situation or environment.

This model also describes differing approaches individuals might adopt to manage stress. Accordingly, coping is a process in which a difficult or threatening situation evokes an emotional response, which is labeled as either positive or negative, e.g. stressful. These emotional responses are interpreted and then "treated," or acted upon, in some way. After interpreting the situational constraints, individuals engage in coping to address the challenge and subsequently re-examine or reappraise their affective states (Folkman & Lazarus, 1980). They may implement problem-focused and/or emotion-focused coping communication to achieve the optimal outcomes (Carver, Scheier, & Wientraub, 1989). In problem-focused coping, people actively try to alter their situation by suppressing competing activities, recruiting assistance, or ameliorating the problem itself. They may also engage in emotion-focused coping by attempting to restructure their affective responses, change their negative mood state, seek emotional support, and the like. Among skilled humor communicators, these patterns may be enhanced by creating an amusing situation via nonverbal displays, witty comments, or generally making light of the situation. Such actions serve to address situational constraints impacting the problem or issue, as well as altering the affective components for themselves and others.

A number of studies have provided support for the link between humor and coping using this transactional framework. For example, Vela, Booth-Butterfield, Wanzer, and Vallade (2013) note that couples can use humor to contend with problems and increase satisfaction in their relationships. Occupational stress relief has been found through humor enactment by nurses (Wanzer et al., 2005), university students (Booth-Butterfield, Booth-Butterfield, & Wanzer, 2007), and even among relationships with partners in law enforcement (Horan et al., 2012).

Figure 6.1 illustrates humor's repeatedly demonstrated coping effects. Following the Folkman and Lazarus framework, humor enactment patterns heighten efficacy in coping, which in turn increases satisfaction/decreases dissatisfaction. Hence there is typically only a weak direct effect between the pattern of humor enactments and the outcome. Rather the humorous orientation increases experienced efficacy to cope with and "handle" various problems, and this efficacy then enhances confidence and positive outcomes.

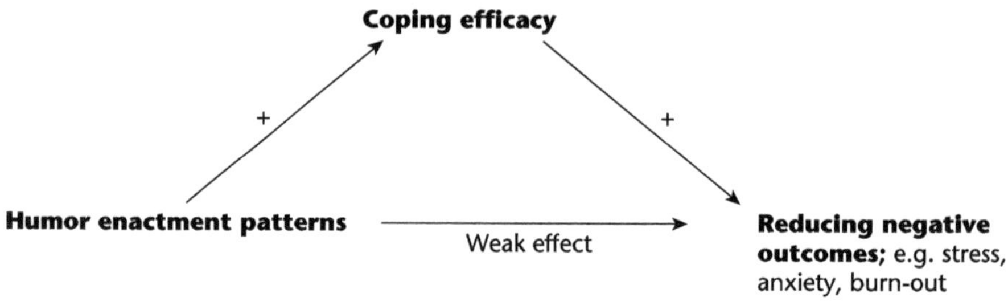

FIGURE 6.1 Path diagram demonstrating the effect of humor enactment patterns on outcomes mediated by coping efficacy.

Understanding "benign violations" as useful to coping

A third way to view humor enactment, and how it may alleviate negative responses to stress, involves the benign violations theory of humor (McGraw, Williams, & Warren, 2014). The benign violations theory is an extension of Incongruity Theory, and builds on work by Veatch (1998). Importantly, it suggests that not just *any* incongruity in an attempt at humor will be perceived as amusing, and it is important the humor enactors understand the boundaries that delineate what makes an incongruity funny in order to avoid mistakes. McGraw and Warren (2010) proposed that an attempt at humor is perceived as amusing when a violation (i.e. a stimulus that is physically or psychologically threatening) simultaneously is interpreted as benign (i.e. non-threatening). For example, a duck walking into a bar is a violation (i.e. of psychological expectations for a duck's behavior), but it is a benign violation in that it doesn't hurt anybody, or cause threat or disgust. However, a joke about the Pope walking into the bar may or may not be perceived as benign by the recipient. If the punchline suggests that the Pope does something inappropriate, it might be perceived as threatening (non-benign), but if he does something inherently moral, just in an unconventional place, the violation is benign. Similarly, workplace humor that could be perceived as intimidating or harassing may or may not be viewed as "benign." As a humor-enactor it becomes important to gauge what will be received as threatening in the workplace. For example, supervisors' jokes about work effort may carry more negative weight and potential to their subordinates – even when not intended as hostile. Teasing from teachers may well be misperceived by students who cannot equally tease in return. The potential for negative consequences is greater the more status-discrepancy there is between interactants at work, and therefore individuals in a lower status position in organizations are less likely to view communication as harmless and amusing.

Further, both physical and psychological distance reduces threat, helping transform a potentially serious violation into a benign violation (McGraw et al., 2014). There appears to be a curvilinear function with time and psychological distance on receivers' reactions. Too close or too soon after a negative event, and receivers are horrified and/or threatened by the source's humor attempt. Too far away and even seemingly exciting events tend to become dull and boring (as in when the source of the amusing tale ends up admitting, "I guess you had to be there").

In summary, this theory suggests that the enactment of humor that might be useful for coping also necessitates a certain level of skill. Specifically, the humor created must not only fulfill the requirements of being incongruous and amusing, it must also appear incongruous and benign to receivers. Violations of these principles might exacerbate rather than reduce stress, and make workplace coping more difficult.

Benefits of workplace humor and application of humor to stressors

The examination of humor's benefits has a long history in the area of instructional communication (Bryant, Comisky, & Zillmann, 1979; Bryant, Crane, Comisky, & Zillmann, 1980; Bryant & Zillmann, 1988; Goodboy, Booth-Butterfield, Bolkan, & Griffin, 2015; Wanzer, 2002), as well as more recent attention from interpersonal/ relational researchers (e.g. Bippus, Young, & Dunbar, 2011; Merolla, 2006). But clearly, humorous enactments have substantive influence in work settings as well. A recent meta-analysis of positive humor use described how humor can benefit both employees and supervisors (Mesmer-Magnus et al., 2012).

Researchers identified scholarship on positive workplace humor to "explore the extent to which positive (coping or affiliative) humor is associated with desirable employer, team, and leader outcomes, as well as the extent to which such humor may buffer the effects of workplace stress on employee burnout" (Mesmer-Magnus et al., 2012, p. 168). In total, 49 studies addressed relationships between supervisor/ employee humor and at least one relevant outcome. Similar to the research on humor and coping with death (Booth-Butterfield et al., 2014), the meta-analysis indicates both intrapersonal and interpersonal benefits for workplace humor. Specifically, when employees use humor at work they experience health benefits such as better health, less stress and burnout, and increased coping efficacy. Employees' humor was positively related to their work performance and workgroup cohesion, but inversely related to work withdrawal. Supervisors' use of humor was correlated positively with employee job satisfaction and workgroup cohesion, and inversely associated with employee work withdrawal (Mesmer-Magnus et al., 2012).

Three key takeaways from the meta-analysis are: 1) positive employee/supervisor humor is correlated with good physical and mental health; 2) positive perceptions of employee/supervisor humor can buffer the negative effects of work stress; and 3) positive employee/supervisor humor can lead to greater productivity. Not surprisingly, the authors recommend that organizations incorporate humor into the workplace in an attempt to reduce stress and increase solidarity and productivity.

Again, most of the benefits of workplace humor as noted by Mesmer-Magnus et al. (2012) were associated with effects in the receiver. Additional work-related coping benefits include a variety of empirically supported advantages for those who regularly enact humor. For example, employees reported increased liking for supervisors who used humor more effectively and greater job satisfaction (Rizzo, Wanzer, & Booth-Butterfield, 1999). Humorous interactions at work tend to lower perceived organizational power discrepancies, and make leadership seem more accessible (Davis & Kleiner, 1989; Vinton, 1989). Humor enactment has been noted to contribute to increases in compliance, learning, attitude shifts, and enjoyment, as well as improving organizational cohesiveness (McIlheran, 2006).

As we encode and communicate humor we experience mood elevation and that action also releases tension/energy, potentially improving breathing processes (Pollack, 2012). Using humor regularly enhances self-efficacy (e.g. Booth-Butterfield et al., 2007). Other studies indicate that engaging in humorous interactions, and being generally open to "funniness" may increase social support, as well as reduce negative somatic symptoms (Booth-Butterfield et al., 2014; Wanzer et al., 1996). Horan et al. (2012) found that humor orientation worked with efficacy to not only decrease stress in law enforcement relationships, but was also associated with fewer negative conflict tactics. All of these findings may also have implications for potential conflict and other workplace interactions.

Limitations on use of humor to alleviate workplace stress

Realistically, humorous communication, no matter how funny it may be, cannot solve every problem at work. Your work life will nearly always involve some level of stressful activation. So it is important to consider humor's help in coping with workplace stress, but not to overestimate the potential.

First, humorous communication cannot overcome massive negative occurrences. It doesn't make them disappear. For example, employing humor assists in the grieving process, and is definitely better than suppressing the urge to communicate with humor (Booth-Butterfield et al., 2014) but humor doesn't entirely eradicate the pain. Job termination, major economic downturns that create financial crises, disastrous business outcomes requiring product recalls, and the like are not to be underestimated. A single humorous story won't suffice. But enactment of humor can certainly help people to cope. Even in circumstances such as warfare, natural disasters, and tragedies such as the terror attack on the World Trade Center, humor has been found to mitigate participants' negative affect (Bonnano, 2004).

Second, some jobs inherently entail greater stress than others, and humor may not be the best way to manage this stress. Law enforcement and military operations are fraught with very real dangers. Many health care providers hold people's lives in their hands, sometimes literally. Certain construction jobs involve dangerous environments, toxic chemicals, and powerful tools. Competitive athletic endeavors often depend on aggressive physical actions. Nevertheless, existing data on humor enactment, even in tense situations, indicates that humor relieves pressures, and can help workers perform their jobs better.

Third, certain dignified or highly serious work contexts may not lend themselves to light-hearted banter. Joking from a funeral director to the bereaved would be inappropriate. Highly symbolic, formal, and religious ceremonies are probably not the place to enact humor. Nevertheless, even in such serious contexts, humor may be implemented to cope among colleagues (rather than the general public) (e.g. Wanzer et al., 1995) or when something goes awry (e.g. spills, trips, unavoidable surprises) to cope with the situational difficulty.

Finally, there is no strong empirical evidence that aggressive humor helps to alleviate stress, or is organizationally beneficial in any other way (e.g. Campbell, Martin, & Wanzer, 2001; Martin et al., 2003). Although we view aggressive humor in media, and may even laugh, as we've established, the workplace is a different venue. Aggressive humor can harm relationships with customers, colleagues, and supervisors. Notably, aggressive humor is more likely among men than women (Cann, Zapata, & Davis, 2009; Martin, et al., 2003; Romero, Alsua, Hinrichs, & Pearson, 2007; Vela & Booth-Butterfield, 2015), which may have additional implications for work-related interactions.

In the few studies indicating somewhat favorable outcomes for aggressive humor, we note that *mildly aggressive humor,* when enacted as teasing or ridicule, may serve as a means of delivering certain types of messages or gaining compliance from employees; however, there is not strong empirical evidence to support the use of this type of humor in the workplace (Romero & Cruthirds, 2006). For example, research by Janes and Olsen (2000) examined young adults' perceptions of peer teasing and ridicule, which they labeled "jeer pressure." The researchers studied whether observing peers being ridiculed and teased in a video was related to college students' fear of failure, creativity, and conformity. Participants viewed one of three videos (i.e. other-ridicule, self-ridicule or no-target humor) and then performed different tasks to assess fear of failure, conformity and creativity. Compared to participants who viewed the self-ridicule or no-target humor video, those in the other-ridicule condition were more conforming in completing their tasks and indicated a greater fear of failure. These findings seem to indicate that observing others being ridiculed or teased can influence individuals to adhere to group norms.

Managers could use lighthearted teasing or ridicule with their employees in an effort to get them to conform to group norms. Romero and Cruthirds (2006) note that "senior members who feel responsible to maintain group integrity can use mild aggressive humor (e.g. good-natured teasing, ridicule, mocking) with new members to shape their behavior" (p. 60). To support this claim, Romero and Cruthirds include an excerpt from an interview with a college baseball player who experienced teasing as a rookie during training camp. This player recounted his experiences of being taunted and yet "holding his own" and proving his worth as a player. He not only proved that he could tolerate the teasing, but also that he was a strong player worthy of respect. While teasing might work in this particular setting, it is important for managers to determine what employees think constitutes "good-natured teasing" in the workplace before attempting to engage in this behavior. The context and relationship with ones' colleagues appear to be important. For example, Robert, Dunne, and Iun (2015) found that when a leader and subordinate have a positive relationship (defined by the subordinate), the leader's use of aggressive humor is positively correlated with the subordinate's job satisfaction. This might suggest that such leaders have a good reading of their receivers, and can enact even aggressive humor in a way that might be perceived as a benign violation by their subordinates, and thus engender positive outcomes. However, when the relationship between the leader and subordinate is low quality, both positive and negative humor (affiliative or aggressive) was associated with low job satisfaction, perhaps because it was perceived as a serious, non-benign violation. To be effective in the workplace, humor has to be well-communicated in a variety of ways. This chapter is not advocating that every employee try to transform into a comedian. But, by understanding factors that impact humorous messages, everyone may be able to improve their enactment of humor and lower stress.

Contextual variables in using humor

You do not want your humorous communication to backfire. No matter how well intentioned, negative responses might make workplace situations even more stressful, tense, risky, or unproductive. There are several aspects about the enactment of humorous communication in work settings to remember:

1. Sometimes adaptive versus maladaptive humor enactments can be a matter of *duration or repetition* – how long does the humor attempt continue? A brief humorous interaction, quip, or nonverbal display may be funny – or at least not obnoxious. However, if humor goes on for too long, if the enactor tries to be funny in every interaction, the humor becomes "lame," predictable, and often inappropriate. Remember that humor relies upon incongruity and surprise perceived in a non-threatening manner, in order to work effectively. Humor is generally only entertaining when it is new, when the anecdote hasn't been related previously, and the surprise is genuine.
2. *Intensity* – how intense is the "kidding?" Humor that is very vivid and extreme may be better communicated at the bar than the office. Comedians and entertainers who make their living in front of audiences tend to employ more intense forms of humor, but those types are typically not appropriate in the workplace. How intense and pointed the humor message is, how directly it is focused on an individual, may mean the distinction between perceived bullying and good-natured kidding.
3. Select the right target for the humor; that means *adapt to your audience.* Potential receivers may not all appreciate the same humor enactments, and while this is always true, it is particularly salient at work. Norms tend to be somewhat more formal, conservative, or legally-bound in work environments, so choose your audience carefully for the best outcome. The same humorous pattern that may be acceptable on the basketball court or the back of one's work truck, might be offensive or credibility-harming in more standard workplace environments. You must recognize that if you need to amend and say, "I was just kidding," your humor was not optimally-received.

4 *Skill in delivery* no doubt makes a difference in how the humor, whether verbal or nonverbal, is perceived. Know yourself. Does your comment sound hostile or charitable? Does the enactor go too far in exaggerating or mimicry? An enactment that is too loud, even if the content is non-threatening, may sound aggressive. Poor skill levels also result in perceptions that the communicator is trying too hard or is "desperate." The best humor communication seems effortless and spontaneous, even if it was truly planned and strategic.

5 *Timing* may make a difference too. Don't "kid" someone or make light of the situation just after they lost a major account or received a negative report. Avoid making jokes when the receiver is tired, stressed out, or overloaded as well. In humor, optimal timing of the communication is imperative. Again the benign violations theory applies – for humor to be effective it must be interpreted as non-threatening. Part of such interpretation includes that the joking message is not communicated too proximally to the negative occurrence (McGraw et al., 2014). For example, in medical situations when a patient is in crisis, or recovery is in question, making light of the situation should be avoided. Individuals may be able to laugh with you after a crisis has passed, but not during.

6 *Individual differences* such as sex, ethnicity, region, age, and the dyadic composition should also be considered when using humor in the workplace or encouraging others to use humor with peers or clients. A substantial body of research indicates that males use humor more often, and in different ways, than do females (e.g. Booth-Butterfield et al., 2014; Horan et al., 2012; Martin, Rich, & Gayle, 2004). In addition, males and females use and appreciate different forms of humor. As mentioned previously, males use more aggressive styles of humor and females use more self-enhancing humor (Romero et al., 2007). Because males create and perform humor more often in the workplace, they will be more receptive to using humor among their peers and clients. Romero et al. (2007) also point out differences in humor styles and humor use based on respondents' age and region of the country. For example, when comparing differences in humor styles among residents from Alaska, NW Texas, Minnesota and SW Texas, the researchers found that respondents from Minnesota reported the most affiliative humor use while SW Texas reported the least humor use.

7 Recognize that *feedback from your humor may be inaccurate or biased*. This means all laughter and chuckling around an organization might not be honest. Employees may respond with an artificial humor reaction in order to be polite, fit in, or honor their supervisors, and this is more likely the higher up in the organizational hierarchy the humorous source is (Gillen & Booth-Butterfield, 2013; see also Galinsky et al., 2006 for discussion).

Future research on stress and humor

Examination of humor enacted to cope with stress in the workplace stimulates ideas and directions for future research in several areas. There is much yet to be learned concerning how humorous messages may be attributed, how men versus women employ humor to cope with stress, potential humor training activities, and areas in which there may be concrete benefits, as well as potential drawbacks for humorous communication.

First, there are some predisposing factors that seem associated with attributions for humor enactment with implications for managing stress. Power differentials, relationship status, and one's own humor orientation have been found to influence interpretations (Banas, Dunbar, Rodriguez, & Liu, 2011; Galinsky et al., 2006; Robert et al., 2015; Wanzer & Frymier, 1999). Thus, it is likely that employees' coping and stress reduction may be related to additional contextual or individual variables, and are in further need of study.

The study of male and female enactment of humor within organizations is a research area with great potential. Numerous studies have found differences in how men versus women employ humor, as well as the types of humor expressed (e.g. Martin et al., 2004).

Sometimes, employees, especially women, may worry about their organizational credibility if they employ and encourage humor. They report concern that they might be viewed as frivolous or not seriously committed to organizational objectives. Indeed, one study indicated that female managers employed different, and more low key, cooperative humor styles compared to male managers (Martin, 2004). However, other studies (e.g. Sculz, Cowan, Cowan, & Brennan, 2004) suggest that women and men may behave very differently when under work stress, and have diverse behavioral outcomes. The existing literature indicates that the intrapersonal and interpersonal benefits of skillfully communicated humor far outweigh any drawbacks for both males and females, but specific patterns of humor and stress communication would be useful to understand more fully.

There is also a need to conduct more physiological measurement studies on stress and humor to determine whether and how enactments lower physical stress levels. Research could extend findings on embodied persuasion/self-validation (Brinol, Petty, & Wagoner, 2011), which suggests that we respond attitudinally and emotionally differently (and potentially more positively) depending on our nonverbal stance, posture, and even nodding and smiling (Rahona, Fernandez, Rolke, Vazquez, & Hervas, 2014). Specifically, Carney, Cuddy, and Yap's (2010) research on power posing showed that a few minutes of power posing led to decreased cortisol levels and increased testosterone levels. This pattern may be extended by giving employees humorous material to read aloud or act out, perhaps decreasing their subsequent stress and cortisol levels at work. An experimental design would assess cortisol levels pre and post to examine whether induced humor enactment helps in reducing stress.

Despite admonitions to undertake improvements in humor in the workplace, the utility and feasibility of humor communication training has yet to be researched extensively (e.g. Vela & Booth-Butterfield, 2015). One study examined the effectiveness of humor training on six patients suffering from depression. While this study was not conducted in the workplace, the results were promising and illustrate the potential of extended training programs. Patients who participated in eight weeks of training to improve humor abilities experienced notable mood improvement and were more capable of using humor to cope (Falkenberg, Buchkremer, Bartels, & Wild, 2011).

Additional research is needed to identify the specific content that should be included in humor training programs as well as the effects of these efforts on employees. One recent study sheds some light on humor content that could be included in corporate training sessions. Pundt and Herrmann (2015) examined the relationship between leaders' use of affiliative and aggressive humor and the quality of their relationships with followers. As expected, leaders' use of affiliative humor improved leader–follower exchanges while use of aggressive humor was negatively related to the quality of leader–follower exchanges. Based on their findings and related work (Robert et al., 2015), effective corporate humor programs should focus on how leaders might use affiliative humor with employees to improve leader–follower exchanges and avoid aggressive humor in the workplace (Martin & Gayle, 1999; Pundt & Herrman, 2015).

As an extension of the difficulty of "training" people to be better humor enactors, researchers also need to examine the potential drawbacks of poorly communicated humor. It seems the advantages of enacting appropriate humor are quite clear. But what about poor enactment? If one is an incompetent communicator, attempts to be funny may exacerbate the stress problems in the workplace. In addition, adding "funniness" to ones' repertoire may be another cognitive burden on an already overloaded system. Scholars in the area of humor need to conduct studies of such issues in order to address or negate negative outcomes.

Conclusion

Ultimately, "work" is something people pay you to do. Why? Otherwise you might not do it. You may not find your employment context the most enjoyable, free, relaxing, fun way to spend major amounts of your time. The underlying premise in this case is that work is necessary, though perhaps stress-inducing, and therefore we need productive communication patterns to manage work-related pressures. Humor provides that mechanism.

When we successfully enact humor, it can improve outcomes in many arenas. Colleagues may be entertained, relieved, like us better, and evidence less stress-contagion. Clients may feel more comfortable and enjoy spending time in our presence. And, as the employee, you yourself may benefit from this external and positive orientation as you encode and communicate messages which produce amusement, entertainment, and positive affect in those around you.

References

Abel, M. (2002). Humor, stress, and coping strategies. *Humor: International Journal of Humor Research*, 15, 365–381.

Alston, S. (2007). Nothing to laugh at: Humour as a means of coping with pain and stress. *Australian Journal of Communication*, 34, 77–89.

Avtgis, T. (2012). Humor in health care. In R. DiCiccio (Ed.), *Humor communication: Theory, impact and outcomes* (pp. 189–201). Dubuque, IA: Kendall Hunt Publishing.

Bakker, A., Westman, M., & van Emmerik, I. (2009). Advancements in crossover theory. *Journal of Managerial Psychology*, 24, 206–219.

Banas, J., Dunbar, N., Rodriguez, D., & Liu, S. (2011). A review of humor in educational settings: Four decades of research. *Communication Education*, 60, 115–144.

Bippus, A., Young, S., & Dunbar, N. (2011). Humor in conflict discussions: Comparing partners' perceptions. *Humor*, 24, 287–303.

Bonanno, G. (2004). Loss, trauma, and human resilience. *American Psychologist*, 59, 20–28.

Booth-Butterfield, M., Booth-Butterfield, S., & Wanzer, M. (2007). Funny students cope better: Patterns of humor enactment and coping effectiveness. *Communication Quarterly*, 55, 299–315.

Booth-Butterfield, M., Wanzer, M. B., Weil, N., & Krezmien, E. (2014). Humorous communication during bereavement: Intrapersonal and interpersonal emotion management strategies. *Communication Quarterly*, 62, 436–454.

Booth-Butterfield, S., & Booth-Butterfield, M. (1991). The communication of humor in everyday life. *Southern Communication Journal*, 56, 205–218.

Brinol, P., Petty, R., & Wagoner, R. (2011). Embodied attitude change: A self-validation perspective. *Social and Personality Psychology Compass*, 5, 1039–1050.

Bryant, J., & Zillmann, D. (1988). Using humor to promote learning in the classroom. *Journal of Children in Contemporary Society*, 20, 49–78.

Bryant, J., Comisky, P., & Zillmann, D. (1979). Teachers' humor in the college classroom. *Communication Education*, 28, 110–118.

Bryant, J., Crane, J. S., Comisky, P. W., & Zillmann, D. (1980). Relationship between college teachers' use of humor in the classroom and students' evaluations of their teachers. *Journal of Educational Psychology*, 72, 511–519.

Buchanan, T., Bagley, S., Stansfield,. R., & Preston, S. (2012). The empathic, physiological resonance of stress. *Social Neuroscience*, 7, 191–201.

Campbell, K. L., Martin, M. M., & Wanzer, M. B. (2001). Employee perceptions of manager humor orientation, assertiveness, responsiveness, approach/avoidance strategies, and satisfaction. *Communication Research Reports*, 18(1), 67–74.

Cann, A., Zapata, C., & Davis, H. (2009). Positive and negative styles of humor in communication: Evidence for the importance of considering both styles. *Communication Quarterly*, 57, 452–468.

Carney, D., Cuddy, A., & Yap, A. (2010). Power posing brief nonverbal displays affect neuroendocrine levels and risk tolerance, *Psychological Science*, 21, 1363–1369.

Carver, C. S., Scheier, M., & Weintraub, J. (1989). Assessing coping strategies: A theoretically based approach. *Journal of Personality and Social Psychology*, 56, 267–283.

Davis, A., & Kleiner, B. H. (1989). The value of humor in effective leadership. *Leadership & Organization Development Journal*, 10, i–iii.

Dillon, K. M., Minchoff, B., & Baker, K. H. (1985). Positive emotional states and enhancement of the immune system. *International Journal of Psychiatry in Medicine*, 15, 13–18.

Eisend, M. (2009). A meta-analysis of humor in advertising. *Academy of Marketing Science Journal, 37(2)*, 191–203.

Falkenberg, I., Buchkremer, G., Bartels, M., & Wild, B. (2011). Implementation of a manual-based training of humor abilities in patients with depression: A pilot study. *Psychiatry Research*, 186, 454–457.

Folkman, S., & Lazarus, R. S. (1980). An analysis of coping in a middle-aged community sample. *Journal of Health and Social Behavior*, 21, 219–239.

Fry, W. F. (1994). The biology of humor. *Humor*, 7, 111–126.

Galinsky, A., Magee, J., Inesi, M., & Gruenfeld, D. (2006). Power and perspectives not taken, *Psychological Science*, 17, 1068–1074.

Ganster, D. C., & Rosen, C. C. (2013). Work stress and employee health: A multidisciplinary review. *Journal of Management*, 39, 1085–1122.

Gillen, H., & Booth-Butterfield, M. (2013). *I'm only laughing because we work together: An examination of status differentials and the use of humor artifice in the workplace.* Paper presented at the annual conference of the National Communication Association, Washington, DC.

Goodboy, A., Booth-Butterfield, M., Bolkan, S., & Griffin, D. (2015). The role of instructor humor and students' educational orientations in student learning, extra effort, participation, and out-of-class communication, *Communication Quarterly*, 63, 44–61.

Graner, J. T., Chandler, R. C., & Wallace, J. D. (2015). Nothing to laugh about: Student interns' use of humor in response to workplace dissatisfaction. *Southern Communication Journal*, 80, 102–118.

Guenter, H., Schreurs, B., Van Emmerik, I. J., Gijsbers, W., & Van Iterson, A. (2013). How adaptive and maladaptive humor influence well-being at work: A diary study. *Humor*, 26, 573–594.

Haggard, D., Robert, C., & Rose, A. (2011). Co-rumination in the workplace: Adjustment trade-offs for men and women who engage in excessive discussions of workplace problems. *Journal of Business Psychology*, 26, 27–40.

Horan, S., Bochantin, J., & Booth-Butterfield, M. (2012). Humor in high stress relationships: Understanding communication in police officers' romantic relationships. *Communication Studies*, 63, 554–573.

Janes, L. M., & Olsen, J. M. (2000). Jeer pressure: The behavioral effects of observing ridicule of others. *Personality and Social Psychology Bulletin*, 26, 474–485.

Kanner, A., Coyne, J., Schafer, C., & Lazarus, R. (1981). Comparison of two modes of stress measurement: Daily hassles and uplifts versus major life events, *Journal of Behavioral Medicine*, 4, 1–39.

Keltner, D., Gruenfeld, D., & Anderson, C. (2003). Power, approach, and inhibition. *Psychological Review*, 110, 265–284.

Kobasa, S. (1979). Stressful life events, personality, and health: An inquiry into hardiness. *Journal of Personality and Social Psychology*, 37, 1–11.

Kohn, P., Lafreniere, K., & Gurevich, M. (1991). Hassles, health, and personality. *Journal of Personality and Social Psychology*, 61, 478–482.

Kuiper, N. A., & McHale, N. (2009). Humor styles as mediators between self-evaluative standards and psychological well-being. *The Journal of Psychology: Interdisciplinary and Applied*, 143, 359–376.

Lazarus, R. S., & Folkman, S. (1987). Transactional theory and research on emotions & coping. *European Journal of Personality*, 1, 141–169.

Martin, D. (2004). Humor in middle management: Women negotiating the paradoxes of organizational life. *Journal of Applied Communication Research*, 32, 147–170.

Martin, D., & Gayle, B. (1999). It isn't a matter of just being funny: Humor production by organizational leaders. *Communication Research Reports*, 16, 72–80.

Martin, D., Rich, C., & Gayle, B. (2004). Humor works: Communication style and humor functions in manager/subordinate relationships. *Southern Communication Journal*, 69, 206–222.

Martin, R. (2001). Humor, laughter, and physical health: Methodological issues and research findings. *Psychological Bulletin*, 127, 504–519.

Martin, R. A., Puhlik-Doris, P., Larsen, G., Gray, J., & Weir, K. (2003). Individual differences in uses of humor and their relation to psychological well-being: Development of the humor styles questionnaire. *Journal of Research in Personality*, 37, 48–75.

McGraw, A. P., & Warren, C. (2010). Benign violations: Making immoral behavior funny. *Psychological Science*, 21, 1141–1149.

McGraw, A. P., Williams, L., & Warren, C. (2014). The rise and fall of humor: Psychological distance modulates humorous responses to tragedy. *Social Psychological and Personality Science*, 5, 566–572.

McIlheran, J. (2006). The use of humor in corporate communication. *Corporate Communications*, 11, 267–274.

Merolla, A. (2006). Decoding ability and humor production. *Communication Quarterly*, 54, 175–189.

Mesmer-Magnus, J., Glew, D. J., & Viswesvaran, C. (2012). A meta-analysis of positive humor in the workplace. *Journal of Managerial Psychology*, 27, 155–190.

Miczo, N. (2012). Humor and message production. In R. DiCiccio (Ed.), *Humor communication: Theory, impact and outcomes* (pp. 35–49). Dubuque, IA: Kendall Hunt Publishing.

Miron-Spektor, E., & Rafaeli, A. (2009). The effects of anger in the workplace: When, where, and why observing anger enhances or hinders performance. In J. J. Martocchio, & H. Liao (Eds.), *Research in personnel and human resources management*, vol. 28 (pp. 153–178). Bingley, West Yorkshire: Emerald Group Publishing Limited.

Motley, M. (1997). COM Therapy. In J. Daly, J. McCroskey, J. Ayres, T. Hopf, & D. Ayres (Eds.), *Avoiding communication*, 2nd edition (pp. 379–400). Cresskill, NJ: Hampton Press.

Pham, L., Taylor, S., & Seeman, T. (2001). Effects of environmental predictability and personal mastery on self-regulatory and physiological processes. *Personality and Social Psychology Bulletin*, 27, 611–620.

Pollack, E. P. (2012). Humor and laughter as medicine: Physiologic impacts and effects. In R. DiCiccio (Ed.), *Humor communication: Theory, impact and outcomes* (pp. 203–214). Dubuque, IA: Kendall Hunt Publishing.

Pundt, A., & Herrmann, F. (2015). Affiliative and aggressive humor in leadership and their relationship to leader-member exchange. *Journal of Occupational & Organizational Psychology*, 88, 108–125.

Rabinowitz, D. (1998). 'The Seinfeld Firing.' *Wall Street Journal*. Retrieved August 17, 2016 from http://www.wsj.com/articles/SB894666378174741500

Rahona, J., Fernandez, S., Rolke, B., Vazquez, C., & Hervas, G. (2104). Overt head movements moderate the effect of depressive symptoms on mood regulation. *Cognition and Emotion*, 28, 1328–1337.

Rizzo, B., Wanzer, M., & Booth-Butterfield, M. (1999). Individual differences in managers' use of humor: Subordinate perceptions of managers' humor. *Communication Research Reports*, 16, 360–369.

Robert, C., Dunne, T. C., & Iun, J. (2015). The impact of leader humor on subordinate job satisfaction: The crucial role of leader-subordinate relationship quality. *Group and Organization Management*. Advance online publication. doi:10.1177/1059601115598719.

Romero, E. J., & Cruthirds, K. W. (2006). The use of humor in the workplace. *Academy of Management Perspectives*, 20, 58–69.

Romero, E. J., Alsua, C. J., Hinrichs, K. T., & Pearson, T. R. (2007). Regional humor differences in the United States: Implications for management. *Humor*, 20, 189–201.

Sculz, M., Cowan, P., Cowan, C., & Brennan, R. (2004). Coming home upset: Gender, marital satisfaction, and the daily spillover of workday experience into couple interactions. *Journal of Family Psychology*, 18, 250–263.

Selye, H. (1976). *Stress in health and disease*. London: Butterworth Publishers Inc.

Veatch, T. (1998). A theory of humor. *Humor*, 11, 161–215.

Vela, L., & Booth-Butterfield, M. (2015). *Can humor skill be improved? Investigating the effect of communication training on adaptive and maladaptive humor styles, knowledge, self-efficacy, and motivation.* Paper presented at the annual conference of the National Communication Association, Las Vegas, NV.

Vela, L., Booth-Butterfield, M., Wanzer, M., & Vallade, J. (2013). Relationships among humor, coping, relationship stress, and satisfaction in dating relationships: Replication and Extension. *Communication Research Reports*, 30(1), 68–75.

Vinton, K. L. (1989). Humor in the workplace: It is more than telling jokes. *Small Group Behavior*, 20, 151–166.

Wanzer, M. B. (2002). Use of humor in the classroom: The good, the bad, and the not-so-funny things that teachers say and do. In J. L. Chesebro, & J. C. McCroskey (Eds.), *Communication for teachers* (pp. 116–125). Boston, MA: Allyn & Bacon.

Wanzer, M. B., & Frymier, A. B. (1999). The relationship between student perceptions of instructor humor and student's reports of learning. *Communication Education*, 48, 48–62.

Wanzer, M. B., Booth-Butterfield, M., & Booth-Butterfield, S. (1995). The funny people: A source-orientation to the communication of humor. *Communication Quarterly*, 43, 142–154.

Wanzer, M. B., Booth-Butterfield, M., & Booth-Butterfield, S. (1996). Are funny people more popular: The relationship of humor orientation, loneliness, and social attraction. *Communication Quarterly*, 44, 42–52.

Wanzer, M. B., Booth-Butterfield, M. & Booth-Butterfield, S. (2005). "If we didn't use humor, we'd cry:" Humorous coping communication in health care settings. *Journal of Health Communication*, 10, 105–125.

Wanzer, M. B., Sparks, L., & Frymier, A. B. (2009). Humorous communication within the lives of older adults: The relationships among humor, coping efficacy, age, and life satisfaction. *Health Communication*, 24, 128–136.

Weinberg, A., & Cooper, C. (2011). The challenge of stress in modern organizations. In R. Contrada, & A. Baum (Eds.), *The handbook of stress science: Biology, psychology, and health* (pp. 151–165). New York: Springer Publishing Company.

Williams, M., & Emich, K. (2014). The experience of failed humor: Implications for interpersonal affect regulation. *Journal of Business and Psychology*, 29, 651–668.

7

HUMOR IN WORKGROUPS AND TEAMS

John Crowe, Joseph A. Allen, and Nale Lehmann-Willenbrock

Humor is an inherently social phenomenon. In the workplace, humor manifests most prominently in teams of employees that work together (e.g. Lefcourt, 2001). Humor in workgroups and teams can be a powerful positive resource and has been linked to a number of positive outcomes. In organizations, humor has the potential to enhance group cohesiveness (Duncan, 1982), improve employee morale (Gruner, 1997), stimulate individual and group creativity (Murdock & Ganim, 1993), create a more positive organizational culture (Clouse & Spurgeon, 1995), and to promote motivation (Crawford, 1994) and productivity (Clouse & Spurgeon, 1995). Thus, the purpose of this chapter is to review how humor in teams might play a key role in driving these workplace outcomes. By discussing what is known about humor in teams, the chapter concludes with ideas for future inquiry in the area of humor in teams, particularly in terms of interaction processes and workplace fun.

Humor in team meetings

Humor is a positive affective experience that is typically shared in a social context with others (e.g. Johnson, 2007). As such, we need to focus on specific social settings for understanding the role and effects of humor in the workplace. In the organizational context, one of the most universal events for examining social interactions among employees and within teams is the workplace meeting. The use of meetings has been increasing in recent years, especially among upper-level managers (Allen & Rogelberg, 2013). In fact, approximately 25 million meetings take place every day in the United States alone (Allen, Lehmann-Willenbrock, & Rogelberg, 2015). Meetings are affective events and an important context for studying socially shared affective experiences (e.g. Rogelberg, Allen, Shanock, Scott, & Shuffler, 2010). In a study conducted on firefighters, a thematic analysis demonstrated that humor was one of eight emergent themes that individuals identified as a good or wanted behavior in a meeting (Crowe, Allen, Scott, & Harms, 2013). Thus, as the interaction in a meeting plays out, the interchange of ideas as well as a variety of shared affective experiences such as conflict, trust, and, of importance to this chapter, humor, may emerge.

Building upon the assumption that humor occurs in meetings as a shared social activity, humor has the ability to strengthen interpersonal dynamics and organizational relationships (Cooper, 2008). According to Holmes (2000), humor contributes to a workplace culture and humor is identifiable in many workplaces. In some research, this function is linked to Brown and Levinson's (1987) concept of humor as a positive face strategy (Rogerson-Revell, 2007). During workplace meetings, one can observe the emergence of humor in process. This includes the elements facilitating humor events, the humor act itself, and subsequent laughter or other reactions (or lack thereof). But first, it is important to understand what makes something funny. We turn our attention now to theories of humor as they are manifest in teams with an eye toward how humor emerges in team meetings and team interaction.

Humor theories in teams

The humor literature contains three primary theories of humor: incongruity theory, relief theory, and superiority theory. According to all of these theories, what is humorous is determined by the interactions among individuals and the behavior elicited by the humorous action. That is, humor occurs through interaction and in many cases, these interactions occur in groups and teams. Thus, we review these theories briefly so as to provide the context for understanding humor in teams.

First, incongruity theory is based on the premise that surprises and novel circumstances are essential for something to be perceived as funny (Meyer, 2000). Incongruity humor functions by establishing an incompatibility between two different sets of expectations, and the sudden resolution of that incompatibility by the recipient (Suls, 1972). Humor, then, can be seen as problem solving which results in pleasure (e.g. laughter) when resolved. This form of humor is found amusing if it is irrational, paradoxical, illogical, incoherent, fallacious, or inappropriate. For example, consider the following joke by comedienne Mackenzie Harms: "What did the 0 say to the 8? Nice belt!" The incongruity is established in the joke's set-up by initiating incompatible schemata in the recipient – in that numbers are used for calculations, and numbers do not talk. The punchline draws on a third schema (i.e. the visual representation of the numbers) to allow the recipient to resolve what previously felt incongruous. The sudden experience of resolution causes pleasure.

Second, relief theory postulates that humor triggers laughter, which, in turn, releases tension (Romero & Pescosolido, 2008). Laughter is a complex body movement that has been found to ease muscle tension, break spasm-pain cycles, clear ventilation and mucus plugs, and increase oxygen and nutrients into tissues, which helps fight infection (Fry, 1992). Laughter has also been linked to elevated pain thresholds (Dunbar, Baron, Frangou, Pearce, van Leeuwen, Stow, Partridge, Macdonald, Barra, & van Vugt, 2011). The work of Hunter Doherty "Patch" Adams relates to these findings. Dr. Adams is both a medical doctor and a clown who believes that laughter, joy, and creativity are an integral part of the healing process. Subsequently, he opened the *Gesundheit! Institute* which combines traditional medicine with performing arts, crafts, nature, agriculture, and recreation in groups.

Third, superiority theory originally suggested that a person laughs about misfortunes of others (*Schadenfreude*), because these misfortunes assert the person's superiority in light of the shortcomings of others. However, more nuanced understandings of the theory suggest that humor is used to gain control (LaFave, Haddad, & Maeson, 1976) and feel superior (Ziv & Labelle, 1984). The mechanism of control can be seen in a joke that goes, "I'm so dumb, the closest I ever got to a 4.0 was my blood alcohol content." This allows others to laugh at the joke teller for not being superior, while simultaneously gaining status by making fun of him- or herself. What is clear in the above examples of the various humor theories is there is a unifying chord to humor: it makes us feel better. However, what people find humorous is as varied as people themselves. In fact, Thomae and Pina (2015) postulate that although humor is common, perceptions of humor are extremely idiosyncratic.

Given these theoretical frameworks for understanding humor, it is important to recognize that humor has the power to make even the most mundane team tasks pleasurable (Holmes, 2006). But because not all people interpret statements considered to be humorous in the same way, we must pay attention to differences in humor types and styles. According to Martin, Puhlik-Doris, Larsen, Gray, and Weir (2003), there are four basic types of humor that arise including affiliative (focused on the enhancement of relationships), aggressive (at the expense of others), self-defeating (at the expense of one's self), and self-enhancing (bolstering the view of one's self) variants. The use of these different humor styles is thought to have implications for psychological well-being and health (Martin et al., 2003). Relatedly, Wanzer, Sparks, and Frymier (2009) found that those who engage in positive humor often exhibit higher self-esteem and lower levels of depression. As such, humor plays a vital role in increasing positive team outcomes. The question, then, is how to facilitate a humorous group interaction. As noted earlier, team meetings are the ideal location for humor to infuse an organization's culture. Thus, we now turn to the positive effects of team humor and then focus on both leader humor behavior and humor through team interaction.

Positive effects of team humor

Oscar Wilde wrote, "If you want to tell people the truth, make them laugh, otherwise they'll kill you." What Wilde is elucidating here is the utility of humor in opening up interpersonal relations. In bringing laughter, the momentary behavioral expression of a shared affection opens a positive socioemotional connection (Ziv, 2010). The research on the effects of humor in the workplace has revealed that humor affects variables ranging from socialization, bonding, stress, burnout, and employee morale to productivity, creativity, and performance (e.g. Mesmer-Magnus, Glew, & Viswesvaran, 2012; Romero & Cruthirds, 2006). Humor also significantly affects team relationships (Cooper, 2008) by allowing individuals to mitigate withdrawal and negative socioemotional behaviors such as burnout (Talbot & Lumden, 2000) by strengthening group cohesion (Walter & Bruch, 2008). Studies have shown humor may reduce burnout by helping employees deal with difficult situations, release tension, regain perspective on their jobs, and facilitate an optimistic reinterpretation of events (Talbot & Lumden, 2000).

In addition to its effects on employees' personal outcomes, humor has been shown to be positively associated with work-related outcomes. Numerous studies have found the positive effects of humor, including improving the quality of team functioning and performance under stress (Bizi, Keinan, & Beit-Hallahmi, 1988), an increase in mental flexibility (Morreall, 1991), and an increase in openness to constructive feedback that motivates teams to stretch beyond their assumed limits (Berg, 1990).

Previous research has suggested that group level humor strengthens organizational outcomes. For instance, group level humor can be used to communicate information or to make a potentially controversial point in a positive way (Ullian, 1976), facilitate higher levels of trust (Hampes, 1999), reduce social distance between group members (Graham, 1995), and assist in creating the group's identity (Weick & Westley, 1996). Research also suggests humor promotes team cohesion via increased group harmony, collegiality, and inter-member attractiveness (Holmes, 2006). Emphasizing shared values (Meyer, 1997) and masking the unpleasant content of messages (Holmes, 2000) has also been shown to facilitate teamwork. It has been suggested that team humor can operate as a social lubricant (Morreall, 1991) that generates positive affect among group members (Robert & Wilbanks, 2012), helping to build group consensus (Coser, 1960), and limiting friction in interactions (Fine & DeSoucey, 2005).

Individual level humor has been shown to increase positive emotions shared among co-workers, which contributes to a positive affect spiral that promotes improved co-worker relationships, member performance, organizational citizenship behaviors, and work satisfaction (Gully, Devine, & Whitney, 1995). These are all factors that are also known to relate to reduced work withdrawal and turnover (Podsakoff, LePine, & LePine, 2007). Humor has also been associated with reduced absenteeism, job satisfaction (Mesmer-Magnus et al., 2012), higher organizational commitment, and lower turnover intentions (Brief & Weiss, 2002). Further, in a study conducted by Priest and Swain (2002), employees were asked to recall good or bad leaders and rate their use of humor. They found that good leaders were reported to use significantly more humor. Given this finding, we now turn our attention to team leaders and the humor they introduce in their teams.

Humor and team leaders

Team leaders are positioned well to have a disproportionately powerful impact on employees' behavior through humor efforts, partly stemming from their own sense of humor (Priest & Swain, 2002). Leaders who are seen as effectively using humor may be more persuasive than their less-humorous counterparts, as humor creates positive affect (Kuiper, McKenzie, & Belanger, 1995), increases liking for the source (Morkes, Kernal, & Nass, 1999), suggests a shared set of personal values (Meyer, 1997), and increases trust in the source (Hampes, 1999). Humor by leaders has been shown to reduce withdrawal behaviors and increase subordinate job satisfaction and commitment in teams (Burford, 1987). For instance, as one of the authors observed, a bank call center was having a team meeting in which everyone congregated around the office cubicles. One of the employees opened her desk drawer to retrieve both an orange and a tangerine while the manager was speaking. The manager stopped what she was saying and joked, "That's amazing! You're growing an orchard in your desk!" – which provoked abrupt laughter. Later that week the manager brought in a potted orange tree. From that point on the orange tree's fruit acted as a unifying experience and when an employee would outperform their metrics he or she would go get an orange.

Supervisor humor may operate by having the dual influence potential of securing power and reducing social distance between supervisors and the teams in their charge (Romero & Cruthirds, 2006). Leader humor may also increase creativity, but may also improve performance by facilitating group learning, helping change behavior, and reducing perceived threat associated with organizational change (Barbour, 1998). According to Dixon (1980), leaders who appropriately used humor inspired their teams to find creative and innovative solutions to complex problems. An example of this can be seen in the film *The Internship* in which the protagonists, Billy and Nick, playfully banter with their team and, in the end, cause the members of their team to each play to his or her strengths, thereby winning the competition. As we see, the use of humor by leaders is associated with increases in unit performance (Avolio, Howell, & Sosik, 1999) and has important implications for team satisfaction with supervisors (Crawford, 1994; Decker & Rotondo, 1999).

In summary, humor theories help explain how humor emerges in teams, how humor produces positive outcomes for teams, and how leaders may serve as one mechanism for facilitating those positive outcomes. The unifying thread through this section is the observation that all this humor behavior occurs through interaction among individuals within their teams. It is to these interactive processes that we now turn.

Humor as a team interaction process

The fact that humor is embedded within social contexts is reflected in most theoretical perspectives on humor as well as definitions of workplace humor. For example, Romero and Cruthirds (2006) define humor in workplace settings as "amusing communications that produce positive emotions and cognitions in the individual, group, or organization" (p. 59), and Cooper (2008) defines it as "any event shared by an agent (e.g. an employee) with another individual (i.e. a target) that is intended to be amusing to the target and that the target perceives as an intentional act" (pp. 766–767). Inherent in these definitions is the notion that humor and laughter are intertwined, as humor is often a trigger for laughter or other responses by the target. Moreover, these perspectives emphasize the crucial role of interactions when considering how humor emerges and is responded to.

However, previous empirical research has tended to neglect the social context in which humor occurs, and research on socially embedded humor in the workplace is particularly sparse (e.g. Mesmer-Magnus et al., 2012). This is an important omission, as humor and laughter are often bound to social settings. For example, we are 30 times more likely to laugh in a group than in isolation (Johnson, 2007). Workplace humor is particularly context-bound, such that jokes among co-workers are often obscure to outsiders (Holmes & Marra, 2002). Hence, to understand why humor and laughter occur and how they may benefit individual and team outcomes, researchers need to consider the conversational context surrounding humor and laughter occurrences. Moreover, when considering humor as it occurs within the team interaction process, researchers can examine how humor might trigger positive team experiences and create a pleasant group mood (e.g. Lehmann-Willenbrock, Meyers, Kauffeld, Neininger, & Henschel, 2011).

Interaction rituals (Collins, 2004) provide a theoretical lens for understanding how humor embedded in dynamic conversations can facilitate collaboration. At the core of any interaction ritual, participants focus their attention upon a common object or activity, explicitly communicate this focus to each other, and become physiologically and emotionally synchronized via cyclical patterns. In the case of humor and laughter, such shared patterns could build positive momentum (Den Hartigh, Gernigon, Van Yperen, Marin, & Van Geert, 2014) and hence promote team functioning.

The notion of shared humor patterns as an interaction process in groups and teams is intuitively appealing. Both humor and laughter should be considered, because positive, successful humor typically requires a social reaction (i.e. laughter). Moreover, humor and laughter are often ingrained in the context of a team's interactions. Consider a team sharing an "insider joke" or laughing at a funny statement during one of their meetings. If you are not part of the team, you probably would not understand what was so funny because joking is so context-specific and tends to refer to subtle group experiences that are difficult to discern by outsiders (e.g. Fine & DeSoucy, 2005; Holmes & Marra, 2002).

In a recent study, we investigated the notion of shared humor patterns in a sample of 54 videotaped team meetings from two medium-sized organizations (Lehmann-Willenbrock & Allen, 2014). We used the act4teams coding scheme (e.g. Kauffeld & Lehmann-Willenbrock, 2012) to slice the entire team meeting interaction into individual behaviors or statements by team members that follow one another over time. To examine how humor patterns emerge, we used lag sequential analysis,

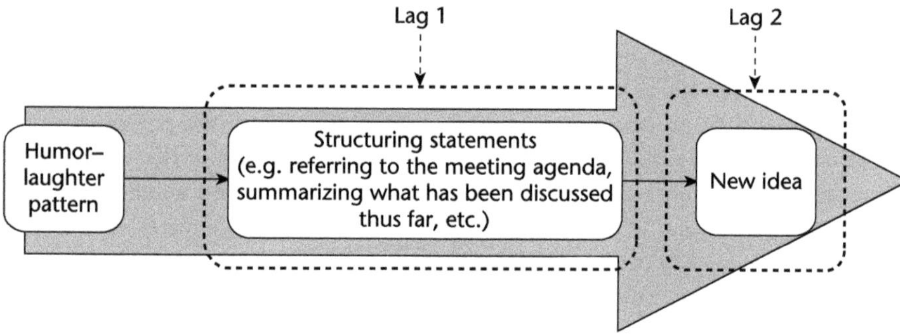

FIGURE 7.1 Lag sequential findings from a behavior-level process analysis of 54 organizational team meetings.

Note: Simplified figure, adapted from Lehmann-Willenbrock & Allen, 2014.

a statistical procedure that tests whether observed behavioral patterns such as humor–laughter are meaningful rather than just occurring by chance (for a detailed description of lag sequential analysis applied to team meeting interactions, see Lehmann-Willenbrock, Allen, & Kauffeld, 2013).

Figure 7.1 shows a simplified summary of our findings. First, as expected, lag sequential analysis revealed that humor typically occurred in humor–laughter patterns. Second, as illustrated in Figure 7.1, we saw that these shared patterns triggered constructive team interactions in the events following a pattern. Immediately after a humor–laughter pattern, teams often used structuring statements, such as referring back to the meeting agenda ("So, let's get back to our topic, which was . . ."), summarizing the discussion ("Alright, so far we've talked about . . ."), or making a procedural suggestion ("Ok, let's talk about . . . next"). After these structuring statements, we saw an increase in new ideas.

The research results, as illustrated by Figure 7.1, imply that shared humor patterns can serve an important function for team problem-solving and creativity processes. Considering that many team meetings have the purpose to solve problems and generate new ideas (e.g. Van Vree, 2011), the finding that humor patterns triggered new ideas within the team interaction process is particularly important. This finding also aligns with previous theorizing on the benefits of positive humor for team functioning (Romero & Pescosolido, 2008) by showing how humor–laughter patterns can trigger helpful communication dynamics, which may then aid team performance more broadly.

Moreover, Figure 7.1 highlights the important role of procedural communication after a humor–laughter pattern occurred. One reason why humor may be helpful in team interactions is because it can break up tension and facilitate communication (e.g. Duncan, Smeltzer, & Leap, 1990; Holmes & Marra, 2002; Meyer, 2000). The breaking up of tension that humor can do in teams is highly consistent with relief theory as previously reviewed. As such, a humor pattern could indicate a shift away from a difficult conversational moment, and a move toward more productive discussion. Yet, such a shift seems to require more than just the occurrence of a humor–laughter pattern. Procedural behaviors, such as referring to the meeting agenda or making suggestions about what to discuss next, can leverage the positive energy from a humor pattern and ensure that the team interaction stays on track (see also Lehmann-Willenbrock, Allen, & Kauffeld, 2013).

As mentioned earlier, the observed humor patterns in these meetings were positively linked to team performance, rated by the teams' supervisors in this study. Interestingly, when we only considered humor occurrences by themselves (rather than emergent patterns of humor and laughter), we saw no significant impact on team performance. This result underscores the need to consider humor as a shared, socially embedded interaction process rather than an isolated phenomenon. Thus, consistent with the theories of humor previously reviewed, it is not enough for humor behaviors to occur, but those behaviors must be found to be humorous by the target. Thus, humor is quite idiosyncratic and the outcomes of humor behavior are not always easily predicted.

Where we go from here

The forgoing discussion of humor in the workplace, its manifestation in interactive processes, and during workplace meetings leads us to the question of where research, inquiry, and application go from here in terms of workplace humor. Given that recent empirical findings show that workplace humor is linked to team performance (Lehmann-Willenbrock & Allen, 2014), researchers and managers in organizations may want to investigate how to promote humor interaction, the positive and uplifting type, in the workplace. Also, because humor appears to emerge in patterns of mutually shared humor and laughter (Lehmann-Willenbrock & Allen, 2014), there needs to be more investigation of humor and laughter as embedded and shared in dynamic social interactions (Klep, Wisse, & Van der Flier, 2011). Several avenues to promote humor and study the process of humor in the workplace are worth considering here.

First, in addition to the conversational dynamics following humor patterns (see Figure 7.1), we have yet to understand the antecedents of humor within the team interaction process. For example, organizational culture may be an important antecedent to humor such that cultures that are more open and psychologically safe may create an environment where playful and positive forms of humor can be used successfully (Robert & Wilbanks, 2012). Additionally, from a leadership perspective, one could imagine different styles of leadership may lend themselves more to the use of humor by leaders and followers. For example, charismatic leaders may use humor as a means to maintain the liking and devotion often associated with that leadership style.

In addition, the specific type of workplace humor needs to be considered (e.g. Romero & Cruthirds, 2006). For example, Lehmann-Willenbrock and Allen (2014) only looked at positive humor in relation to team performance. It may be that put-down humor or negatively based sarcasm may have the opposite effect, though technically still a humor style. Moreover, whether humor actually helps team functioning may be driven not only by micro-temporal contingencies (such as necessary procedural statements in order to focus after a humor occurrence, see Figure 7.1), but also by the macro-temporal context in which humor occurs (e.g. early versus later in a team's life, when considering newly formed teams who collaborate over a period of time). For instance, because team meetings have become a standard procedure in many contemporary organizations (e.g. Liker, 2006), Lehmann-Willenbrock and Allen (2014) hypothesized and found that extended humor patterns meaningfully related to team performance over time, highlighting the potential of humor as a positive team resource.

One potential antecedent to workplace humor that needs investigation is workplace fun (Karl, Peluchette, Hall, & Harland, 2005). Specifically, Karl and colleagues investigate how fun at work promotes positive attitudes and behaviors in the workplace (see Karl, Peluchette, Hall, & Harland, 2006). Workplace fun appears to promote positive perceptions of service quality, and such experiences may very well promote humor patterns in interaction, both between employees in an organization and between employees and customers, clients, and other stakeholders (Karl, Peluchette, Harland, & Rodie, 2010). In the few, but growing number of studies on workplace fun, humor has not received attention in terms of its role in creating an environment where workplace fun can or would occur. Although workplace fun could cause humor behavior, it may also be that humor behavior causes workplace fun. Perhaps humor is a subset of "fun" in the workplace along with things like novelty of events (i.e. nontypical workplace activities) and breaks in routine (i.e. work activities that disrupt normal workflow). Because precious little is known about how fun impacts humor in the workplace, a processual study of groups interacting may prove an important starting point. For example, if a workplace introduces fun activities into the work environment, recording such events and analyzing the group or team interaction would give insights into the effects of such events on humor behavior. Then a comparison could be made between workplace fun events and, for example, routine meetings to see if humor occurs with greater or lesser frequency during workplace fun events.

Second, workplace humor can be intertwined with gender issues. For example, Martin (2004) conducted qualitative interviews and found that female middle managers used humor in their meetings and in casual discourse in order to solve the paradox between being a woman and being a manager. Rather than rational facts statements, humor is ambiguous or incongruous by definition (Lynch, 2002), which may present a particularly useful tool for women in managerial positions. Innovative quantitative methodologies to examine such questions might integrate multi-level explanatory variables (e.g. individual gender; humor styles; team size) and time-series modeling (e.g. turn-taking behavior; problem-solving behavior within the interaction process; for a recent application of such methodology, see Lehmann-Willenbrock, Chiu, Lei, & Kauffeld, 2016).

Third, the ways in which humor and laughter are shared during team conversations may hinge upon status differences (Robinson & Smith-Lovin, 2001).

Laughter reactions can be "upward," such that team members laugh at their leaders' jokes but not necessarily vice versa. In that case, hierarchy might undermine the facilitative function of humor and laughter for group functioning. Hierarchy may also play a role in the intensity of laughter reactions to humor. Moreover, "contagious" humor and laughter may be shaped by team leaders, similar to findings on interpersonal positive affect sharing between team leaders and followers (Van Kleef, Homan, Beersma, Van Knippenberg, Van Knippenberg, & Damen, 2009). It is also possible that laughter in response to leader humor might not be as diagnostic as laughter in response to co-worker humor due to the relative social pressure to respond to leader humor. Lag sequential analysis can test these ideas at the micro-level of behaviors following one another over time (e.g. Lehmann-Willenbrock et al., 2013), while also accounting for hierarchical differences between team leaders and team members.

Conclusion

Humor is not an isolated event, but a shared social experience that unfolds during interactions between individuals, often in groups and teams. Because humor is quite often a group or team process, we tend to observe an actor engaging in behavior that they believe will elicit laughter. Hence, we have argued that a focus on the fine-grained interaction dynamics that trigger humor and emergent patterns that result from humor may yield the most fruitful continuation of the investigation of humor in the workplace. With the prevalence of meetings in the workplace, future research should focus on team meetings as a context for examining the antecedents and consequences of humor in team interactions.

References

Allen, J. A., & Rogelberg, S. G. (2013). Manager-led group meetings: A context for promoting employee engagement. *Group & Organization Management*, 38, 543–569.

Allen, J. A., Lehmann-Willenbrock, N., & Rogelberg, S. (2015). An introduction to the Cambridge handbook of meeting science. In J. Allen, N. Lehmann-Willenbrock, & S. Rogelberg (Eds.), *The Cambridge handbook of meeting science* (pp. 3–11). New York: Cambridge University Press.

Avolio, B. J., Howell, J. M., & Sosik, J. J. (1999). A funny thing happened on the way to the bottom line: Humor as a moderator of leadership style. *Academy of Management Journal*, 42, 219–227.

Barbour, G. (1998). Want to be a successful manager? Now that's a laughing matter! *Public Management*, 80, 6–9.

Berg, D. H. (1990). Let's get serious. . . about humor. *Journal for Quality and Participation*, 1, 80–83.

Bizi, S., Keinan, G., & Beit-Hallahmi, B. (1988). Humor and coping with stress: A test under real-life conditions. *Personality and Individual Differences*, 9, 951–956.

Brief, A. P., & Weiss, H. M. (2002). Organizational behavior: Affect at work. *Annual Review of Psychology*, 53, 279–307.

Brown, P., & Levinson, S. (1987). *Politeness: Some universals in language usage*. Cambridge: Cambridge University Press.

Burford, C. (1987). Humor of principals and its impact on teachers and the school. *Journal of Educational Administration*, 25, 29–54.

Clouse, R. W., & Spurgeon, K. L. (1995). Corporate analysis of humor. *Psychology: A Quarterly Journal of Human Behavior*, 32, 1–24.

Collins, R. (2004). *Interaction ritual chains*. Princeton, NJ: Princeton University Press.

Cooper, C. (2008). Elucidating the bonds of workplace humor: A relational process model. *Human Relations*, 61, 1087–1115.

Coser, R. (1960). Some social functions of laughter: a study of humor in a hospital setting. *Human Relations*, 12, 171–181.

Crawford, C. B. (1994). Theory and implications regarding the utilization of strategic humor by leaders. *Journal of Leadership & Organizational Studies*, 1, 53–68.

Crowe, J., Allen, J., Scott, C., & Harms, M. (2013, July). After action reviews: Perspective from those who engage. Research presented at the Interdisciplinary Network for Group Research Conference, July 11–13, 2013, Atlanta, GA.

Decker, W. H., & Rotondo, D. M. (1999). Use of humor at work: Predictors and implications. *Psychological Reports*, 84, 961–968.

Den Hartigh, R. J. R., Gernigon, C., Van Yperen, N. W., Marin, L., & Van Geert, P. L. C (2014). How psychological and behavioral team states change during positive and negative momentum. *PLoS ONE*, 9, e97887.

Dixon, N. F. (1980). Humor: A cognitive alternative to stress? In I. G. Sarason, & C. D. Spielburger (Eds.), *Stress and anxiety* (pp. 281–289). Washington, DC: Hemisphere.

Dunbar, R., Baron, R., Frangou, A., Pearce, E., van leeuwen, E., Stow, J., Partridge, G., Macdonald, I., Barra, V., & van Vugt, M. (2011). Social laughter is correlated with an elevated pain threshold. *Proceedings of the Royal Society of London B: Biological Sciences*. doi:10.1098/rspb.2011.1373.

Duncan, W. J. (1982). Humor in management: Prospects for administrative practice and research. *Academy of Management Review*, 7, 136–142.

Duncan, W. J., Smeltzer, L. R., & Leap, T. L. (1990). Humor and work: Applications of joking behavior to management. *Journal of Management, 16,* 255–278. doi:10.1177/014920639001600203.

Fine, G. A., & DeSoucey, M. D. (2005). Joking cultures: Humor themes as social regulation in group life. *Humor*, 18, 1–22.

Fry, W. (1992). The physiological effects of humor, mirth, and laughter. *Journal of the American Medical Association*, 267, 1857–1858.

Graham, E. E. (1995). The involvement of sense of humor in the development of social relationships. *Communication Reports*, 8, 158–170.

Gruner, C. R. (1997). *The game of humor: A comprehensive theory of why we laugh*. New Brunswick, NJ: Transaction.

Gully, S. M., Devine, D. J., & Whitney, D. J. (1995). A meta-analysis of cohesion and performance: Effects of levels of analysis and task interdependence. *Small Group Research*, 26, 497–520.

Hampes, W. P. (1999). The relationship between humor and trust. *Humor*, 12, 253–259.

Holmes, J. (2000). Politeness, power and provocation: How humour functions in the workplace? *Discourse Studies, 2,* 159–185.

Holmes, J. (2006). Sharing a laugh: Pragmatic aspects of humor and gender in the workplace. *Journal of Pragmatics*, 38, 26–50.

Holmes, J., & Marra, M. (2002). Having a laugh at work: How humor contributes to workplace culture. *Journal of Pragmatics*, 34, 1683–1710.

Johnson, S. (2007). What's so friggin' funny? Nothing—laughter is simply how we connect. Retrieved January 3, 2016, from http://discovermagazine.com/2007/brain/laughter

Karl, K., Peluchette, J., Hall, L., & Harland, L. (2005). Attitudes toward workplace fun: A three-sector comparison. *Journal of Leadership & Organizational Studies*, 12, 1–17.

Karl, K., Peluchette, J., Hall, L., & Harland, L. (2006). Attitudes toward workplace fun among public sector employees. *Journal of Contemporary Business Issues*, 14, 26–33.

Karl, K., Peluchette, J., Harland, L., & Rodie, A. (2010). Perceptions of service quality: What's fun got to do with it? *Health Marketing Quarterly*, 27, 155–172.

Kauffeld, S., & Lehmann-Willenbrock, N. (2012). Meetings matter: Effects of team meeting communication on team and organizational success. *Small Group Research*, 43, 130–158.

Klep, A., Wisse, B., & Van der Flier, H. (2011). Interactive affective sharing versus non-interactive affective sharing in work groups: Comparative effects of group affect on work group performance and dynamics. *European Journal of Social Psychology*, 41, 312–323.

Kuiper, N. A., McKenzie, S. D., & Belanger, K. A. (1995). Cognitive appraisals and individual differences in sense of humor: Motivational and affective implications. *Personality and Individual Differences*, 19, 359–372.

LaFave, L., Haddad, J., & Maeson, W. A. (1976). Superiority, enhanced self-esteem and perceived incongruity humor theory. In A. J. Chapman, & H. C. Foot (Eds.), *Humor and laughter: Theory, research and applications* (pp. 63–91). New York: Wiley Press.

Lefcourt, H. M. (2001). *Humor: The psychology of living buoyantly*. New York: Kluwer Academic.

Lehmann-Willenbrock, N., Allen, J. A., & Kauffeld, S. (2013). A sequential analysis of procedural meeting communication: How teams facilitate their meetings. *Journal of Applied Communication Research*, 41, 365–388.

Lehmann-Willenbrock, N., & Allen, J. A. (2014). How fun are your meetings? Investigating the relationship between humor patterns in team interactions and team performance. *Journal of Applied Psychology*, 99, 1278–1287.

Lehmann-Willenbrock, N., Chiu, M. M., Lei, Z., & Kauffeld, S. (2016). Positivity as a dynamic team phenomenon: A statistical discourse analysis. *Group & Organization Management*. Advance online publication. doi:10.1177/1059601116628720.

Lehmann-Willenbrock, N., Meyers, R. A., Kauffeld, S., Neininger, A., & Henschel, A. (2011). Verbal interaction sequences and group mood: Exploring the role of planning communication. *Small Group Research*, 42, 639–668.

Liker, J. (2006). *The Toyota way fieldbook*. New York: McGraw-Hill.

Lynch, O. (2002). Humorous communications: Finding a place for humor in communication research. *Communication Theory*, 12, 423–445.

Martin, D. M. (2004). Humor in middle management: Women negotiating the paradoxes of organizational life. *Journal of Applied Communication Research*, 32, 147–170.

Martin, R. A., Puhlik-Doris, P., Larsen, G., Gray, J., & Weir, K. (2003). Individual differences in uses of humor and their relation to psychological well-being: Development of the humor styles questionnaire. *Journal of Research in Personality*, 37, 48–76.

Mesmer-Magnus, J., Glew, D. J., & Viswesvaran, C. (2012). A meta-analysis of positive humor in the workplace. *Journal of Managerial Psychology*, 27, 155–190.

Meyer, J. C. (1997). Humor in member narratives: uniting and dividing at work. *Western Journal of Communication*, 61, 188–208.

Meyer, J. C. (2000). Humor as a double-edged sword: Four functions of humor in communication. *Communication Theory*, 10, 310–331.

Morkes, J., Kernal, H. K., & Nass, C. (1999). Effects of humor in task-oriented human-computer interaction and computer-mediated communication: a direct test of SRCT theory. *Human-Computer Interaction*, 14, 395–435.

Morreall, J. (1991). Humor and work. *Humor*, 4, 359–373.

Murdock, M. C., & Ganim, R. M. (1993). Creativity and humor: Integration and incongruity. *Journal of Creative Behavior*, 27, 57–70.

Podsakoff, N. P., LePine, J. A., & LePine, M. A. (2007). Differential challenge stressor-hindrance stressor relationships with job attitudes, turnover intentions, turnover, and withdrawal behavior: A meta-analysis. *Journal of Applied Psychology*, 92, 438–454.

Priest, R. F., & Swain, J. E. (2002). Humor and its impact on leadership effectiveness. *Humor*, 15, 169–189.

Robert, C., & Wilbanks, J. E. (2012). The wheel model of humor: Humor events and affect in organizations. *Human Relations, 65,* 1071–1099.

Robinson, D. T., & Smith-Lovin, L. (2001). Getting a laugh: Gender, status, and humor in task discussions. *Social Forces*, 80, 123–158.

Rogelberg, S. G., Allen, J. A., Shanock, L., Scott, C., & Shuffler, M. (2010). Employee satisfaction with meetings: A contemporary facet of job satisfaction. *Human Resource Management*, 49, 149–172.

Rogerson-Revell, P. (2007). Humour in business: A double-edged sword. A study of humour and style shifting in intercultural business meetings. *Journal of Pragmatics*, 39, 4–28.

Romero, E., & Cruthirds, K. W. (2006). The use of humor in the workplace. *Academy of Management Perspectives*, 20, 58–69.

Romero, E., & Pescosolido, A. (2008). Humor and group effectiveness. *Human Relations*, 61, 395–418.

Suls, J. M. (1972). Two-stage model for the appreciation of jokes and cartoons: Information-processing analysis. In J. H. Goldstein, & P. E. McGhee (Eds.), *The psychology of humor* (pp. 81–100). San Diego, CA: Academic Press.

Talbot, L. A., & Lumden, D. B. (2000). On the association between humor and burnout. *Humor: International Journal of Humor Research*, 13, 419–428.

Thomae, M., & Pina, A. (2015). Sexist humor and social identity: The role of sexist humor in men's in-group cohesion, sexual harassment, rape proclivity, and victim blame. *Humor*, 28, 187–204.

Ullian, J. A. (1976). Joking at work. *Journal of Communication*, 26, 129–133.

Van Kleef, G. A., Homan, A. C., Beersma, B., Van Knippenberg, D. V., Van Knippenberg, B., & Damen, F. (2009). Searing sentiment or cold calculation? The effects of leader emotional displays on team performance depend on follower epistemic motivation. *Academy of Management Journal*, 52, 562–580.

Van Vree, W. (2011). Meetings: the frontline of civilization. *The Sociological Review*, 59, 241–262.

Walter, F., & Bruch, H. (2008). The positive group affect spiral: A dynamic model of the emergence of positive affective similarity in work groups. *Journal of Organizational Behavior*, 29, 239–261.

Wanzer, M. B., Sparks, L., & Frymier, A. B. (2009). Humorous communication within the lives of older adults: The relationships among humor, coping efficacy, age, and life satisfaction. *Health Communication*, 24, 128–136.

Weick, K., & Westley, F. (1996). Organizational learning: Affirming an oxymoron. In S. Clegg, C. Hardy, & W. Nord (Eds.), *Handbook of organizational studies* (pp. 440–458). Thousand Oaks, CA: Sage.

Ziv, A. (2010). The social function of humor in interpersonal relationships. *Society*, 47, 11–18.

Ziv, A., & Labelle, F. (1984). *Personality and sense of humor*. New York: Springer Publishing Company.

8

HUMOR IN JOB SEARCH AND RECRUITMENT

Serge P. da Motta Veiga

As noted by various scholars (e.g. Barber, 1998; Chapman, Uggerslev, Carroll, Piasentin, & Jones, 2005), attracting qualified applicants is an extremely important human resource management practice. The importance of selection practices depends a lot on the quality of the applicant pool, as well as whether the top applicants accept job offers (e.g. Boudreau & Rynes, 1985; Murphy, 1986). From an individual applicant's perspective, an applicant's intentions and behaviors toward a specific potential employer (e.g. applying for a job with this employer, intentions to accept a job offer if one is made by this employer) are components of the applicant's job search process, which typically involves multiple possible employers (Boswell, Zimmerman, & Swider, 2012; Kanfer, Wanberg, & Kantrowitz, 2001). Not surprisingly, studies examining organizational attraction have examined the influence of firms' recruitment practices, and job and organizational attributes, on the firms' ability to attract the best applicants (e.g. Collins, 2007; Turban & Cable, 2003). Thus, as individuals conduct their job search they are exposed to various recruitment practices and obtain information about job and organizational attributes, which may influence their job search activities.

This chapter explores the notion that humor might influence job search and recruitment processes and outcomes. Indeed, the use of humor could become an integral part of the strategies used by companies to attract and recruit potential employees, while it also can influence the way job seekers navigate their search for employment. Since a firm's recruitment processes influence an applicant's reaction to that firm and also may influence the applicant's job search processes, the use of humor during these processes can influence job search processes, recruitment processes, and the overall outcomes of both processes, namely whether an offer is made to an applicant, and whether the applicant accepts it.

Although an extensive amount of research examining applicant attraction has taken an organizational perspective (e.g. Barber, 1998; Chapman et al., 2005), it is critical to note that applicants' intentions and behaviors are also important aspects of the job search process (e.g. Schreurs, Derous, van Hooft, Proost, & De Witte, 2009). That is, job seekers are *active* information processors whose attitudes and behaviors towards organizations are dynamic; they change with additional input from organizations, and shape the way job seekers view the whole job search process. Specifically, an organization's recruitment practices not only influence applicants' attraction to the firm (e.g. Barber, 1998; Collins, 2007), but also impact applicants' subsequent job search processes and behaviors. For example, the use of humor in an interview by the recruiter may not only influence the applicant's attraction to the firm as a potential employer, but might also influence the applicant's subsequent job search behaviors and the expectations they form about other employers.

Job search and recruitment are "two sides of the same coin" (da Motta Veiga & Turban, forthcoming). On one side, recruiting applicants is an essential human resource management practice for organizations looking to recruit and select the best potential applicants. On the other side, job seekers are attracted to apply for jobs at specific organizations.

Job search is typically defined as behaviors designed to learn about and pursue job openings with the ultimate goal of receiving and accepting a job offer (Boswell et al., 2012), and involves various activities engaged in by the job applicant. The job search process is considered a stressful, self-regulated process with the job seeker's goal to find suitable employment (Boswell et al., 2012; Kanfer et al., 2001). Job search behavior is typically operationalized by assessing the frequency of job search activities, such as revising one's resume, completing applications, or by the overall effort exhibited by the job seeker (Blau, 1994; Boswell et al., 2012; Saks & Ashforth, 2002). Job search behaviors, whether the seeker received an offer, and how many job offers were received, are the most studied job search processes and outcomes. Evidence indicates that job search behaviors are predicted by job seeker personality characteristics, job search self-efficacy, self-esteem, financial need and employment commitment, and social support (Kanfer et al., 2001). Furthermore, since the job search is a stressful, self-regulated process, research has also focused on the regulation of affect, stress, and motivation as influencing persistence during the job search process (e.g. da Motta Veiga & Gabriel, 2016; da Motta Veiga & Turban, 2014; Song, Uy, Zhang, & Shi, 2009).

Recruitment is defined as the organizational practices that influence the number and quality of individuals that apply for vacant positions (e.g. Barber, 1998; Chapman et al., 2005; Rynes, 1991). Specifically, Barber (1998) suggested that the recruitment process includes three phases: generating applicants, maintaining applicant status, and influencing job choice. In the generating applicants phase, organizations are attempting to attract quality applicants who will apply for positions. During the maintaining applicant status phase organizations are attempting to keep applicants interested in the firm as applicants are being exposed to the organization's selection practices (i.e. interviews, site visits). When a job offer is made, the organization attempts to influence job choice such that applicants will accept the job offer. In general, the recruitment (applicant attraction) literature has examined predictors of important individual-level recruitment outcomes such as organizational attraction, job pursuit, and job choice (Barber, 1998; Chapman, et al., 2005; Rynes, 1991). Specifically, in their meta-analysis, Chapman et al. (2005) found that recruitment outcomes were predicted by job/organization characteristics, recruiter behaviors, applicant perceptions of the recruiting process, perceived fit, and hiring expectancies.

The scope of this chapter encompasses facets of the job search and recruitment processes that can be influenced by the use of humor by organizations, their recruiters, and by job seekers. In the remainder of the chapter, I explore the important role humor can have in influencing job search processes and outcomes (i.e. the applicant's perspective). For example, humor can perhaps help job seekers cope with the stress associated with the job search (Song et al., 2009). Furthermore, humor can also serve as an impression management tool to help job seekers obtain higher interview success, and ultimately secure more job offers.

I also explore whether and how the use of humor can influence recruitment processes and outcomes (i.e. the organization's perspective) directly or indirectly via other predictors (e.g. recruitment ads, recruiter behaviors). For example, humor can perhaps be used by recruiters to signal the culture of the organization to potential applicants, and as such, to help them identify whether such an organization would be a good fit or not (Kristof-Brown, Zimmerman, & Johnson, 2005). Furthermore, humor can also influence whether job applicants decide to accept or reject an offer made by an organization. Finally, I discuss how future research could integrate the impact of humor into both job search and recruitment simultaneously. Throughout the chapter, I pay more attention to the potential positive role of humor in both the job search and recruitment processes, but remain mindful of some of its downsides as well.

Humor and job search

The role of humor in organizations has received some interest both theoretically and empirically in recent years (Cooper, 2005, 2008; Robert & Wilbanks, 2012; Robert & Yan, 2007; Romero & Pescosolido, 2008). However, there is still a limited amount of empirical research on humor in organizations, and existing empirical research is typically driven by popular notions of humor. In the job search literature, in particular, the role of humor on job search processes and outcomes has not been studied yet. Furthermore, since one of the primary barriers to "mainstreaming" research on humor has been the difficulty situating humor phenomena within more established and well-developed organizational literatures, it seems that the humor and job search literatures are ripe for such research to occur.

The literature on humor suggests that people are motivated to use humor for many reasons. One of those reasons is that humor is thought to act as stress relief (Graham, Papa, & Brooks, 1992) and to help people cope with work-related stress (Abel, 2002). Since the job search is a relatively complex and ambiguous process in which job seekers engage in activities to find a job (Wanberg, Kanfer, & Rotundo, 1999), the conceptualization of humor as a behavior that might help reduce the perceived stress associated with job seeking can be viewed from both a problem-focused and emotion-focused coping perspective. The purpose of problem-focused coping is to change the stressful relationship between the individual and a specific situation (e.g. job search) by acting on the situation or oneself (Carver, 2011). On the other hand, emotion-focused coping is oriented toward managing the emotions that accompany the perception of stress, such as distracting oneself (Carver, 2011; Folkman & Moskowitz, 2004). As such, one mechanism that can help resolve job search stress would be to use humor as a coping mechanism.

It would be interesting for future research to examine whether, how, and to what extent the use of humor in job search can help job seekers cope with the process both by helping them adapt their behaviors (i.e. problem-focused coping), but also providing a well-needed break or distraction (i.e. emotion-focused coping) (e.g. Trougakos, Beal, Green, & Weiss, 2008). An example of both problem- and emotion-focused coping would be for job seekers to share their bad experiences in a humorous way with fellow job seekers or career counselors in order to learn from their mistakes while also laughing at themselves (i.e. providing a distraction). Notably, scholars have conceptualized and examined job search behaviors as a type of problem-focused coping behavior (McKee-Ryan, Song, Wanberg, & Kinicki, 2005; Song et al., 2009; Wanberg, 1997). Perhaps using humor in job search could be a behavior that helps job seekers jump the hurdles of the process, while simultaneously helping them manage inevitable negative emotions.

Another avenue for future research examining the role of humor in job search would be to examine whether humor can serve as an impression management tool in helping job seekers obtain interviews and even job offers. Indeed, Cooper (2005) suggested that humor can be a type of ingratiatory behavior in the workplace. Evidence also strongly indicates that impression management influences job search outcomes such as interview success, second-round interviews and job offers (Bolino, Kacmar, Turnley, & Gilstrap, 2008; Stevens & Kristof, 1995; Tsai, Chen, & Chiu, 2005). As such, perhaps the use of humor as an impression management tool can help job search outcomes such as interview success and job offers. Interestingly, Glenn (2010) investigated the role of shared laughter in job interviews, and found that laughter is not always shared and sometimes these laughter asymmetries serve to reinforce the "power distance" between the interviewer and interviewee. As such, it is critical for future research to delineate whether and how humor is used as ingratiatory behavior, and what type of humor is used.

Finally, I also encourage future researchers to examine the influence of humor in recruitment practices, such as recruitment ads, on subsequent job search behaviors. Indeed, although this might overlap with the recruitment literature and the following section of this chapter, the use of humor in recruitment practices can influence the amount of time and effort job seekers want to invest in applying to specific organizations. Relatedly, perhaps job seekers who value the use of humor at work might dedicate their time and effort to applying to companies who portray themselves, through their recruitment ads or recruiter behaviors, as having a climate that supports humor use (Robert & Wilbanks, 2012). This would also be consistent with the person–organization fit literature, which suggests that job applicants seek organizations that share their same characteristics or values (Kristof, 1996; Kristof-Brown et al., 2005). Interestingly, though, it will also be important to account for the type of humor used and context in which the humor is used. For example, a company that portrays itself as having a carnival-like atmosphere might not appeal to many job seekers, whereas a company that indicates that humor is an integral part of their laid-back, friendly culture might appeal to a greater number of job seekers.

Humor and recruitment

In the recruitment literature, the role of humor on recruitment processes and outcomes has received very limited attention. In the only study that was somewhat related to the role of "humor" in recruitment, Goltz and Giannantonio (1995) indicated that job applicants made significantly more positive inferences regarding organizational characteristics when recruiters were friendly versus unfriendly, and that recruiter friendliness influenced applicants' attraction to the job. However, that study did not specifically examine humor, but rather recruiter friendliness. As such, the recruitment literature seems to provide an established and well-developed organizational literature within which the role of humor can be examined and integrated.

One interesting avenue for future work would be to understand whether and how organizations could use humor as a recruitment tool, for example, by introducing humor in recruitment ads or by using humor in recruiter behaviors. Interestingly, there is extensive research looking at the role of humor in marketing, especially in advertising (for a meta-analysis see Eisend, 2009). Humor has been shown to positively influence the impact of advertising, although some research has shown that sometimes humor can also inhibit ad outcomes (Cline, Altesch, & Kellaris, 2003). In terms of recruitment, the use of humor might align with the organization's desire to signal to potential applicants, through its recruitment ads or recruiter behaviors, that the organization supports humor use at work.

To pursue this avenue, future research could draw from signaling theory to examine the role humor can have in recruitment ads and recruiter behaviors. Signaling theory proposes that individuals interpret available information as providing signals about what is unknown (for a recent review see Connelly, Certo, Ireland, & Reutzel, 2011). Since job applicants do not have complete information about an organization, they interpret available information as signal(s) about the job and organization (Rynes, 1991). For example, evidence suggests that reputation provides a signal about the job and organization, which subsequently influences job pursuit intentions (Turban & Cable, 2003). Furthermore, recruitment behaviors may be interpreted as providing information about an organization such that an unfriendly recruiter may signal an unfriendly environment (Taylor & Bergmann, 1987). In summary, signaling theory has been used to examine various recruitment predictors such as organizational reputation and attractiveness, recruiter behaviors and traits, and recruitment delays (Cable & Turban, 2001; Collins, 2007; Turban &

Cable, 2003). Perhaps, the use of humor during recruitment could serve as a signal to potential job applicants about the organization's culture and values.

Future research could thus extend prior work by using signaling theory to examine whether, and how, the use of humor in recruitment ads and/or recruiter behaviors influences various recruitment outcomes, such as applicant attraction, whether job applicants accept an offer from this organization, intention to remain with the organization, etc. Organizations could use these signals to indicate that they have a humorous work environment, and that job applicants who are interested in being in an environment that is supportive of, and perhaps even conducive to, humor use might be more attracted to such organizations and pursue employment. As mentioned earlier, there are opportunities for future research to also integrate the person–organization fit literature (Kristof, 1996) when examining whether and how humor influences recruitment practices. Indeed, while organizations send signals about their values, job applicants receive those and interpret them for fit with their own values (Kristof-Brown et al., 2005). Even if that humor is not successful, and as long as it is not offensive it could act as a signal to job applicants about the value that the organization puts on humor and related qualities, such as friendliness and cohesiveness.

Another avenue for future research would be understanding whether, and how, the use of humor at any point during the recruitment process influences the ultimate goal of getting a job offer accepted (or rejected) by a top applicant. Indeed, although humor can play a positive role at various stages of the process, when can humor make or break the deal? When is too much humor too much? When is it a bad time to use humor? It would be interesting to answer these questions from an organization's perspective of trying to recruit top applicants. Furthermore, these questions could very well apply to job seekers as well. When should they use or avoid humor? For example, should they use humor or not when negotiating a job offer? Companies such as Glassdoor.com present researchers with rich databases, which include information about the recruitment process, including whether applicants received an offer or not, and whether they accepted it or not. Furthermore, the website also contains information (content data) about the recruitment process itself (e.g. friendly recruiter, slow process, etc.). Using websites and databases such as Glassdoor.com could help answer some of the questions above.

Finally, both recruitment and job search can be perceived as persuasion processes: the applicant is trying to persuade the potential employer to give them an offer, while the organization is trying to persuade the applicant to accept their offer. The elaboration likelihood model (ELM; Petty & Cacioppo, 1986; Roberson, Collins, & Oreg, 2005; Turban, Forret, & Hendrickson, 1998) might provide a useful lens through which to view humor's role in the persuasion process. At the core of the ELM is the notion that persuasive messages are processed along either a peripheral route, which involves limited cognitive effort and reliance on shortcuts and signals, or along a central route, involving more focused attention and effort at evaluating the quality of persuasive arguments (Petty & Cacioppo, 1986). People who are less motivated or able to process persuasive arguments are likely to employ the peripheral route, whereas individuals who are motivated and able to evaluate persuasive arguments employ the central route. The value of humor, for both job seekers and recruiters, might be dependent on whether humor is used in a context in which the other party is engaging in peripheral- or central-route processing. Light humor that is used primarily to generate positive affect and good feelings in the other party might be ineffective in persuasion if a party is employing central-route processing. For example, the context of an informal unstructured interview might make both the job seeker and recruiter engage in peripheral processing of information about the other party. Humor used in such a context might influence both parties' judgments in that they might simply rely on the "feeling" they get from the other party, rather than evaluating the quality and decision-relevance of persuasive messages. In contrast, structured interview contexts generally indicate that interviewers are motivated to engage in careful scrutiny of information from job seekers. This might suggest that humor use by job seekers might backfire if the interviewer perceives the job seeker to be avoiding providing relevant answers to structured job relevant questions. That being said, even central-route processing might benefit from humor if the humor itself is relevant to the organization's decision. For example, humor might be used as a way of signaling an organization's or applicant's values, or might be used as a subtle way of conveying information that might be otherwise difficult to communicate in a direct manner (e.g. salary demands).

Integrating humor, job search, and recruitment

Throughout the chapter, I have opened the door for future humor research to take either an individual (i.e. job search) or organizational (i.e. recruitment) approach. However, applicants and organizational representatives influence each other throughout the job search and recruitment processes, with these reciprocal effects being strongest in interviews. Indeed, considerable evidence indicates recruiter behaviors influence applicant attraction (Chapman et al., 2005). For example, when recruiters are seen as friendly, applicants tend to report greater attraction to the firm (Turban & Dougherty, 1992). Extending prior research, future work could thus investigate the influence of recruiters' use of humor not only on applicant attraction, but also on job search intentions and behaviors.

It would be interesting to consider whether, and how, applicants and recruiters (or other organizational representatives) influence each other, especially since humor is a dyadic process with reactions (i.e. laughter, smile, smirk, etc.) and responses (Robert & Wilbanks, 2012). For example, emotional contagion theory suggests that individuals have a tendency to experience emotions that are similar to, and influenced by, those of others (Barsade, 2002; Hatfield, Cacioppo, & Rapson, 1994; Kelly & Barsade, 2001). Since evidence indicates that applicants' positive emotions influence the likelihood of obtaining a call-back interview (Burger & Caldwell, 2000; Turban, Stevens, & Lee, 2009), and that humor is related to positive affect (Goel & Dolan, 2007; Sy, Côté, & Saavedra, 2005), perhaps humor interactions during job interviews could help generate more positive affect and increase the interview experience for both parties. This would be consistent with emotional contagion theory, and with research on interpersonal affect regulation (Niven, Holman, & Totterdell, 2012; Niven, Totterdell, Holman, & Headley, 2012), which suggests that people engage in various interpersonal behaviors (including humor) in order to regulate others' emotions.

More broadly, future work might investigate whether and how applicant personality characteristics, including humor styles or propensity to use humor, influence recruiter behaviors and outcomes. For example, in a study examining service interactions, customer personality traits influenced displays of positive emotions by the service provider in a very brief interaction (Tan, Foo, & Kwek, 2004). Specifically, service providers displayed more positive emotions to customers higher on agreeableness and lower on negative affectivity, with this display of positive emotions resulting in increased customer satisfaction. Perhaps future research could extrapolate these findings and extend them to the influence of personality traits on the use of humor in dyadic interactions. Research might also examine how applicant humor styles and propensity to use humor influence recruiter behaviors, which then influence applicant attraction. In summary, future research that examines applicant and interviewer use of humor during the initial interview is warranted, perhaps using dyadic data analysis techniques (Kenny, Kashy, & Cook, 2006).

To bridge the gap between the job search and recruitment literatures by introducing the important role humor can have in these processes, future work could utilize additional research methodologies, such as multilevel (e.g. examining job applicants across multiple organizations' processes), or repeated measures (e.g. following applicants throughout one recruitment process). For example, several recent studies that have examined job seekers' emotions, behaviors, and motivations daily or weekly over time, have provided valuable insight into job search behaviors (e.g. da Motta Veiga & Gabriel, 2016; da Motta Veiga & Turban, 2014; Song et al., 2009). Similarly, it could be interesting to pursue research examining the role of humor in influencing job search behaviors, and job search and recruitment processes and outcomes, over time. For example, by collecting multiple measures throughout the job search and recruitment processes, organizations could understand why and when the use of humor leads applicants to change their intentions and perceptions about the organization, and vice versa.

Another promising methodological development in the job search and recruitment literatures would be to use qualitative data from job seekers and recruiters, using interviews or focus groups. For example, a qualitative study of applicants may provide insight into how the use of humor influences applicants' search for jobs, including how they cope with the process, and how potential employers' use of humor in recruitment activities influence job search behaviors. I encourage research that simultaneously examines applicants' perceptions of, and reactions to, potential employers and how such perceptions influence job search activities. Specifically, qualitative analysis might be better able to deal with nuances that are inherent in humor use, including nuances in timing, content, and reactions to humor, which might not be easily captured in some quantitative methodologies (e.g. surveys).

Conclusion

Although researchers have expressed some interest in the study of humor in organizations, very few empirical studies on the topic have been published in the organizational literature. As mentioned earlier, perhaps the primary barrier to "mainstreaming" research on humor has been the difficulty situating humor phenomena within more established and well-developed organizational literatures.

This chapter proposes ways to integrate existing humor research and theoretical approaches with the job search and recruitment literatures, both independently and simultaneously. This approach offers both theoretical and empirical opportunities for future work to answer many questions, and contribute to all three literatures. Indeed, humor can help job seekers cope with the stress associated with the process, and manage recruiters' and interviews' impressions. Humor can also help organizations signal to these same job seekers that their work environment is supportive of humor, and hopefully help make the job search and recruitment processes more fun and less dreadful.

References

Abel, M. H. (2002). Humor, stress, and coping strategies. *Humor*, 15, 365–381.

Barber, A. E. (1998). *Recruiting employees: Individual and organizational perspectives*. Thousand Oaks, CA: Sage.

Barsade, S. G. (2002). The ripple effects: Emotional contagion and its influence on group behavior. *Administrative Science Quarterly*, 47, 644–675.

Blau, G. (1994). Testing a two-dimensional measure of job search behavior. *Organizational Behavior and Human Decision Processes*, 59, 288–312.

Bolino, M. C., Kacmar, M., Turnley, W. H., & Gilstrap, J. B. (2008). A multi-level review of impression management motives and behaviors. *Journal of Management*, 34, 1080–1109.

Boswell, W. R., Zimmerman, R. D., & Swider, B. W. (2012). Employee job search toward an understanding of search context and search objectives. *Journal of Management*, 38, 129–163.

Boudreau, J. W., & Rynes, S. L. (1985). Role of recruitment in staffing utility analysis. *Journal of Applied Psychology*, 70, 354–366.

Burger, J. M., & Caldwell, D. F. (2000). Personality, social activities, job-search behavior and interview success: Distinguishing between PANAS trait positive affect and NEO extraversion. *Motivation and Emotion*, 24, 51–62.

Cable, D., & Turban, D. (2001). Establishing the dimensions, sources and value of job seekers' employer knowledge during recruitment. In G. Ferris (Ed.), *Research in personnel and human resource management*, vol. 20 (pp. 115–163). Greenwich, CT: JAI Press.

Carver, C. S. (2011). Coping. In R. J. Contrada, & A. Baum (Eds.), *The handbook of stress science: Biology, psychology, and health* (pp. 221–229). New York: Springer Publishing Company.

Chapman, D. S., Uggerslev, K. L., Carroll, S. A., Piasentin, K. A., & Jones, D. A. (2005). Applicant attraction to organizations and job choice: A meta-analytic review of the correlates of recruiting outcomes. *Journal of Applied Psychology*, 90, 928–944.

Cline, T. W., Altesch, M. B., & Kellaris, J. J. (2003). When does humor enhance or inhibit ad responses? *Journal of Advertising*, 32, 31–45.

Collins, C. J. (2007). The interactive effects of recruitment practices and product awareness on job seekers' employer knowledge and application behaviors. *Journal of Applied Psychology*, 92, 180–190.

Connelly, B. L., Certo, S. T., Ireland, R. D., & Reutzel, C. R. (2011). Signaling theory: A review and assessment. *Journal of Management*, 37, 39–67.

Cooper, C. D. (2005). Just joking around? Employee humor expression as an ingratiatory behavior. *Academy of Management Review*, 30, 765–776.

Cooper, C. D. (2008). Elucidating the bonds of workplace humor: A relational process model. *Human Relations*, 61, 1087–1115.

da Motta Veiga, S. P., & Gabriel, A. S. (2016). The role of self-determination motivation in job search: A dynamic approach. *Journal of Applied Psychology*, 101, 350–361.

da Motta Veiga, S. P., & Turban, D. B. (2014). Are affect and perceived stress detrimental or beneficial to job seekers? The role of learning goal orientation in job search self-regulation. *Organizational Behavior and Human Decision Processes*, 125, 193–203.

da Motta Veiga, S. P., & Turban, D. B. (forthcoming). Who is searching for whom? Integrating applicant attraction and job search research. In U.-C. Klehe, & E. A. J van Hooft (Eds.), *The Oxford handbook of job search and job loss*. New York: Oxford University Press.

Eisend, M. (2009). A meta-analysis of humor in advertising. *Journal of the Academy of Marketing Science*, 37, 191–203.

Folkman, S., & Moskowitz, J. T. (2004). Coping: Pitfalls and promise. *Annual Review of Psychology*, 55, 745–774.

Glenn, P. (2010). Interviewer laughs: Shared laughter and asymmetries in employment interviews. *Journal of Pragmatics, 42,* 1485–1498.

Goel, V., & Dolan, R. J. (2007). Social regulation of affective experience of humor. *Journal of Cognitive Neuroscience*, 19, 1574–1580.

Goltz, S. M., & Giannantonio, C. M. (1995). Recruiter friendliness and attraction to the job: The mediating role of inferences about the organization. *Journal of Vocational Behavior*, 46, 109–118.

Graham, E. E., Papa, M. J., & Brooks, G. P. (1992). Functions of humor in conversation: Conceptualization and measurement. *Western Journal of Communication*, 56, 161–183.

Hatfield, E., Cacioppo, J. T., & Rapson, R. L. (1994). *Emotional contagion: Studies in emotion and social interaction*. New York: Cambridge University Press.

Kanfer, R., Wanberg, C., & Kantrowitz, T. (2001). Job search and employment: A personality-motivational analysis and meta-analytic review. *Journal of Applied Psychology*, 86, 837–855.

Kelly, J., & Barsade, S. (2001). Mood and emotions in small groups and work teams. *Organizational Behavior and Human Decision Processes*, 86, 99–130.

Kenny, D. A., Kashy, D. A., & Cook, W. L. (2006). *Dyadic data analysis*. New York: Guilford Press.

Kristof, A. L. (1996). Person–organization fit: An integrative review of its conceptualizations, measurement and implications. *Personnel Psychology*, 49, 1–49.

Kristof-Brown, A. L., Zimmerman, R. D., & Johnson, E. C. (2005). Consequences of individuals' fit at work: A meta-analysis of person–job, person–organization, person–group, and person–supervisor fit. *Personnel Psychology*, 58, 281–342.

McKee-Ryan, F. M., Song, Z., Wanberg, C. R., & Kinicki, A. J. (2005). Psychological and physical well-being during unemployment: A meta-analytic study. *Journal of Applied Psychology*, 90, 53–76.

Murphy, K. R. (1986). When your top choice turns you down: Effect of rejected job offers on the utility of selection tests. *Psychological Bulletin*, 99, 133–138.

Niven, K., Holman, D., & Totterdell, P. (2012). How to win friendship and trust by influencing people's feelings: An investigation of interpersonal affect regulation and the quality of relationships. *Human Relations*, 65, 777–805.

Niven, K., Totterdell, P., Holman, D., & Headley, T. (2012). Does regulating others' feelings influence people's own affective well-being? *Journal of Social Psychology*, 152, 246–260.

Petty, R. E., & Cacioppo, J. T. (1986). *Communication and persuasion: Central and peripheral routes to attitude change*. New York: Springer-Verlag.

Roberson, Q. M., Collins, C. J., & Oreg, S. (2005). The effects of recruitment message specificity on applicant attraction to organizations. *Journal of Business and Psychology*, 19, 319–339.

Robert, C., & Wilbanks, J. E. (2012). The wheel model of humor: Humor events and affect in organizations. *Human Relations*, 65, 1071–1099.

Robert, C., & Yan, W. (2007). The case for developing new research on humor and culture in organizations: Towards a higher grade of manure. *Research in Personnel and Human Resource Management*, 26, 205–267.

Romero, E., & Pescosolido, A. (2008). Humor and group effectiveness. *Human Relations*, 61, 395–418.

Rynes, S. L. (1991). Recruitment, job choice, and post-hire consequences: A call for new research directions. In M. D. Dunnette, & L. M. Hough (Eds.), *Handbook of industrial and organizational psychology*, vol. 2, 2nd edition (pp. 399–444). Palo Alto, CA: Consulting Psychologists Press.

Saks, A. M., & Ashforth, B. E. (2002). Is job search related to employment quality? It all depends on the fit. *Journal of Applied Psychology*, 87, 646–654.

Schreurs, B., Derous, E., van Hooft, E. A. J., Proost, K., & De Witte, K. (2009). Predicting applicants' job pursuit behavior from their selection expectations: The mediating role of the theory of planned behavior. *Journal of Organizational Behavior*, 30, 761–783.

Song, Z., Uy, M. A., Zhang, S., & Shi, K. (2009). Daily job search and psychological distress: Evidence from China. *Human Relations*, 62, 1171–1197.

Stevens, C. K., & Kristof, A. L. (1995). Making the right impression: A field study of applicant impression management during job interviews. *Journal of Applied Psychology*, 80, 587–606.

Sy, T., Côté, S., & Saavedra, R. (2005). The contagious leader: Impact of the leader's mood on the mood of the group members, group affective tone, and group processes. *Journal of Applied Psychology*, 90, 295–305.

Tan, H. H., Foo, M. D., & Kwek, M. H. (2004). The effects of customer personality traits on display of positive emotions. *Academy of Management Journal*, 47, 287–296.

Taylor, M. S., & Bergmann, T. J. (1987). Organizational recruitment activities and applicants' reactions at different stages of the recruitment process. *Personnel Psychology*, 40, 261–285.

Trougakos, J. P., Beal, D. J., Green, S. G., & Weiss, H. M. (2008). Making the break count: An episodic examination of recovery activities, emotional experiences, and affective delivery. *Academy of Management Journal*, 51, 131–146.

Tsai, W. C., Chen, C. C., & Chiu, S. F. (2005). Exploring boundaries of the effects of applicant impression management tactics in job interviews. *Journal of Management*, 31, 108–125.

Turban, D. B., & Cable, D. M. (2003). Firm reputation and applicant pool characteristics. *Journal of Organizational Behavior*, 24, 733–751.

Turban, D. B., & Dougherty, T. W. (1992). Influences of campus recruiting on applicant attraction to firms. *Academy of Management Journal*, 35, 739–765.

Turban, D. B., Forret, M. L., & Hendrickson, C. L. (1998). Applicant attraction to firms: Influences of organizational reputation, job and organizational attributes and recruiter behaviors. *Journal of Vocational Behavior*, 52, 24–44.

Turban, D. B., Stevens, C. K., & Lee, F. K. (2009). Effects of conscientiousness and extraversion on new labor market entrants' job search: The mediating role of metacognitive activities and positive emotions. *Personnel Psychology*, 62, 553–573.

Wanberg, C. R. (1997). Antecedents and outcomes of coping behaviors among unemployed and reemployed individuals. *Journal of Applied Psychology*, 82, 731–744.

Wanberg, C. R., Kanfer, R., & Rotundo, M. (1999). Unemployed individuals: Motives, job-search competencies, and job-search constraints as predictors of job seeking and reemployment. *Journal of Applied Psychology*, 6, 897–910.

9
HUMOR CONSULTING

John Morreall

In 1989, after studying and teaching about the benefits of humor for a decade, I took the show on the road by doing talks and seminars for business and medical groups. At that time, people like me were not called "humor consultants." In that era of *just in time* and *do more with less*, claiming expertise on humor in the workplace would have been like saying that you manufacture square wheels. Humor is a kind of play, and for most people then – and quite a few even now – play is the opposite of work. So "humor in the workplace" sounded like a contradiction-in-terms.

Overcoming the old prejudice

Opposition to humor and play has a long history in Western culture, especially in the United States, and so it took decades for humor consultants to be taken seriously. The Puritans of New England were the original American workaholics. According to their theology, all human beings are born depraved and deserving of hell, but a few have been chosen by God to be saved. One indication that you may be among the *elect* is that you are successful in your work. To assuage their fears about damnation, the Puritans embraced a *work ethic* in which idleness and play were suspect. When their cousins back home ruled England under Oliver Cromwell in the 1650s, they outlawed comedy and other plays, shut down pubs, banned most sports, and outlawed the celebration of Christmas. The Puritans in Massachusetts criminalized the celebration of Christmas from 1659 to 1681. Only partly tongue-in-cheek, H. L. Mencken defined a "Puritan" as "someone who is desperately afraid that, somewhere, someone might be having a good time" (Albrecht, 2006, p. 73).

The Puritans' work ethic was a cornerstone of American culture for four centuries, passed on by parents and teachers. In its book of rules, a Methodist boarding school in the 1780s put it this way:

> We prohibit play in the strongest terms . . . The student shall rise at five in the morning summer and winter . . . The students shall be indulged with nothing which the world calls play. Let this rule be observed with strictest nicety, for those who play when they are young will play when they are old.

Even today, the standard way to praise children is to say "Good work" and "Good job" – not just when they load the dishwasher but when they play the piano, paint a colorful picture, or score a home run. In school, their teachers systematically suppress laughter and playfulness. "We're here to get our work done . . . Get serious . . . Act your age . . . Are you trying to be funny?" are the standard put-downs. And so, while pre-schoolers laugh hundreds of times a day, most adults are down to a dozen or so. What is suppressed in schools is not just humor, but other valuable traits such as imagination, creative problem-solving, and the enjoyment of challenging work.

In the 1800s, as the Industrial Revolution drew millions into cities to toil ten to 12 hours a day, six days a week, in drab, dangerous factories, the work ethic, with its suppression of humor and play, was a godsend for factory owners. In manufacturing well into the twentieth century, workers were expected to endlessly repeat simple, monotonous tasks requiring no skill. Frederick W. Taylor's 1911 industrial handbook *The Principles of Scientific Management* told factory managers how to divide big jobs, like building a machine, into hundreds of small, mindless tasks that could be learned in a few minutes. No one brought up the subject of job satisfaction. Only slightly better was *The Management Handbook* of 1922: one of its 2,281 pages was devoted to employee morale.

The suppression of humor and play in the workplace lasted through most of the twentieth century. "When we are at work," Henry Ford said, "we ought to be at work. When we are at play, we ought to be at play. There is no use trying to mix the two" (Benyon, 1980, p. 40). At his factories through the 1940s, laughter was a disciplinary offense. Managers banned workers at the River Rouge Plant from talking with each other, even during lunch, and treated humming and whistling as evidence of goldbricking. One Ford worker, John Gallo, was fired for being "caught in the act of 'smiling'" (Sward, 1948, pp. 312–313). Earlier, he had been reprimanded for "laughing with the other fellows," and slowing down the assembly line for "maybe half a minute."

Though few of us any longer work in factories, the Puritans' work ethic lingers on. That is evident in all that has been said about our "workaholism." Americans are allotted many fewer weeks of vacation time than workers in other industrialized nations, for example, and yet, on average, they take only half of their paid vacations.

Funny business: The new appreciation of humor

In the last 25 years, fortunately, many traditional prejudices against humor have been overcome. Since 1989, academics have had the International Society for Humor Studies with its journal *Humor: International Journal of Humor Research.*

Meetings of the Association for Applied and Therapeutic Humor attract hundreds of professionals in medicine, psychotherapy, and counseling. Hundreds of articles about the benefits of humor have been published in psychology, business, and medical journals, and there are dozens of books offering tips for incorporating humor into various workplaces.

Humor consultants around the world now do keynotes, seminars, and training sessions, relating humor to themes such as stress reduction, change management, team-building, and creative problem-solving. I have done over 500 programs in North America, Europe, and Japan for organizations like AT&T, IBM, and the IRS. At IBM's Advanced Business Institute (now called the Executive Business Institute), I've done over a dozen presentations. In a February 6, 1999 *The New York Times* article, "Serious Talk about Funny Business," Marion Atwater, program director at IBM's Institute, said that just five years earlier, "We never would have featured a humorist because it wouldn't have been in sync . . . If you go back and say, 'What were the audience expectations, late 80's, early 90's?' it wasn't step back and have a laugh, it was get in your Porsche and drive as fast as you can." Especially receptive to the lessons of humor consultants, *The Times* article pointed out, are computer companies, because they undergo "change, change, change all the time," according to Carol Schoenfeld, director of executive education programs at the IBM Institute.

One company that embraced humor early is Adaptec, manufacturer of interface and storage devices for computers. 20 years ago they decided that their annual reports to stockholders were boring, so the format of their 1995 report was an action comic book. On the cover were a business man and woman with inset illustrated text touting "The Amazing Feats of: IOware Man," a blond version of Superman; Adaptra, a masked superwoman holding computer cables in each of her six hands; and Bottleneck Buster, a green creature shaped like a muscular bottle. The banner at the bottom proclaimed, "IN THIS ISSUE: Data transfer triumphs! Adaptec IOware products blast off into the 21st century with dynamic new solutions!" Naturally, the report contained all the usual financial information, news about products, etc., but the clever format attracted much more attention than annual reports usually receive. In the business press, Adaptec got lots of free publicity – so much, in fact, that their 1996 report was designed to look like a child's first reading book. Titled *A B C & D: All About Being Connected to Data*, the cheerful yellow cover featured child-like drawings of a boy and girl, Wally and Molly. On an early page, Wally is shown trying to connect his computer with the Internet but failing miserably because he doesn't have Adaptec equipment. On the next page Molly effortlessly succeeds using Adaptec devices. The pages with financial information start with a drawing of a school tablet with the words in crayon "1 trillion." Under that is "+ 2 trillion" with a heavy line under it, and below that "3 trillion." Toward the end of the book is a page with child-like drawings of two men smiling and waving, John J. Adler, Chairman of the Board; and F. Grant Saviers, President and CEO.

In the last two decades, many corporations have made humor and play part of their corporate culture. Famous examples include Southwest Airlines and Ben &

Jerry's Ice Cream. Several companies, including Google, Hewlett-Packard, and Price Waterhouse, have created special humor rooms or play rooms in their office complexes. The old Digital Equipment Corporation even had a "Grouch Patrol" to spot joyless colleagues and cheer them up. The Chicago comedy troupe The Second City regularly trains business groups in improvisational comedy as a way of developing skills in teamwork and creative problem-solving.

Even traditionally staid businesses, like banking and insurance, are putting humor to work, as in Capital One's TV commercials with the tag line "What's in your wallet?", GEICO's commercials featuring the gecko with the British accent, and Progressive Insurance's ads with the character Flo. Bankrate.com, a company that publishes current loan rates at hundreds of banks, might seem to be immune to humor, but one of their print ads in national magazines is a photo of an obviously pregnant bride about to cut the wedding cake with her unhappy groom. The caption: "Only 2% of condoms actually fail. Every percent counts. bankrate.com."

The best known corporate executive to embody the new appreciation of humor and play is Herb Kelleher of Southwest Airlines. The cover of *Fortune* magazine's May 2, 1994 issue showed him flying through the air wearing a World War I leather aviator's helmet but without an airplane. The caption read: "IS HERB KELLEHER AMERICA'S BEST CEO? He's wild, he's crazy, he's in a tough business. And he has built the most successful airline in the U.S." In the story, Kelleher articulated Southwest's corporate philosophy this way: "What we are looking for, first and foremost, is a sense of humor . . . We don't care that much about education and expertise, because we can train people to do whatever they have to do. We hire attitudes." One of the questions in job interviews at Southwest is: "Can you remember a time when you were in a tight spot, but you got out of it with your sense of humor?"

Southwest has occasionally gotten into trouble with the Federal Aviation Administration, as when they were ordered to stop singing the pre-flight safety announcement to the tune of the theme song from *The Beverly Hillbillies*. And flight attendants still sometimes insert lines like these into their safety announcements:

> In case of a sudden loss of cabin pressure, oxygen masks will descend automatically. If you're traveling with a small child, put your own mask on first and then the child's mask, if they've been good.

A newer airline, kulula of South Africa, embraces humor in a bolder way. One of their print ads says, "Fourth Wife Flies Free." The design of the exterior of their Boeing 737 jets has the theme "Flying 101." Under the captain's window is printed "the big cheese." On the right side is an arrow pointing to a "black box (which is actually orange)," and under the entry door it says, "the door's always open . . . unless we're at 41,000 feet." Under the wings, next to the wheels, it says, 'landing gear (comes standard with supa-fly mags)."

Management studies show that executives with a good sense of humor advance faster and further, and top business schools such as Wharton now evaluate applicants on their sense of humor. An encouraging study done in 1985 by Richard Cronin, head of an executive search firm, asked the Fortune 500 CEOs and deans of leading business schools how they viewed the role of humor in business. The responses showed 97 percent agreement on three points: 1) humor is important in business; 2) most executives don't show enough humor; and 3) when hiring, they give preference to people with a good sense of humor. More recently, an article by Margery Weinstein in *Training* magazine titled "Hard Truths about Soft Skills" discussed a nationwide survey conducted online by Harris Interactive with 2,076 hiring managers and human resource (HR) professionals across many industries. Employers were asked, "If you had two equally qualified candidates, which factors would make you more likely to consider one candidate over another?" The factor chosen by the greatest number of managers and HR professionals was "The candidate with the better sense of humor."

A May 2, 2013 article in *Forbes* listed "10 Reasons Why Humor Is a Key to Success at Work":

1. People will enjoy working with you.
2. It is a potent stress-buster.
3. It is humanizing.
4. It puts others at ease.
5. Ha + ha = aha! [Humor promotes creative thinking and problem-solving.]
6. It helps build trust.
7. It boosts morale.
8. People who use humor tend to be more approachable.
9. It can allow your company to stand out.
10. It can increase productivity.

In my book *Laughing All the Way* (Morreall, 2015), I add another ten benefits:

11. Laughter is medically healthy in several ways.
12. Humor enhances creative problem-solving.
13. It helps us manage change.
14. It makes persuasive messages like advertising more effective.
15. It's a core skill in leadership.
16. It makes training more effective.
17. It improves customer service.
18. It's the fastest way to de-fuse conflict.
19. It's effective in negotiation.
20. It makes meetings tolerable, even fun.

A good indication of how the lessons of humor consultants are catching on is the number of companies that have added humor and fun to their mission statements. The human resources consulting firm William M. Mercer found that of nearly 300 employers surveyed, eight percent wrote in their mission statement that they needed to incorporate humor or fun into the workplace. Binney & Smith, makers of Crayola Crayons, saw an increase in sales from $92 million to $242 million in six years, in part because they created a program to make the workplace more fun.

Since the Puritan work ethic started in New England, it's encouraging to read the updated corporate philosophy of New England Securities, a subsidiary of MetLife. Its first three principles are:

1. Take risks. Don't play it safe.
2. Make mistakes. Don't try to avoid them.
3. Take initiative. Don't wait for instructions.

And the last four:

10. Try easier, not harder.
11. Stay calm!
12. Smile!
13. Have fun!

The diversity of humor consultants

In the new field of humor consulting, there are no educational or other standards established, as there are, say, in accounting or tax law. Consultants range from seasoned experts like Paul McGhee who have Ph.Ds. and have published academic books on humor, to business people who simply got interested in humor and developed a funny talk about its benefits.

Different consultants emphasize different things and have different styles of presentation. A few provide considerable background in the psychology of humor, using frameworks such as the incongruity theory, relief theory, and superiority theory of humor. But most consultants go light on psychological theories and heavy on funny stories, quips, and exercises. Business clients generally expect humor consultants to be funny and entertaining, and not sound like professors. For one of my seminars, at Cisco Systems, for example, I teamed up with Bob Mankoff, Cartoon Editor of *The New Yorker* and a doctoral student in psychology who studies humor and creativity. He illustrated connections between humor and creativity by drawing and analyzing cartoons, and then we broke up into small groups to play a version of *The New Yorker* Cartoon Caption Contest, which he invented.

Some clients want more from a consultant than a presentation, and they even like to have interactive exercises. Most consultants recommend various play activities that can be scheduled after they leave, such as Dress Like Your Favorite Movie Star Day. Consultants also work with clients to create customized events. For instance, I was once asked by a group of hospitals in New Jersey to create programs for them as they made the transition to a new computer system. They had chosen the new software carefully and had scheduled training sessions, but they wanted to do something more to assure staff that the new system would be an improvement. What we designed was a special ceremony for the first part of a morning, a combination funeral and birth – the funeral for the old computer system and the birth for the new one.

Staff gathered in an auditorium for a continental breakfast, after which the lights went down. From the back of the room came the sounds of a slow New Orleans-style jazz funeral procession. Six mourners carried a casket with the nickname of the old computer system painted on the side. When they reached the front of the room, they placed the casket on a white mound lit by a spotlight. The lead mourner, in a black stovepipe hat, gave a funny eulogy about how at first the old computer system had seemed efficient, but over time its shortcomings became annoying. When his eulogy was over, the pallbearers lowered the casket into the hole in the mound. There was laughter all around the room.

Just then the lights came up, and from the back of the room a woman looking nine months pregnant came waddling up the aisle, yelling "It's time, it's time." She walked up to the mound and then behind it. Next was the sound of a baby's cry, and from the hole in the mound sprung Tom Pirelli, CEO of the new software company, dressed only in a large diaper and an oversized baby bonnet. He walked to the microphone and gave a short talk about how getting a new computer system is like having a baby. You'll eventually love it, but it may take a while! The hospital staff embraced his stunt and funny talk, and over the coming months, as they adjusted to the new computer system, they often remembered the funeral/birth ceremony. When they made a mistake or encountered a glitch on their computer, instead of getting stressed out, they pictured Tom Pirelli in his diaper and bonnet.

Most humor consultants who offer keynotes and seminars have created at least a handful of programs with titles emphasizing different benefits. The three most general headings for these I call *health*, *mental flexibility*, and *social benefits*. These are discussed in detail in my books *Humor Works* (Morreall, 1997) and *Laughing All the Way* (Morreall, 2015). Here we can summarize the main benefits.

Health

Reader's Digest presents jokes, funny stories, and visual gags under the heading "Laughter, the Best Medicine," and the Book of Proverbs 17:22 says that "A merry heart does good like a medicine." The seventeenth-century British physician Thomas Sydenham wrote that "the arrival of a good clown into a village does more for its health than twenty asses laden with drugs." But through most of history, such ideas were treated as mere folklore by medical professionals. Only in the twentieth century did anyone test the medical benefits of humor. In his 1928 article Laughter and Health, Dr. James Walsh observed that laughter after surgery promotes healing and reduces pain. But another 40 years went by before Dr. William Fry of Stanford University Medical School started doing controlled experiments. Then in 1979 a book by a magazine editor rather than a doctor got thousands of people interested in the medical benefits of humor. This was Norman Cousins' *Anatomy of an Illness as Perceived by the Patient.* Cousins had been afflicted with ankylosing spondylitis, a severe form of arthritis in which the slightest movement caused him great pain. When his doctors gave him a 1-in-500 chance of recovery, he decided to take matters into his own hands. It was stress and tension that had gotten him into this disease, he reasoned, so relaxation and laughter would get him out of it. His friend Allen Funt, creator of the *Candid Camera* TV program, brought over clips from the show as well as funny movies. Cousins quickly discovered that a few minutes of hearty laughter brought him hours of freedom from pain. That allowed him to get much needed sleep. Within weeks, his blood sedimentation rate – a measure of inflammation – was declining, and months later he had beaten the disease. In writing about his recovery, Cousins acknowledged that this was not a controlled experiment and that laughter was not the only thing that helped. His general claim was that our emotions have a lot to do with our health, especially with our ability to fight off disease. That struck a chord not just with ordinary readers but with physicians. Thanks to Cousins' inspiration, experimental research was done over the next three decades, creating the new field of psychoneuroimmunology to study the relation of the mind (psycho), nervous system (neuro), and immune system.

Cousins' experience of pain reduction after laughter has been thoroughly tested. In one experiment, subjects are told to immerse their arms in ice water for as long as they can stand the pain. Those who joke about the procedure are typically able to keep their arms in the water longer than those who take it seriously (Zweyer, Velker, & Ruch, 2004).

Laughter also provides a workout for the heart and lungs. According to Dr. William Fry (Fry & Savin, 1988), in hearty laughter we take in six times more oxygen than when we are simply having a conversation. And while heart rate and blood pressure increase during hearty laughter, they drop to below normal after laughter stops. According to Dr. Fry's research, they then stay below normal for up to 45 minutes. Hearty laughter also brings relaxation: after it stops, muscle tension is below normal.

Perhaps the most promising benefit of humor is its boosting of the immune system. We live surrounded by bacteria and viruses that can cause infection, and within our bodies, the number of microbes is ten times the number of our own cells. Fortunately, our bone marrow, lymph glands, spleen, thymus, and liver produce substances to eliminate the harmful ones. "Natural killer cells" patrol our bloodstreams, eliminating disease-causing microbes and cancer cells. Germ-fighters called immunoglobulins in our nasal passages and throats protect us from respiratory infections. Taken collectively, the activity of these and other protections is called the immune system, and mirthful laughter enhances its effectiveness. In the research of Drs. Lee Berk and Stanley Tan (Berk et al., 1989), subjects who watched funny videos experienced an increase in immune system activity including B lymphocytes; T lymphocytes; immunoglobulin A, G, and M; natural killer cells; and gamma interferon.

The psychologist Steven Sultanoff (1997) extends the concept of the immune system from substances in our blood to our responses to potentially threatening experiences. "Just as our physical immune system protects us from toxins in our environment," he writes, "our psychological immune system protects us from the toxins generated from psychological stressors we experience in the world around us" (p. 1). He adds "Humor helps to sustain the psychological immune system by altering how we feel, think, and behave" and concludes that "by changing one's biochemistry, thoughts, feelings, and behaviors, humor can help build physical and emotional resilience as it stimulates the production of physical and psychological antibodies" (p. 1).

A fuller treatment of the links between sense of humor and resilience is presented by Herbert M. Lefcourt (2000). Like Sultanoff, Lefcourt integrates the psychological with the physical in explaining how humor moderates the negative effects of negative experiences. Indeed, both physically and mentally, as I have often argued, humor is the opposite of stress. Levels of the stress chemicals epinephrine (adrenaline), noradrenaline, cortisol, and DOPAC go down in laughter, as do feelings of loss of control. As Sigmund Freud pointed out, when we joke and laugh about a problem, we get the feeling – realistic or not – that we have done something about it.

Studies by Rod Martin and Herbert Lefcourt (1983) suggest that people with a better sense of humor do not undergo as great a mood disturbance when things don't go well. They also score higher on tests of self-esteem measuring "actual-ideal discrepancy." When asked to describe themselves as they are, and as they would like to be, they show a fairly small difference, while those prone to stress and depression show a large difference. Humor thus supports mental health generally.

Mental flexibility

The second heading under which I group the benefits of humor is mental flexibility. This is my umbrella term for rebounding from failure, disappointment, and mistakes; coping with change; questioning standard ideas; seeing problems from new perspectives; and thinking creatively. Humor promotes mental flexibility in two ways.

First, it blocks negative emotions, especially the stress emotions of fear and anger. I can't be terrified of you or enraged by you, and laughing with you at the same time. Negative emotions are centered in the brain's limbic system, which we have in common with other mammals. In negative emotions we tend to re-act rather than act autonomously, and in simple, automatic ways like fighting and fleeing. Humor, by contrast, is centered in the cerebral cortex, the higher, more uniquely human part of the brain responsible for rational and creative thinking. When faced with a problem, if we keep our cool and laugh rather than feeling fear or anger, we're better able to think our way rather than feel our way through the problem.

The second way that humor promotes mental flexibility is by violating our expectations in a pleasurable way. According to the incongruity theory of humor, being amused is related to enjoying something odd or abnormal. So when we are creating or looking for humor, we think in non-standard, non-rigid ways. Consider this line from a routine by Ken Littleton Crow, a Native American comedian who was also a paraplegic: "There are advantages to being in a wheelchair, though. Wherever you go, you've got a seat, and a pair of shoes will last you twenty years." By rewarding us with the pleasure of laughter, humor prompts us to be emotionally resilient and creative in our thinking.

Creativity is widely talked about, but not always understood. Many people think of it as a kind of intelligence, but creative people don't stand out on IQ tests. Nor, as commonly thought, is creativity a special skill, such as a singer's perfect pitch. What makes some people creative is certain ways of thinking and certain attitudes about their work and their lives. They are experimental, playful, and willing to take risks. Most of us were this way as young children, but then we started school. As many studies have shown, schools systematically suppress creativity (Sternberg, 2012). Experts cite four "creativity killers" in standard education: surveillance, evaluation, rewards, and competition. As Ann Lewin-Benham, director of the Capital Children's Museum, has said about standard schools, "If we conspired to stamp out creativity in children, we could not be doing a better job" (in Perlmutter & Kaufman, 1991). Another educator, Neil Postman, quipped that children enter school as question marks and leave as periods.

In discussing humor and creativity, especially in problem-solving, most consultants talk about reframing – seeing things in one way, and then shifting to seeing them another way. "Humor is by far the most significant behavior of the human brain," creativity expert Edward de Bono (1993, p. 8) wrote, since it "shows how perceptions set up in one way can suddenly be reconfigured in another way. This is the essence of creativity." Consider this quip from Mae West, a comic actress and screen-writer in the 1930s: "Marriage is a great institution – but I'm not ready for an institution." The first time we hear the word "institution," we think of something like "social custom." But the second time, we think of something like "mental hospital." That reframing is jolting, and if we enjoy the jolt, we laugh.

Reframing can be merely entertaining, but it can also be useful. Just before Walt Disney opened Disneyland in 1955, he ran out of money to finish the landscaping. The trees and shrubs that had been put in had small signs in front of them with their Latin botanical names. So Disney had the sign makers put signs in front of the weeds with their botanical names, too. Disneyland opened and no one noticed the unfinished landscaping.

In the 1980s, American Airlines was losing money on the late-night flights that business people call "red-eyes" – until they did some reframing. Adopting the name of a popular radio show, they called the flights "Midnight Specials" and they served champagne and snacks. Business increased by 70 percent.

To bring out the natural links between humor and creative problem-solving, many consultants use brainstorming exercises. As we generate new ideas, we naturally come up with incongruous ideas that make us laugh, and our delight in those new ideas further stimulates our creativity. In brainstorming sessions, it is common for gentle laughter to emerge in the first few minutes, as the creative juices begin to flow, and then for laughter to get stronger and more frequent as people loosen up and think more creatively. One of the small-group exercises I do is "A Better Bathroom":

> Think of thirty improvements on the standard bathtub/shower.
>
> Money is no object, and neither is technical feasibility.
>
> There are no wrong answers, so do not judge anyone's ideas, but write down every one of them.

When most groups start off, they produce predictable ideas such as "self-cleaning" and "scald-proof." But as their minds loosen up, they think of things like "walls with holograms of exotic scenery," "a distorting mirror that makes you look fantastic," and even "Brad Pitt." The longer the brainstorming goes on, the more creative – and the funnier – the ideas get.

Social benefits

In discussing the medical and psychological benefits of humor, we have focused on individuals, but laughter and humor are primarily social experiences. As Robert Provine showed in *Laughter: A Scientific Investigation* (2001), we are 30 times more likely to laugh when we are with others than when we are alone. According to a widely accepted theory, human laughter evolved from "play signals" in lower apes. In interactions like tickling and playful chasing, which could be taken seriously, as threatening, the relaxed mouth and panting-like sounds of laughter sent the message "This is just for fun." Today's workplaces are full of potentially threatening social interactions in which humor can serve as a social lubricant. In my seminars we discuss examples such as warning, criticizing, evaluating, announcing bad news, apologizing, handling complaints, and defusing conflict. We also discuss the benefits of humor in communication generally, such as that it gets and holds attention, creates rapport, and is remembered. That makes humor useful in training and education, and in sales and marketing.

All of the social benefits of humor we have been discussing make it essential for the new kind of empowering leader that is valorized today. In the hands of a skilled leader, humor shows confidence, awareness of what's going on, control of the situation, self-control, humility, mental flexibility, and a constructive attitude toward mistakes.

An important subtopic in the social benefits of humor is the differences between women's humor and men's. Traditional male humor was often competitive, like football and war. It has a target who is humiliated, and in practical jokes, even physically harmed. Women don't often play practical jokes, and their humor tends to be compassionate and supportive rather than competitive. When they kid one another about mistakes and misfortunes, it is usually to reassure her that "that has happened to all of us" rather than to mock her.

As some traditional male humor shows, not all humor is beneficial. Most consultants distinguish between healthy and unhealthy kinds of humor, and offer tips for avoiding and correcting unhealthy kinds. The healthy kinds typically allow everyone involved to laugh and relax, while the unhealthy kinds pit those laughing against victims who are embarrassed or offended.

The future of humor consulting

As a field that has existed for less than three decades, its future is hard to predict. Adding to the uncertainty is the low priority that humor training has in most businesses and professions. During the recession of 2008–2009, all the humor consultants I know saw a significant reduction in the number of requests they received. What makes humor consulting more than a fad, however, are the linkages between humor in the workplace and such solid topics as health, stress reduction, change management, creative thinking, good morale, and conflict resolution. To the extent that humor consultants show persuasively how humor fosters these benefits, the field should continue and flourish.

Seven humor consultants

With the great variety among humor consultants, we have been making generalizations rather than universal statements. A good way to complete the general picture of humor consulting is to consider short profiles of some of the most successful consultants.

Paul M. McGhee, Ph.D.

One of the most respected consultants, McGhee was a pioneer in humor research, laying the groundwork for the current interest in its psychological and medical benefits. After receiving his Ph.D. in developmental psychology in 1968, he did 22 years of research on humor and laughter as a university professor. In 1989, he left his academic career to become a full-time consultant, offering programs on humor, health, and stress management to corporations, hospitals, and other professional organizations. He calls his business The Laughter Remedy. Among his 13 books is *Humor as Survival Training for a Stressed-Out World: The 7 Humor Habits Program.* His humor skills training program is based on the principle that if we practice finding humor in the small negative events in our lives, our sense of humor will be there to sustain us during crises.

Joel Goodman, Ed. D.

Perhaps the most widely known humor consultant, Goodman founded the Humor Project in 1977. Through it he has done annual conferences and programs on all seven continents. He and the speakers in his Speakers Bureau have presented for over three million people. Goodman's best known book is *Laffirmations: 1,001 Ways to Add Humor to Your Life and Work* (Health Communications, 1995). He is editor of *Laughing Matters* magazine. The HUMOR Project has provided grants to over 475 schools, hospitals, and human service agencies to help them develop services and resources that tap the positive power of humor.

Karyn Buxman, R.N., M.S.N.

Trained as a nurse, Buxman early on got interested in the health benefits of humor and its importance in health care. She now bills herself as a "neurohumorist" – someone who studies and does presentations on the effects of humor on the brain. Most of her clients are medical groups and business organizations. She is the author of *Amazed and Amused: How to Survive and Thrive as a Health Care Professional* (What's So Funny About Publishing, 2012), and creator of the *What's So Funny About . . .?* series, which includes books on nursing, heart disease, and diabetes, with future volumes on Alzheimer's, Parkinson's, depression, chronic obstructive pulmonary disease (COPD), multiple sclerosis, asthma, and breast cancer. She is currently writing a book on humor in leadership, and she edits the *Journal of Nursing Jocularity*.

Patty Wooten, R.N.

Like many other humor consultants with medical backgrounds, Wooten got started in the "therapeutic humor" movement. Trained as a nurse and a hospital clown, she was a charter member of the Association for Applied and Therapeutic Humor in the 1980s. Most of her clients are still medical groups. She specializes in presentations for nurses that help them renew their commitment to the profession. Her website calls this "nurse retention and renewal." Her clown persona Nancy Nurse is

> a wild, red-headed clown, armed with a combat belt of weapons, such as bedpans, urinals, enema buckets, and over-sized syringes . . . Her stethoscope is made from a garden hose and a toilet plunger, which is great to use on those big-hearted patients . . . it can also be used to relieve constipation!

A more recent clown persona is Nurse Kindheart, "every patient's dream of the perfect nurse." She and Shobi Dobi (Shobhana Schwebke), another hospital clown, have created the comedy act Kindheart and Krapinka as part of a nurse retention program. Wooten is the author of *Compassionate Laughter: Jest for your Health* (Commune-A-Key, 1996); co-author of *The Hospital Clown a Closer Look: What Hospitals Need to Know About Clowns, What Clowns Need to Know About Hospitals* (Jest Press, 2000); and editor of *Heart, Humor, and Healing: Quotes of Compassionate Comedy* (Commune-a-Key, 1994).

Steve Wilson, M.A.

Billing himself as "America's Joyologist and Cheerman of the Bored," Wilson came to humor consulting from his work as a clinical psychologist and counselor. After Dr. Madan Kataria became well known for starting laughter clubs in India, Wilson founded the World Laughter Tour to spread the movement around the globe. At laughter club meetings, people begin with performed laughter, chanting "Ho, ho, ha-ha-ha" and clapping their hands, which then turns into real laughter. "Fake it, fake it, until you make it" is their motto. Wilson's book *Good-Hearted Living* (Steve Wilson Co., 2003) is a "guide to the important practices that laughter club members use to be happier, to have less stress and more laughter, and to make the world a better place." Wilson's other books include *The Art of Mixing Work and Play* (Steve Wilson Co., 1992), *Super Humor Power* (Ohio Professional Counseling, 1992) and *CHILL! 271 Tips, Practices & Secrets for Staying Healthy, Happy & Sane Under Pressure* (Steve Wilson Co., 1998)

Malcolm Kushner, J.D.

With a background in communication studies and the practice of law, Kushner started doing presentations on humor in 1982. He calls himself "America's favorite humor consultant." His book *The Light Touch: How to Use Humor for Business Success* (Simon & Schuster, 1990) is one of the best of the genre, with many examples of humor in business. He currently has two popular programs: "Jest For Success: Using Humor As A Communication Tool," and "Leading with Laughter: How U.S. Presidents Use Humor to Relate, Motivate and Communicate – and How You Can Too!"

Bob Basso, Ph.D.

A writer, producer, theater director, professor, and former TV news director, *People* magazine called Basso "America's number one fun motivator." His eight books include *Lighten Up, Corporate America!* (New Breed, 1986), *555 Ways to Put More Fun in Your Life* (Globe Pequot, 1994), *Confessions of an American Speaker: If B. S. Were Concrete, I'd be Route 66* (Sligo, 1999), and *This Job Should Be Fun: The New Profit Strategy for Managing People in Tough Times* (iUniverse, 2000), co-written with Judi Klosek, an attorney who specializes in preventive litigation in the workplace.

References

Albrecht, S. (2006). *Tough training topics: A presenter's survival guide.* San Francisco, CA: John Wiley & Sons.

Benyon, H. (1980). *Working for Ford.* Harmondsworth: Penguin.

Berk, L. S., Tan, S. A., Fry, W. F., Napier, B. J., Lee, J. W., Hubbard, R. W., Lewis, J. E., & Eby, W. C. (1989). Neuroendocrine and stress hormone changes during mirthful laughter. *American Journal of the Medical Sciences*, 289(6), 390–396.

Cousins, N. (1979). *Anatomy of an illness as perceived by the patient*. New York: Norton.

De Bono, E. (1993). *Serious creativity: Using the power of lateral thinking to create new ideas*. New York: Harper Business.

Fry, W. F., & Savin, W. M. (1988). Mirthful laughter and blood pressure. *Humor*, 1, 49–62.

Lefcourt, H. M. (2000). *Humor: The psychology of living buoyantly*. New York: Springer.

Martin, R., & Lefcourt, H. M. (1983). Sense of humor as a moderator of the relation between stressors and moods. *Journal of Personality and Social Psychology, 45,* 1313–1324.

Morreall, J. (1997). *Humor works*. Amherst, MA: Human Resource Development Press.

Morreall, J. (2015). *Laughing all the way: Your sense of humor—don't leave home without it*. Carlsbad, CA: Motivational Press.

Perlmutter, A. H., & Kaufman, P. (1991). Creative beginnings (DVD). In C. Tatge, A. H. Perlmutter, P. Kaufman, & L. Sonne (Producers) and C. Tatge (Director), *The creative spirit*. New York: Ambrose Video.

Provine, R. R. (2001). *Laughter: A scientific investigation*. New York: Penguin Books.

Sternberg, R. J. (2012). The assessment of creativity: An investment-based approach. *Creativity Research Journal*, 24, 3–12.

Sultanoff, S. (1997). Survival of the witty-est: Creating resilience through humor. *Therapeutic Humor*, 11(5), 1–2.

Sward, K. (1948). *The legend of Henry Ford*. New York: Russell & Russell.

Zweyer, K., Velker, B., & Ruch, W. (2004). Do cheerfulness, exhilaration, and humor production moderate pain tolerance? A FACS study. *Humor*, 17, 85–199.

10

PARADOXES IN WORKPLACE HUMOR RESEARCH

Theory, culture, and the messy work of moving forward

Christopher Robert and Scott U. Seyrek

This volume had two primary goals: 1) to provide the reader with a thorough understanding of our existing knowledge-base about workplace humor as represented across literature from a broad array of disciplines; and 2) to provide food-for-thought to researchers and practitioners who wish to pursue new avenues of research on workplace humor, and/or creatively apply what we know about humor to everyday workplace problems. It is our sincere hope that we have accomplished these goals, and that this volume will be a useful resource for both researchers and practitioners.

At the same time, the completion of this volume also represents a good opportunity for us, as scholars, to engage in some introspection about the value, validity, and importance of the study of humor at work. At the center of this soul-searching is a somewhat uncomfortable question: with only a handful of exceptions, why has humor at work received so little attention in the organizational literature, and particularly in the most influential and widely-read publications in the field? Indeed, if humor is so important across a wide variety of workplace contexts (as represented by the topics addressed in the preceding chapters), and people generally feel that workplace humor is a "crucial," "vital," "essential," and "necessary" feature of the workplace (as argued in Chapter 1), then why have organizational scholars largely ignored it?

We argue that at the core of this disconnect between humor's importance and the lack of attention it has been paid in the organizational literature are two paradoxes that characterize the way we think about humor, which might limit scholars' inclination to focus on workplace humor as an important phenomenon. The first paradox is "humor is simultaneously everywhere, and nowhere." This paradox reflects the fact that although humor inserts itself into so many contexts by virtue of its flexibility and widespread use in interpersonal communication, it nearly always plays second fiddle to other phenomena that receive our primary attention and focus. As a result, whereas many workplace phenomena are more readily conceptualized as focal constructs that are important in their own right and worthy of attention (e.g. leadership, teams, personality), when humor is considered at all, it is more likely to be thought of as playing a supporting role.

The second paradox is "humor is extraordinarily complex, but also very simple." This paradox reflects the fact that although the cognitive, motivational, and social processes that contribute to the enactment and perception of humor are extremely complex, people seldom give humor much conscious attention. The subjective experience of humor is that it is just something that naturally occurs in social interactions. We use and respond to humor so often, and with seemingly such little effort, that we are often not consciously aware of the complex processes that give rise to humor or our responses to it. The automatic and effortless manner in which humor is woven into our lives might lead us to believe that humor is simple, and well-understood (Martin, 2007). Why study something that we already implicitly understand?

In the remainder of this chapter we flesh-out these two paradoxes. Our goal is to draw attention to them in order to acknowledge them as hurdles that impede not only scholarly attention to humor as a topic worthy of study in its own right, but by extension, our ability to draw on research in order to inform management practice. By acknowledging and embracing these paradoxes, we believe that scholars can make a more effective case for the continued examination of humor as an important phenomenon in its own right, and as a deliciously complex human behavior that permeates and deeply impacts the workplace.

Paradox 1: Humor is everywhere and nowhere

For many of the core areas of study within the organizational sciences, it is not very difficult to make the case that the topic is important, and worthy of scholarly attention. Take, for example, leadership, motivation, and personality. Leaders are widely believed to have significant effects on followers and institutions, so it is not difficult to convince anyone that leadership should be studied. Motivation lies at the core of why people do what they do, and has been of central concern in philosophy and literature for thousands of years: also an easy sell. The study of personality within organizations is a relatively recent undertaking, but understanding the foundations of stable individual differences in how people think, feel, and behave is vital for predicting and explaining both individual and interpersonal behavior. As such, it is relatively easy to make a case for the relevance of studying these, and many other topics. When someone says "I study leadership," people implicitly understand both *what* is being studied, and *why*.

The study of humor in organizations is a lot more ambiguous. While people know *what* humor is, it is not as intuitively obvious *why* it is important. The most typical arguments for why we should care about humor in the workplace typically cast humor in a supporting role, and as a modifier of some other phenomenon of primary interest. For example, the study of leadership is a focal construct, whereas leaders' use of humor might modify leader effectiveness or follower behavior. Stress has clear implications for employee health and well-being, and humor might help alleviate stress and support coping. Indeed, most of the chapters in this volume cast humor in a supporting role, or as the background to a more prominent and recognizable foreground. In fact, because humor is such a common and flexible human behavior, it is challenging to identify an area of study within the realm of organizational behavior for which humor cannot be hypothesized to have some role.

This is the crux of the paradox: humor can be seen as extending its tendrils into nearly every other micro-level organizational phenomenon, but yet, because it is always cast as the secondary rather than the focal construct, in a supporting role rather than the lead, or as background to the foreground of other popular constructs, it is easy for humor to fade from view. Because it is ubiquitous in human interactions and across workplace contexts (i.e. it is "everywhere") it is hidden from our conscious awareness: it hides in plain sight. In this regard, it is difficult to generate significant traction for the study of workplace humor in its own right.

Complicating this issue is the fact that humor is also not a unitary construct that lends itself easily to definition: it cannot be pigeonholed. As soon as one starts discussing how humor might play a role in context X, someone shouts out "but what about humor in context Y! Isn't that important?" We suggest that one way of addressing the paradox of being everywhere but nowhere is by explicitly acknowledging and embracing the notion that humor can in fact play unique and interesting roles in multiple workplace contexts. And while its ability to play multiple roles is interesting in its own right, it is also important to allow scholars to focus on humor's role in specific contexts. By studying humor in leadership, we are not minimalizing humor's impact on stress processes or its contribution to personality. This approach explicitly embraces a "many small effects" type of model. That is, rather than demonstrating that humor has dramatic effects (e.g. the relationship between cognitive ability and job performance), the field might prosper by viewing humor's impact in terms of its cumulative impact across multiple workplace contexts. Humor "works" by subtly impacting many interpersonal phenomena as well as individual cognition and behavior.

A useful model for thinking about how research and practice on humor might develop going forward is the literature on mood and emotion, or "affect." As Brief and Weiss (2002) note, with the exception of a brief period of interest in the 1930s, the study of affect at work was largely dormant until the 1980s. They suggest that interest in affect in organizations likely grew out of broader interest in affect that was growing more generally in psychology. Scholarly interest in humor at work might follow a similar course, developing from a broader interest in humor in psychology and other disciplines (e.g. anthropology, communications, sociology), and extending into the organizational domain. Although some traction of this sort might be developing, we do not believe that the level of scholarly activity directed toward humor at work is coming close to approaching the level of activity that was focused on affect at work in the 1980s and 1990s.

Humor and affect are also similar in that both tend to be cast in supporting roles, or as impacting other focal constructs and processes. For example, moods and emotions have been examined with respect to their impact in groups and teams, leadership, job stress, reactions to organizational rewards and justice perceptions, creativity, helping behavior, negotiation, job satisfaction, and work withdraw behavior (Brief & Weiss, 2002). Indeed, the broad range of phenomena in which affect has been implicated led to something of an identity crisis in the field, and difficulty making sense of affect's disparate findings and implications. As Elfenbein (2007) noted in the article in which she outlined a comprehensive theoretical integration of emotion in organizations "the explosion of research in this area [affect] has been a boon, but it has also been a mess" (p. 316). Interestingly, though, out of the "mess" that developed over decades, a strong consensus has coalesced around the notion that affect is an important construct with many different and consequential effects on people and organizational processes (e.g. Elfenbein, 2007; Lyubomirsky, King, & Diener, 2005). Affect is everywhere, and affect is important because it is a salient feature of human experience that impacts multiple interpersonal, behavioral, and cognitive processes.

Research on humor at work has not yet reached a critical volume at which a consensus can be reached that humor's many small effects and supporting roles justify the conclusion that humor at work is important in its own right. However, we believe that the trajectory of research on humor at work might follow a similar path as affect at work. What is needed is a willingness on the part of scholars to endure a certain amount of "messiness" in the burgeoning literature, and to accept the fact that a critical mass of research on humor must be developed before humor at work, like affect at work, can become a foreground rather than background construct.

Paradox 2: Humor is extraordinarily complex, but also very simple

Scholars' hesitancy to dive into research on humor at work might be related to the tension represented in this paradox. People believe humor is pleasurable, positive, light, and fun, and that it generally makes people feel good. Indeed, the physiological basis for the experience of amusement derived from humor is fairly straightforward, and suggests that the pleasure experienced from the brain's cognitive processing of the incongruities embedded in humor links to pleasure centers in the brain (see Robert & Yan, 2007). We don't consciously know how it happens, but the feeling is very real. If forced to analyze the complexities of humor, most people will acknowledge that humor can sometimes be used in a hostile or aggressive manner, and that such humor should be avoided: negative humor is a buzz-kill. This kind of commonsense approach is intuitively appealing, and leads to rather straightforward implications for the workplace: encourage positive humor, and discourage negative humor in the workplace, and it will make people feel better (Robert, Dunne, & Iun, 2015).

Moreover, people might actually be unconsciously concerned about the implications of overthinking humor. As E. B. White (1941) famously quipped, "humor can be dissected, as a frog can, but the thing dies in the process and the innards are discouraging to any but the pure scientific mind" (p. xvii). Isn't it enough to know that we like humor, that we enjoy being around people with whom we share humor, and that it seems to brighten our day? Perhaps a good look at the proverbial "frog's innards" of humor will deprive us of humor's magical properties.

Perhaps such a clinical approach to humor in one's everyday life might result in over-analysis and the diminishment of humor. We doubt it though. In fact, as scholars and scientists, perhaps it is our duty to explicate and appreciate the elegance and beauty of the frog's innards. We must assert without fear of contradiction that humor is a wonderfully complex phenomenon that human beings have learned to mold and shape for a wide variety of purposes, and therefore it *should* be studied and understood.

Scholars have begun to chart the boundaries of humor's impact on peoples' lives, both inside organizations and otherwise, but much like Elfenbein's (2007) characterization of the emotion literature, the literature on humor in organizations is "a mess." In the remainder of this section we attempt to bring a little bit of order to the messiness that currently characterizes research on humor at work. In particular, we want to highlight some of the ways in which the field might continue to break out of the simple "positive humor is good and negative humor is bad" conventional wisdom that still currently seems to pervade management thinking. To do this, we review existing contributions and highlight the role of theoretical mechanisms that might help guide future research. In addition, we highlight what we believe to be one of the more challenging (and messy) issues for humor research – the role of culture in shaping humor processes and outcomes.

Theoretical mechanisms

General theories of humor

Perhaps the most important requirement for moving the literature on humor at work forward is useful theory that can help predict and explain how humor functions in workplace contexts. With regard to general theories of humor that explain how humor works, or "what makes something funny," the most influential overarching theoretical framework is incongruity theory (e.g. Suls, 1972). Briefly, *incongruity theory* proposes that the perception of humor is driven by incongruities between knowledge representations or schemata represented in a humorous stimulus (e.g. a joke or funny comment) that are subsequently resolved by somehow linking the two incongruous elements together in a novel manner. The cognitive process of holding two incongruous schemas within conscious awareness at the same time, and then suddenly discovering a link between them, is thought to create a sudden "a-ha!" moment that is experienced as pleasure. Indeed, recent neuropsychological research has provided support for the underlying theoretical process proposed by incongruity theory (see Robert & Wilbanks, 2012, for a discussion of that literature).

A number of more recent theoretical formulations have elaborated on some of the basic premises underlying incongruity theory. In his book *What's so funny*? Murray Davis (1993) provides perhaps the most comprehensive and colorful description of the role of incongruity in understanding humor, as he expands upon how humorists leverage incongruities within our cultural and social worlds to both build-up and destroy social order. Moreover, Davis describes how other theories of humor (e.g. superiority theory, tension relief theory, see Lynch, 2002) can essentially be subsumed under the broader umbrella of incongruity theory. Indeed, given the comprehensive nature of his treatment of humor and incongruity in society, we are somewhat shocked that Davis' book has received relatively little attention in the broader literature on humor, and almost no attention in the (albeit small) literature on humor in organizational contexts. We highly recommend his book to scholars who wish to gain a deeper appreciation of humor's complexities.

Two other theoretical formulations also build on the basic framework of incongruity theory. First, Wyer and Collins (1992), in their *theory of humor elicitation*, develop a number of principles regarding how incongruities are established, and how the process of incongruity resolution either does or does not result in the experience of amusement. Interestingly, while the Wyer and Collins' (1992) paper and Davis' (1993) book are presented very differently, and it is unlikely that the authors were aware of each other's work as they were published at about the same time, they are remarkably consistent in their underlying ideas about how humor is generated. Moreover, the principles described by Davis and formalized by Wyer and Collins have been supported by subsequent neuropsychological research that was able to leverage more recent technology that can examine brain activity (see Robert & Yan, 2007). Notably, although these theories were developed to describe humor more generally, and not just in organizational contexts, their focus on the motivational and cognitive components of humor perception have great applicability to the workplace. For example, both Davis (1993) and Wyer and Collins (1992) focus on the role of motivated information processing in humor perception: i.e. that people's desire to perceive the world in a particular way influences how they process humor stimuli such as jokes or humorous comments. This type of approach is extremely relevant to the workplace, where existing relationships between co-workers, leaders and subordinates, customers and clients, etc., might impact individuals' motivations to create and interpret others' humor. Therefore, these theories might be extremely useful for understanding not just successful humor, but why humor fails in various interpersonal contexts.

The other theory that builds upon incongruity theory is McGraw and Warren's *benign violations* theory (McGraw & Warren, 2010; McGraw, Warren, Williams, & Leonard, 2012). This theory proposes that "violations" are a necessary component of attempts at humor, but they are only perceived to be funny if they are "benign," rather than threatening to the individual's core sense of self or their perception of how the world ought to be. This theory, which the authors support in a series of clever experiments, is clearly also consistent with Davis' (1993) assertion that individuals do not tend to appreciate incongruities and their resolution when the incongruities imply a threat to their closely-held core beliefs systems (e.g. jokes about priests for someone with closely-held Catholic beliefs). Again, the benign violations perspective might be useful in organizational contexts where the contextual conditions in which humor is used are likely to render some of the violations at the center of humor to be benign in some audiences and not in others. For example, a supervisor's joke about the quality of a subordinate's work might be benign to the supervisor, and even to a subordinate who knows their supervisor generally respects their work. However, such a joke might be perceived as threatening, and not benign, to an individual who is concerned that he or she might be fired. Indeed, the distinction between benign versus threatening humor might be extremely useful for understanding what constitutes "negative" humor in the workplace.

Theories of humor at work

Relatively little theory has been developed specifically to address humor in the workplace. One exception is Cooper's (2008) *relational process model* (see also Chapter 2). The relational process model suggests that humor is used within dyadic interpersonal contexts, and can stimulate positive affect through four specific mechanisms; reinforcing positive affect between the two individuals, increasing perceived similarity, encouraging closeness through greater self-disclosure, and reducing the salience of hierarchical differences between members of the dyad. Importantly, this theory ties humor to affect, and positive affect in particular, which can potentially link humor phenomena to the wide variety of phenomena studied in conjunction with workplace affect. Moreover, the four interpersonal mechanisms proposed to generate positive affect are highly measurable and might be tested empirically in a relatively straightforward manner.

The only other theory of which we are aware that specifically examines humor in the workplace context is Robert and Wilbanks' (2012) *wheel model of humor*. The wheel model, which, like Cooper's (2008) model, also portrays positive affect as a central construct driving humor's effects, was developed to account for the notion that humor likely has lots of small effects that might accumulate over time. The wheel model suggests that humor impacts positive affect, which might be "caught" by other members of a group through emotional displays and emotional contagion processes. Such contagion is hypothesized to result in the development of a climate that is supportive of continued humor use, more positive affect, etc. To some extent, both the wheel model and the relational process model are valuable in that they highlight positive affect as a key mediating mechanism that drives humor's presumed effects. However, we believe the wheel model is also valuable in that it highlights the notion that humor is perhaps best viewed as a cumulative and inherently social process, which impacts groups of individuals in small ways over time, rather than as a discrete behavior that should be studied in isolation.

Recent notable research

A small number of recent studies have also applied a variety of theoretical perspectives to the study of humor, and we thought it worthwhile to review some of these to provide the reader with a sense of the breadth and types of theories and frameworks that have been used at the cutting edge of this emerging research area. Notably, these empirical studies have begun to abandon straightforward demonstrations of the "positive humor is good and negative humor is bad" framework that still dominates management thinking on the topic, and which served as the backdrop for earlier humor research that employed correlational research methods to examine relationships between humor variables and relevant workplace outcomes (e.g. leader humor and subordinate job satisfaction). Although correlational research has been important for building the case that humor is indeed related to a range of workplace outcomes such as cohesiveness, job satisfaction, job performance, coping, burnout, stress, and job withdrawal (see Mesmer-Magnus, Glew, & Viswesvaran, 2012 for a meta-analysis), it has been less helpful in enriching our understanding of the underlying theoretical mechanisms that drive humor's effects. To compensate for this weakness, more recent literature has typically focused on using theory to develop and test models that either frame humor as part of a mediated process, or a moderated process (or both).

One such example is the work by Huo, Lam, and Chen (2012). In this paper, the authors focused on the use of aggressive humor by supervisors, and predicted that aggressive humor by supervisors would cause employee strain, which in turn would cause a number of negative individual behaviors. In addition to this mediated relationship, Huo et al. (2012) leveraged attribution theory to predict that if an individual's supervisor frequently used aggressive humor with other peers (rather than primarily with the focal employee), the focal employee would have somewhat less strain, due to the attribution that the supervisor's aggressive humor was caused by the supervisor's own character (and thus applied to all subordinates), rather than specifically directed at the subordinate because of something he or she did wrong. So, in addition to supporting theory about the process by which humor impacts individuals, the authors supported a contextual hypothesis describing the moderating impact of the social context (i.e. how much aggressive humor the supervisor uses with others) on the relationship between aggressive humor and strain.

Lehmann-Willenbrock and Allen (2014) also explicitly examined both mediating and moderating effects that drive humor (see also Chapter 7). They predicted and found that humor episodes, or "patterns" involving humor and laughter in teams, would impact team performance through their effect on positive team communication patterns. Importantly, though, they also found that job insecurity represented a boundary condition for this effect in that in teams with high insecurity, humor patterns were not related to team performance.

Other research has examined the mediating and moderating processes that impact the relationship between leader humor and subordinate job outcomes. Pundt and Herrmann (2015) found that affiliative humor was positively related to leader-member exchange quality (LMX) and that aggressive humor was negatively related to LMX, and that identification with the leader mediated the positive relationship between affiliative humor and LMX. Cooper (2002) examined a similar hypothesis, and found that some dimensions of LMX mediated the relationship between leader humor frequency and both turnover intentions and organizational citizenship behaviors (see also Chapter 2). Similarly, Gkorezis, Petridou, and Xanthiakos (2014) found that LMX mediated the relationship between positive leader humor and (lower) organizational cynicism.

Robert, Dunne, and Iun (2015) took a somewhat different perspective on LMX, and instead cast it as a moderator of the relationship between leader humor and subordinate job satisfaction. They found that the affiliative and aggressive styles of leaders were positively associated with subordinate job satisfaction when LMX was positive, but they were negatively associated with subordinate job satisfaction when LMX was negative. They concluded that the impact of leader humor has more to do with how subordinates interpret their leader's humor than the actual content of the humor itself. This conclusion is also consistent with findings of a recent study by Kim, Lee, and Wong (2016) which found that affiliative humor was negatively related to social distance, and more strongly so when the subordinate was high in affective trust for the supervisor (similar to high LMX). The findings of these studies suggest that if the subordinate perceives a bad relationship with his or her leader, the leader's use of both positive and negative humor reduces subordinate outcomes, whereas when the relationship is positive, both positive and negative humor might have positive effects. It is certainly possible that leader member exchange quality is both an outcome of leader humor, and impacts subordinates' interpretation of leader humor.

Given the scope of contexts in which humor might play a role in organizations, we argue that a broad range of theoretical perspectives might be applicable in addition to those noted above. For example, Janet Holmes (2000) has applied *politeness theory* (Brown & Levinson, 1987) from a communications perspective to describe how humor might function as a face-saving strategy. Miron-Spektor, Efrat-Treister, Rafaeli, and Schwarz-Cohen (2011) employed *regulatory focus theory* (Higgins, 1997) to describe how replacing anger with sarcastic humor might reduce individuals' tendencies toward narrowed cognitive focus. Researchers might also examine humor from a "resource" perspective, perhaps by leveraging *regulatory resource theory* (e.g. Baumeister, Bratslavsky, Muraven, & Tice, 1998), *conservation of resources theory* (Hobfoll, 2001), or *job demands-resources theory* (Demerouti, Bakker, Nachreiner, & Schaufeli, 2001). A resources perspective might augment the approach of focusing on humor's impact on affect (casting affect as a personal resource). However, a resource perspective could also explain how humor can help to build social resources, and perhaps even cognitive resources associated with flexibility and creativity.

Generally speaking, we wish to encourage theoretical pluralism in addressing humor phenomena in the workplace. It is our hope that in doing so, the "mess" that might be created by multiple approaches to humor at work, and a wide array of findings, might allow future theorists to build a more comprehensive theory of humor at work that accurately reflects the many different ways that humor impacts workplace phenomena.

Humor and culture

The observation that the creation and appreciation of humor is highly dependent on culture is not particularly new or earth-shattering. Incongruity theory and its variations can somewhat easily account for cultural differences (Robert & Yan, 2007). Specifically, culture influences individuals' knowledge structures (what we know, how we think things are related to other things), and thus, the likelihood that incongruities will be perceived when two different knowledge structures or schema are elicited within humor. Political jokes, for example, typically require that individuals have an insider's perspective on a culture's political system and/or the character of certain politicians. Similarly, ethnic jokes often rely on stereotypes about outgroups that differ from culture to culture (Davies, 2002). The fact that the content of humor is different in each cultural group is inherently interesting and worthy of study, because it can be traced to the culture's philosophical, sociological, and historical underpinnings, and viewed as a window into the culture (e.g. Kazarian, 2011). However, the fact that the content of humor created by people from different cultures varies is well-established, and not very interesting in and of itself.

But there are a number of issues related to culture and humor use that are quite interesting and have important implications for research on humor in the workplace. In particular, to what extent is humor a universal phenomenon: do people from different cultures tend to use the same types of humor (although with varying content) and for the same reasons? Do they prefer certain styles of humor, which might be more or less relevant to different outcomes (e.g. the use of sarcasm is frowned upon in some cultures, but supported in others)? Are people from different cultures more or less likely to use humor to achieve certain goals (e.g. to diffuse conflict)? And, does humor have the same status in all cultures? That is, are people more or less likely to utilize humor in one culture versus another, based on differences in the underlying value assigned to humor by a culture?

Past research on humor and culture

Tentative answers to some of these questions have been addressed in the psychological literature. For example, a number of studies have examined whether measures of humor operate similarly in different cultures. This literature generally suggests that measures of humor use or style tend to have similar measurement properties across cultures, indicating that different types of humor such as aggressive, affiliative, self-defeating and coping humor are recognized across cultures. Chen and Martin (2007), for example, found that Martin, Puhlik-Doris, Larsen, Gray, and Weir's (2003) humor styles questionnaire (HSQ) and Martin and Lefcourt's (1983) coping humor scale had similar measurement properties across Chinese and Canadian samples. Similarly, Saroglou and Scariot (2002) found that a French translation of the HSQ had similar measurement properties in a Belgian sample, and Kazarian and Martin (2004) found similar measurement properties of the HSQ across Lebanese, Canadian, and Belgian samples. Examining other measures, Nevo, Nevo, and Yin (2001) found strong similarities across participants from the US, Singapore, and Israel with regard to laughter, smiles, and joke telling.

Cross-cultural differences in mean levels of humor use have also been detected. For example, Chen and Martin (2007) found that Chinese participants scored lower than Canadians on aggressive humor use, and Kazarian and Martin (2004) found that Lebanese participants scored lower than Canadians on self-enhancing and affiliative humor. Nevo et al. (2001) found that Singaporean students tended to rely less on humor to cope with difficulty, and that Singaporean humor patterns reflected more conservative values (e.g. more restricted use of sexual humor). Some research has also shown that humor styles have different patterns of relationships with other humor styles or with other outcome variables across cultures. For example, Kazarian and Martin (2011) found that the affiliative and aggressive humor styles were positively correlated among Canadian participants, but uncorrelated among Lebanese and Belgian participants. This suggests perhaps a tendency for Canadians to joke and tease with one another in both affiliative and aggressive ways, which Belgians and Lebanese might not do. They also found that self-defeating humor was negatively correlated with well-being in the Canadian and Belgian samples, but not in the Lebanese sample. Such results suggest that there might be important cultural differences in how and when people use humor, and in the effects of humor for individuals. By extension, these cultural differences suggest that some of humor's many potential effects in organizational contexts might be more or less absent in some cultures than in others, and this possibility has important practical implications for the applied value of humor in work contexts.

Recent work by Yue (2010, 2011) is also intriguing in this regard. Based on in-depth examinations of the philosophical and historical roots of Chinese culture, as well as primary data from Chinese and Mongolian samples, Yue demonstrates that the Chinese perspective on humor is ambivalent at best, and likely considerably less positive than the perspective that many Westerners have about humor. He argues that while Chinese people report that they value humor in general, and that humor has been rehabilitated somewhat since the 1980s, they do not tend to rate themselves high on sense of humor. He suggests that Chinese people tend to think that humor is immature, shallow, and lowbrow, and not an important characteristic of "orthodox" Chinese personality. Similar remarks have been made about the Japanese view of humor (Cortazzi, 2007). The idea that humor is undesirable, or even a possible character flaw in some cultures, appears to stand in contrast to the strong value that is seemingly placed on the sense of humor in some cultures (e.g. the US and the UK). As E. B. White (1941) observed "Whatever else an American believes or disbelieves about himself, he is absolutely sure he has a sense of humor."

This work raises an intriguing question about humor in cross-cultural contexts (e.g. in multi-national organizations with a culturally diverse workforce, in cross-cultural interactions with customers, or during cross-cultural negotiations). Specifically, if some individuals place significant value on the use of humor while others perceive it to be degenerate, interactions in which one party attempts to infuse humor might be characterized by discomfort and strained relationships, and the intent of the humorist to forge a stronger relationship might backfire. On the other hand, humor might be a powerful tool for bridging gaps between people (including gaps caused by cultural differences), and it might be worthwhile to identify conditions under which humor is likely to be effective in cross-cultural interactions.

Humor themes study

To begin to explore some of these issues, we recently completed a study to determine peoples' perceptions of the role of humor in the workplace. We wanted to explore three things. First, we wanted to get a sense for participants' qualitative view of workplace humor. These results were discussed in Chapter 1. Respondents typically felt very strongly, and positively, about humor's role in their day-to-day lives at work, using terms like "essential," "crucial," "vital," and "necessary" to describe workplace humor. Second, we wanted to determine which themes or categories people would generate when asked to describe humor's role at work. And third, we wanted to compare the frequency of these humor themes across a number of cultural groups, to help understand how different groups of people perceive humor's possible uses: are the themes the same, and to what extent do people from different cultures discuss those themes unsolicited when they think about humor at work?

Our design was simple. Respondents were recruited through Mechanical Turk, and asked to write a paragraph in response to the following prompt:

> Think about the role that humor plays in your day-to-day experiences at work. This can be humor among co-workers, or with supervisors, managers, customers or clients: or it can refer to your own humorous attitude toward your job. Please write a paragraph or two describing what humor at work means to you; how or why it is important, and how or why it impacts your day-to-day work life.

We obtained a sample of 100 respondents from the US, 85 respondents who described themselves as ethnically Chinese (i.e. from China, Taiwan, Hong Kong, or ethnically Chinese from Singapore), and 30 respondents from India. All participants completed the response to the prompt in English, and wrote responses ranging in length from about 75 to 150 words.

Both authors examined responses from the US sample independently, and attempted to generate an exhaustive list of themes raised by respondents in response to the prompt. After meeting and resolving discrepancies by combining or separating categories, we agreed on a set of 15 different themes that we believe captured all of the different responses described in our US participants' open-ended descriptions. A list and brief description of those themes is presented in Table 10.1. Based on that list, we then examined the responses from the Chinese and Indian samples, and categorized each theme raised in each response into one of the 15 categories. No themes appeared in the Chinese or Indian responses that could not be categorized into one of the 15 themes identified using the U.S. sample. Table 10.2 provides a summary of the percent of respondents who raised a given

TABLE 10.1 Content coded themes from open-ended question about the role of humor at work

1	**Positive mood**: Humor encourages positive mood and makes work more enjoyable (helps people maintain a positive attitude, makes the work more enjoyable/fun, boosts morale).
2	**Reduces tension**: Humor helps people cope with daily stressors, reduces tension, keeps people relaxed.
3	**Cope with customers**: Humor allows people to vent and deal with rude or difficult customers, often through sharing humor about customers/making fun of customers with co-workers.
4	**Response to difficulty**: Humor can help people cope with difficulties at work (tragedy, psychological pain) and can be a healthy coping response.
5	**Boredom/monotony**: Humor takes the edge off boring work and makes it more tolerable, makes the day go faster/gets one through the day.
6	**Support customer interaction**: Humor helps support positive and effective relationships with customers, clients, patients (external constituents).
7	**Supports teamwork**: Humor helps co-workers bond and promotes good co-worker relationships, and camaraderie.
8	**Promotes productivity**: Humor can help make people more productive/efficient by promoting focus (i.e. off-task behavior energizes on-task behavior).
9	**Must monitor content**: Content of humor must be monitored to ensure that it's tasteful, sensitive, "clean," doesn't cross the line of propriety, and adheres to contextual considerations.
10	**Work withdrawal**: Humor among organizational members limits work withdrawal – absenteeism, turnover, tardiness, etc.
11	**Diffuse conflict/improve communication**: Humor improves communication among people, reduces generational/age-related/hierarchical differences among people, and helps to diffuse or manage conflict through honesty and reduced tension.
12	**Hierarchical differences**: Humor is used between co-workers and shouldn't be/isn't between co-workers and supervisors, isn't/shouldn't be used with clients/customers.
13	**Skills and abilities**: Humor encourages different perspectives/creativity and improves critical thinking .
14	**Meaning**: Humor helps individuals improve their lives in ways meaningful to them, and improves the way they perceive the world around them.
15	**Physical and psychological health**: Humor promotes a healthy lifestyle by having a positive impact on the physical and mental condition of individuals.

TABLE 10.2 Frequency of themes by group

Themes	*American (N = 100)*	*Ethnic Chinese (N = 85)*	*Indian (N = 30)*
	%	%	%
Positive mood	44	50.6	60
Reduces tension	49	45.9	50
Cope with customers	9	5.9	3.3
Response to difficulty	13	4.7	6.7
Boredom/monotony	49	38.8	13.3
Supports customer interaction	15	15.3	10
Supports teamwork	48	57.6	56.7
Promotes productivity	15	17.6	26.7
Must monitor content	20	16.5	10
Work withdrawal	11	7.1	10
Diffuse conflict/improve communication	15	23.5	33.3
Hierarchical differences	5	4.7	6.7
Skills and abilities	1	3.5	16.7
Meaning	11	15.3	16.7
Physical and psychological health	4	14.1	10

theme in their responses, broken down by culture. Responses typically mentioned multiple themes (typically 2–4).

Our analysis of themes suggests a number of similarities and differences across cultural groups. In terms of similarities, some categories were typical across all respondents: people in all three cultural groups frequently indicated that humor helps boost or maintain a positive mood, that it relieves tension, and supports teamwork. Some categories were less frequently represented in general, but were similarly represented (in terms of percentage) in each culture: participants indicated that humor helps support interactions with customers, it can reduce work withdrawal (i.e. absenteeism and turnover), it can reduce the perception of hierarchical differences, and that it can provide people with meaning by helping make sense of the world around them.

Our results also indicated a number of differences across the three groups. For example, although participants from the US and China both frequently mentioned that humor can help take the edge off boring work (about 50 percent and 40 percent of respondents from the US and China mentioned this, respectively), only 13 percent of Indian respondents mentioned this theme. To be honest, we can't really come up with a good explanation for this difference, but it seems interesting! Also, about one-third of Indian respondents and about one-quarter of Chinese respondents noted that humor can help diffuse conflict and improve communication, while only 15 percent of US respondents noted this feature. This perhaps reflects the stronger emphasis on collective values in China and India, where people might be more sensitive to the potential value of humor as a tool for maintaining in-group harmony (Robert & Yan, 2007).

Some of the themes had to do less with why people use humor, but rather, were posed as caveats to workplace humor use. For example, about 17 percent of Indian respondents thought it important to mention that people often vary in their skill or ability to use humor, while this was mentioned much less frequently by US and Chinese respondents. Also, about 20 percent of US respondents noted that it was important for employees to closely monitor the content of their humor; frequencies for this category were slightly lower in China (17 percent) and India (10 percent).

Although the samples are somewhat small (especially for India), and the use of Mechanical Turk as a source for participants raises issues of generalizability, these cross-cultural data provide a useful glimpse into peoples' perceptions of humor in the workplace. They indicate that there are some strong similarities in peoples' perceptions of humor's role in the workplace, but also some differences that might have important implications for research and practice. In particular, similarities in perceptions about humor's role as a positive mood inducer, and as supporting teamwork and relieving tension, suggest that interventions or encouragement of humor directed at such issues might be particularly likely to be successful, at least across the cultures examined in this sample. However, some of the differences suggest that peoples' expectations regarding humor use might not align across all contexts, perhaps making humor use in some interpersonal contexts awkward or strained.

Conclusion

If you engage people about the topic of humor at work, it is striking how excited and interested they are about the topic. This is true for researchers, business people, practitioners, and basically anyone who has ever held a job. People seem to recognize that humor affects peoples' interactions and experiences in many ways, and, cumulatively, has a meaningful impact on their lives. Yet despite some exemplary contributions to this small literature, there is a disconnect between the interest and excitement about the topic and the amount of attention that it has been paid by researchers.

In this chapter we argued that this disconnect is driven by two paradoxes. First, we argued that "humor is everywhere and nowhere." We suggested that because humor touches people in so many ways, and is implicated in a wide variety of processes, it suffers from an identity crisis. Much like the literature on affect in organizations a couple of decades ago, we believe that the literature on humor might best move forward by embracing the ambiguity, and encouraging a wide variety of theoretical and methodological approaches to examining humor across a broad range of contexts. It will fall to future researchers and theorists to make sense of the "mess" that will result, and to establish workplace humor as a meaningful phenomenon.

The second paradox is that "humor is extraordinarily complex, but also very simple." This paradox reflects the notion that although the experience of humor is generally quite simple (i.e. it is usually positive and feels good), the underlying processes which drive humor's effects are likely much more complex. As with the first paradox, the way to address the second paradox is to take it head on. Going forward, researchers will need to abandon simplistic approaches to workplace humor (i.e. positive humor is good, and negative humor is bad), and to carefully develop theoretical frameworks that help us understand how humor phenomena are related to other work phenomena. Doing so will help legitimize the scientific study of humor, but also, in the spirit of Kurt Lewin's assertion that nothing is as useful as a good theory, might prove invaluable in guiding applied efforts to integrate humor effectively into the workplace.

Toward that end, we spent some time in the remainder of this chapter discussing some of the theoretical advances that have been made concerning humor, and discussed the thorny issue of the relationship between culture and humor. Our hope is that this chapter might provide both guidance and encouragement to researchers who want to study humor, but might not know where to start. Please start anywhere.

References

Baumeister, R. F., Bratslavsky, E., Muraven, M., & Tice, D. M. (1998). Ego depletion: Is the active self a limited resource? *Journal of Personality and Social Psychology*, 74, 1252–1265.

Brief, A. P., & Weiss, H. M. (2002). Organizational behavior: Affect in the workplace. *Annual Review of Psychology*, 53, 279–307.

Brown, P., & Levinson, S. (1987). *Politeness: Some universals in language usage.* Cambridge: Cambridge University Press.

Chen, G. H., & Martin, R. A. (2007). A comparison of humor styles, coping humor, and mental health between Chinese and Canadian university students. *Humor*, 20(3), 215–234.

Cooper, C. D. (2002). *No laughing matter: The impact of supervisor humor on leader-member exchange (LMX) quality* (unpublished doctoral dissertation). University of Southern California, Los Angeles, CA.

Cooper, C. D. (2008). Elucidating the bonds of workplace humor: A relational process model. *Human Relations*, 61, 1087–1115.

Cortazzi, H. (2007). A Japanese sense of humor? *The Japan Times*. Retrieved from http://www.japantimes.co.jp/opinion/2007/03/27/commentary/a-japanese-sense-of-humor/#.Vw6rSHkUWUm

Davies, C. (2002). *The mirth of nations.* New Brunswick, NJ: Transaction.

Davis, M. S. (1993). *What's so funny? The comic conception of culture and society.* Chicago, IL: University of Chicago Press.

Demerouti, E., Bakker, A. B., Nachreiner, F., & Schaufeli, W. B. (2001). The job demands-resources model of burnout. *Journal of Applied Psychology*, 86, 499–512.

Elfenbein, H. A. (2007). Emotion in organizations: A review and theoretical integration. *Academy of Management Annals*, 4, 315–386.

Gkorezis, P., Petridou, E., & Xanthiakos, P. (2014). Leader positive humor and organizational cynicism: LMX as a mediator. *Leadership & Organizational Development Journal*, 35(4), 305–315.

Higgins, E. T. (1997). Beyond pleasure and pain. *American Psychologist*, 52, 1280–1300.

Hobfoll, S. E. (2001). The influence of culture, community, and the nested-self in the stress process: Advancing conservation of resources theory. *Applied Psychology: An International Review*, 50, 337–370.

Holmes, J. (2000). Politeness, power and provocation: How humor functions in the workplace. *Discourse Studies*, 2(2), 159–185.

Huo, Y., Lam, W., & Chen, Z. (2012). Am I the only one this supervisor is laughing at? Effects of aggressive humor on employee strain and addictive behaviors. *Personnel Psychology*, 65, 859–885.

Kazarian, S. S. (2011). Humor in the collectivist Arab Middle East: The case of Lebanon. *Humor*, 24(3), 329–348.

Kazarian, S. S., & Martin, R. A. (2004). Humor styles, personality, and well-being among Lebanese university students. *European Journal of Personality*, 18, 209–219.

Kim, T. Y., Lee, D. R., & Wong, N. Y. S. (2016). Supervisor humor and employee outcomes: The role of social distance and affective trust in supervisor. *Journal of Business and Psychology*. Advanced online publication. doi: 10.1007/s10869–015–9406–9.

Lehmann-Willenbrock, N., & Allen, J. A. (2014). How fun are your meetings? Investigating the relationship between humor patterns in team interactions and team performance. *Journal of Applied Psychology*, 99(6), 1278–1287.

Lynch, O. (2002). Humorous communications: Finding a place for humor in communication research. *Communication Theory*, 12, 423–445.

Lyubomirsky, S., King, L., & Diener, E. (2005). The benefits of frequent positive affect: Does happiness lead to success? *Psychological Bulletin,* 131(6), 803–855.

Martin, R. A. (2007). *The psychology of humor: An integrative approach.* Amsterdam: Academic Press.

Martin, R. A., & Lefcourt, H. M. (1983). Sense of humor as a moderator of the relation between stressors and moods. *Journal of Personality and Social Psychology*, 45(6), 1313–1324.

Martin, R. A., Puhlik-Doris, P., Larsen, G., Gray, J., & Weir, K. (2003). Individual differences in uses of humor and their relation to psychological well-being: Development of the humor style questionnaire. *Journal of Research in Personality, 37,* 48–75.

McGraw, A. P., & Warren, C. (2010). Benign violations: Making immoral behavior funny. *Psychological Science*, 21, 1141–1149.

McGraw, A. P., Warren, C., Williams, L. E., & Leonard, B. (2012). Too close for comfort, or too far to care? Finding humor in distant tragedies and close mishaps. *Psychological Science*, 25, 1215–1223.

Mesmer-Magnus, J., Glew, D. J., & Viswesvaran, C. (2012). A meta-analysis of positive humor in the workplace. *Journal of Managerial Psychology*, 27, 155–190.

Miron-Spektor, E., Efrat-Treister, D., Rafaeli, A., Schwarz-Cohen, O. (2011). Others' anger makes people work harder not smarter: The effect of observing anger and sarcasm on creative and analytic thinking. *Journal of Applied Psychology*, 96(5), 1065–1075.

Nevo, O., Nevo, B., & Yin, J. L. S. (2001). Singaporean humor: A cross-cultural, cross-gender comparison. *Journal of General Psychology*, 128(2), 143–156.

Pundt, A., & Herrmann, F. (2015). Affiliative and aggressive humor in leadership and their relationship to leader-member exchange. *Journal of Occupational and Organizational Psychology*, 88(1), 108–125.

Robert, C., & Wilbanks, J. E. (2012). The wheel model of humor: Humor events and affect in organizations. *Human Relations*, 65, 1071–1099.

Robert, C., & Yan, W. (2007). The case for developing new research on humor and culture in organizations: Towards a higher grade of manure. In J. J. Martocchio (Ed.), *Research in personnel and human resource management*, vol. 26 (pp. 205–226). Amsterdam: Elsevier.

Robert, C., Dunne, T. C., & Iun, J. (2015). The impact of leader humor on subordinate job satisfaction: The crucial role of leader-subordinate relationship quality. *Group and Organization Management*. Advance online publication. doi: 10.1177/1059601115598719.

Saroglou, V., & Scariot, C. (2002). Humor styles questionnaire: Personality and educational correlates in Belgian high school and college students. *European Journal of Personality*, 16, 43–54.

Suls, J. M. (1972). A two-stage model for the appreciation of jokes and cartoons: An information-processing analysis. In J. H. Goldstein, & P. E. McGhee (Eds.), *The psychology of humor* (pp. 81–100). New York and London: Academic Press.

White, E. B. (1941). Preface. In E. B. White, & K. S. White (Eds.), *A subtreasury of American humor*. New York: Coward-McCann.

Wyer, R. S., & Collins, J. E. (1992). A theory of humor elicitation. *Psychological Review*, 99(4), 663–688.

Yue, X. D. (2010). Exploration of Chinese humor: Historical review, empirical findings, and critical reflections. *Humor*, 23(3), 403–420.

Yue, X. D. (2011). The Chinese ambivalence to humor: Views from undergraduates in Hongkong and China. *Humor*, 24(4), 463–480.

INDEX

For Product Safety Concerns and Information please contact our EU
representative GPSR@taylorandfrancis.com
Taylor & Francis Verlag GmbH, Kaufingerstraße 24, 80331 München, Germany

www.ingramcontent.com/pod-product-compliance
Ingram Content Group UK Ltd.
Pitfield, Milton Keynes, MK11 3LW, UK
UKHW011017180926
475701UK00004B/798

9781138232365